NORTH COAST RUN

MEN AND SHIPS OF THE
N.S.W. NORTH COAST

NORTH COAST RUN

MEN AND SHIPS OF THE
N.S.W. NORTH COAST

MIKE RICHARDS

TURTON & ARMSTRONG

ISBN   0 908031 67 X

Published by: Turton & Armstrong
              21 Lister Street,
              Wahroonga
              New South Wales 2076
              Australia
              Telephone (02) 9489 6719

Star Printery, Sydney

Convicts loading wool aboard PS "Grafton" at Port Macquarie in the late 1860s.
Acknowledgement: Ian Goulding, Mid North Coast Maritime Museum.

Contents

AUTHOR'S NOTE

When I commenced to collect material for this book over thirty years ago, it was for my own pleasure and enlightenment that I did so. I did not really expect that it would be published, but one thing led to another, and when part of it was privately produced in 1967 I believed that the material therein was as complete and accurate as I could make it.

Subsequently I have obtained a wealth of additional information, often from those who, having read the first booklet, were able to offer first hand accounts regarding events on the North Coast.

One must, of course, be particularly careful when writing a book of this nature, as errors can easily be allowed to creep in, especially when so many cases arise in which more than one vessel bore the same name. Thus we have three "Bellingers", two "Ulmarras", two "Fitzroys", two "Japs", three "Nambuccas", two "Ramornies", two "Wollongbars", two "Wyrallahs", and so on. To further confuse the issue, many of these pairs were wrecked—sometimes in the same area.

Where doubt can arise, I have specifically stated which vessel was concerned, together with all the available facts, and in several cases I have described the often similar loss of the namesake later on. To further clarify this matter, I have added the suffix "2" or "3" to the name of the later vessel, but in no case that I know was the suffix actually applied to the real ship.

As no list of names of all coastal ships exists today—if one ever did—my list in this book (see Appendix One) is not guaranteed to be in any way complete. Undoubtedly there were more vessels, which are now completely forgotten, while many more do not come within the scope of the book. I believe that the list of vessels **OWNED** by the N.C.S.N. Co. is complete, but it is quite possible that one or two of them had a namesake of which I am not aware.

The events recounted are true; every attempt has been made to ensure authenticity and, while no guarantee is given that the book tells the whole truth, at least it contains "nothing but the truth".

The book is partly a collection of memories and recollections of numbers of ex-Company employees, who have gone to great trouble to assist me in many ways. To all of them, I would say "Thank You' —without your help this story of the coastal boats would probably have died at birth.

Alas, several friends whom I respected and admired, and who gave much of their time in assisting me, have passed away; others are in failing health. This book will be their memorial.

MICHAEL RICHARDS

Metric and Decimal Quantification

Where appropriate these systems have been used, but in order to preserve mood, particularly in quotations, the obsolete forms have been retained.

The 'crack' steamer of her day — the famous 'Agnes Irving' landing goods at Lawrence about 1870. She was later wrecked at Grassy Head, Macleay River, 26 Dec 1879.
Acknowledgement: Clarence River Historical Society.

CHAPTER ONE

From Humble Beginnings

The story of Steam Navigation in Australian waters had its beginning in the year 1831, when Sydney folk awoke one morning to find a lovely little steamship anchored in the Harbour. She was the "Sophia Jane", commanded by Lieut. Edward Biddulph, R.N.; she had sailed out from the United Kingdom via the Cape and the Colony's first newspaper rhapsodized:-

"…she was built in 1826 by Messrs Barnes & Miller, pupils of the celebrated James Watt, the only ones to carry on this work for themselves. The whole of her deck is unimpeded (as all vessels of this kind) and its length is 126 feet, her breadth 20 feet, her burthen 256 tons (150 tons nett register); and her power 50 horse. In smooth waters she will travel 8 miles per hour. She draws only 6 feet of water and could easily be made to draw only five."

"She was originally constructed for the almost exclusive accommodation of passengers, and her apartments are of the finest description. Hitherto, her principal employment has been in the carrying of passengers between England and France, and to various parts of the British Isles. She has three separate cabins—one for the gentlemen, one for the ladies, the other for steerage passengers. In the gent's cabin 16 beds can be made up, in the ladies' cabin 11 and in the steerage 20, while extra beds can be made up in emergency making in all 54."

Originally intended for service to Calcutta, where wood was the cheapest fuel, she was also capable of burning coal. She cost £8,000 to build, and was valued at £7,500 when she arrived in Australian waters. Unusual among her crew was a top-hatted gentleman with the curious title of "Engineer", and she also carried a full set of spares for the machinery. She was, so it is said, one of the fastest steamers built up to that time, and she had often demonstrated her power by being used as a tug.

After the trip out from the "Old Country" a fairly comprehensive refit was in order. That completed (and her paddle wheels shipped), she gave on the 11th June, 1831, a convincing demonstration of the advantages of steam power in the confined waters of the Harbour. The Governor of the Colony, with other distinguished guests, went aboard early for breakfast with the Captain, after which the "Sophia Jane" sailed around Dawes Point, Darling Harbour and Goat Island. Later in the day, she made a public excursion to Middle Harbour, sailing soon after 11 a.m. So fast was she in relation to the lumbering "Tea Waggons", which the locals knew well, that she was abreast of Pinchgut (Fort Denison) almost before the astonished passengers realised that they had sailed.

They were still marvelling at this wonder when they found themselves at the Heads. Their excitement is difficult to comprehend until we compare the "Sophia Jane" and her performance in 1831 to the world's first hovercraft almost exactly 130 years later and remember the effect this revolutionary vehicle had on the amazed people who first saw it. In actual fact the "Sophia"'s 8 m.p.h. was much less than a Manly ferry's service speed of around 11 knots. From the Heads, where she picked up the pilot, the little "Sophia Jane" raced up Middle Harbour, going about 5 or 6 miles inland,

1

in weather which was comparable to the best that Sydney has to offer, until she reached the head of navigation, near where the present Roseville Bridge is situated. At this point she put about, and once more ploughed her way seawards. Lunch, a sumptuous cold collation, was served at 2 p.m. under the direction of Mr. Bax of the Australian Hotel.

No sooner had the guests sat down for the meal than they noticed a "peculiar motion", the vessel rolling in a most regular and agreeable manner. No particular notice was taken, however, until on returning to deck they found themselves several miles outside the Heads. She returned to Sydney in quick time, although opposed by both wind and tide. She travelled from the Heads to Fort Macquarie in 26 minutes, the previous "record" of 42 minutes for the passage having been set by a sailing vessel with both wind and tide in her favour. The "Sophy" proceeded to Kissing Point then back to Sydney Cove.

The following day, she sailed for Newcastle, leaving Sydney at 7.15 in the morning and arriving at the King's Wharf at 3.13 the same afternoon. She then proceeded up the Hunter to Morpeth (then called Green Hills), taking 3½ hours for the river passage. The next day she came down the river to Newcastle in just 3 hours, and did the "60 mile" run back to Port Jackson in 7 hours 40 minutes.

In these days of instant power for any purpose, we tend to overlook the great significance of the foregoing paragraphs. Until May 1831 there was no such thing as powered transport in this country, and precious little anywhere else. Steam had been used in Britain for pumping water for over a century it is true—Newcomen's "Atmospheric" engine dates from 1705, and Watt's improvements thereto from 1763, while rotary motion came in 1781.

The first practical steamboat, however, was the tug "Charlotte Dundas" built by William Symington, and tried in the Forth and Clyde Canal in 1802. A Watt double acting condensing engine, placed horizontally, acted directly by a connecting rod on the crank of a shaft at the stern, which carried a revolving paddle-wheel. The trial was successful, but steam towing was abandoned for fear of injuring the banks of the canal. Ten years were to elapse before Henry Bell built the "Comet" with side paddle-wheels, which ran as a passenger steamer on the Clyde; meanwhile the American, Robert Fulton, outfitted a steamer on the Hudson River in 1807 and brought steam navigation for the first time to commercial success. Engineers were slow to realise the economics of high pressure steam and even in 1835 it was usual for the pressure in marine boilers to be no more than 4 or 5 pounds per square inch above the pressure of atmosphere. Thus steam navigation (which pre-dated railways: Trevithick 1804; Stephenson 1829) came to Australia only 29 years after it was first used successfully anywhere in the world, and 23 years before the first Railways in the country.

1831 must have been a vintage year for maritime innovations, for not only did the "Sophia Jane" arrive here, but an enterprising few had already seen that the future of sea transport lay in steam and had done some local experimenting. A small paddle boat, the "Surprise", had already been launched and was being fitted out for the run to Parramatta, but she was poorly designed and the paddles caused her to roll in a frightening manner. She was therefore withdrawn from

"William The Fourth"—First successful Australian Built Steamer.
(Acknowledgement: Maritime Services Board, N.S.W., from a Painting by John Allcot.)

service and passes from our story somewhat under a cloud. She was sold and went to Hobart Town where she did give useful service for a while.

Local shipwrights, however, did not make a habit of building failures, nor did they allow one setback to discourage them. In May, 1831, the keel was laid, at Clarencetown on the Williams River, of a vessel even more remarkable than the "Sophia Jane". She was in fact building at the time the "Sophy" arrived, and it seems to have been sheer bad luck that robbed her of a better place in history as the "Sophia Jane" rather overshadowed her.

Mr. Joseph Hickey Grose, a leading Sydney merchant, had ordered a steamer to be built locally, before the first rumours were received that the "Sophia Jane" was coming to Australia, and he placed the order with two Scottish migrants, Messrs Marshall and Lowe, who had recently arrived in the Colony. They set up a shipbuilding yard at Clarencetown mainly because suitable timber for shipbuilding grew close by.

The vessel was christened on the 22nd October of the same year, when she slid down the ways and took the water for the first time. The name given her was "William the Fourth". After fitting out she sailed to Sydney, arriving a month later and there her engines, which had been imported from Fawcett & Co. in England, were installed by the Phoenix Foundry at Blackwattle Bay. Mr. Pattison (of the Phoenix Foundry) improved the engines while installing them, but they were never very powerful. Indeed "The Billy", as the vessel came to be called, never exceeded 8 knots. However, the engines were jet condensing and this was quite a modern feature for the time. "The Billy" was a small ship, considerably smaller than a modern tug. She was 80 feet long on deck, 15 feet wide amid-ships (20 feet over the paddle box sponsons), while from the keel to the flush deck was 7 feet, the after cabin had 6 feet 6 inches' head room. She was planked in flooded gum 1¾ ins thick while her decks were 2 ins colonial pine and she was schooner rigged. She took nearly ten hours for the 60-mile run and her master for the maiden voyage was Captain Taggart who was well known as the commodore of the Hunter River passenger trade. The maiden voyage was made in mid-February, 1832, and she ran mostly to Newcastle for the next three years, occasionally making a few trips up the Hawkesbury River to Windsor and to the tiny settlement of Gosford.

In 1832 she visited Port Macquarie and she ran "as required" to many ports between Eden and Grafton before joining the Grafton S.N. Co. in 1857.

Another fine steamer came from the yard of Marshall & Lowe in 1835. This vessel had been ordered in 1834 by a new concern, the Hunter River Packet Association, and was to be of 200 tons. The cost was to be about £8,150. The hull was built, again mostly of flooded gum, but this time the decks were of Norway pine. She was quite large, being 134 feet long and 38 feet in the beam. An unusual feature was that her paddle boxes were enclosed by the deck; that is, they did not protrude at the sides like those of other steamers. She also had six enclosed cabins for family groups, as well as the usual Ladies' cabin and steerage. Of very light draught, she drew only seven feet when carrying 150 tons of cargo. She was fitted with two engines, of 40 h.p. each, and was particularly advanced for her time. This vessel was called "Ceres". Unfortunately she was totally lost when she hit a reef near Norah Head after running for a mere six months. This disaster forced her owners into liquidation, a poor reward for such a fine effort.

The second English-built steamer to reach these shores was the "James Watt". She had been built for the Liverpool-Glasgow trade in 1824 by Humble & Hunry of Liverpool and registered 141 tons. Owing to some miscalculation she was not a success on that run, nor any other in British waters. She was luxuriously appointed, and very well engined, but was a coal-eater even by the standards of those days, while her draft had been under-estimated by her builders, and she was consequently slow and uneconomical. She was purchased and imported to Australia by T. Street in 1834. In December, 1838, she was owned by T. Street & J. H. Grose. She was placed in various trades without much success but is historic in that she was the first steamer to visit Melbourne in July, 1837. She was also the first steamer to visit Moreton Bay.

After trying the Clarence River Trade, she was sold in October, 1842, to R. Scott & Partners who kept her for four years before selling her to the Hunter River S.N. Co. in August 1846. Only five months later her engine was removed and she was broken up in disgust in 1847.

The "Tamar" came to N.S.W. from Launceston, as she had proved too big to be successful with the limited trade offering in the Tamar River at the time. Of only 88 tons and built by McMillan of Greenock in 1833, she was sold in 1835 and lengthened by 28 feet the following year. In March, 1843, she went to R. Scott & Partners, who later became the Hunter River S.N. Co. She had a long life of 40 years, finally being wrecked at 4 p.m. on the 11th February, 1873, at Norah Point, while owned by J. & A. Brown.

The Clarence River, where the north coast trade was centred for many years, is reputed to have been discovered by a runaway convict named Craig, who in 1827 made his escape from Moreton Bay penal colony and, living with friendly Aborigines for seven or eight years, gradually wended his way south, until, in 1834 or 5, he had the good fortune to be granted a free pardon and a place in history as one of the country's pioneer explorers.

It happened, so the story goes, that Craig met a stockman or Government surveyor in the bush south of the Clarence River and, in the course of conversation, was told that a team of bullocks had "gone bush" from Port Macquarie, and that if any convict found and returned them to their owner he would be given a free pardon. Craig of course used the knowledge he had gained from the natives and, finding the lost animals, returned them to Port Macquarie and so earned his freedom.

Craig was next seen in Sydney where his tales of a big river up north led the Government to send a revenue cutter, the "Prince George" to verify his reports, but owing to the surf breaking on the bar she did not enter the river, returning instead to Sydney. Craig had also spoken of the vast stands of timber to be found growing in the area and this prompted private citizens to send their own expeditions to the river for cedar.

Messrs Francis Girard of Sydney and Thomas Small of Kissing Point both sent small sailing vessels with timber getters aboard to capitalise on this timber. Mr Small's vessel the "Susan" was the first vessel to cross the bar, in 1838, and her party camped first at the present site of Maclean and then went on to Woodford Island. Mr. Girard's ship the "Taree" also crossed the bar, and her party made camp at Tyndale. Later these men were to become the first farmers on the river, both grazing cattle and Mr. Girard's property "Waterview" became the first run on the river.

Settlement followed quickly, and soon another enterprising pair,

Messrs Phillips and Cole had established a shipbuilding yard and timber business on the present site of South Grafton. In August 1839, Mr. Joseph Hickey Grose, builder of "The Billy" sent a steamer, the "King William" (not to be confused with "The Billy") from Sydney with orders to explore the river's upper reaches.

This vessel became the first steamer to enter the Clarence River, having been brought out from London by Mr. Grose in 1838. "King William" was built in 1830 at Blackwall (London) and was 81 tons. On board the "King William" were the Deputy Surveyor-General and a number of colonists who were desirous of taking up land for farming and grazing. A writer who was aboard, describing the trip said in a letter, from which I quote:—

"The vessel crossed the bar in two fathoms of water – the approach is around a beautiful grassy hill forming the south head. Exploring slowly up the river, Susan Island was reached on the 29th and on the afternoon of the 30th the steamer brought us to the foot of a rapids 85 miles from the heads.

"In commemoration of so large a steamer navigating so far into the interior, (she is 140 feet long) the mount under which she lay was named "King William's Mount". A little above this point is the confluence of the two branches, both navigable for boats (for) a considerable distance from the junction."

So says the report. A month later the "King William" was lost on Nobby's at the entrance to Newcastle.

This correspondent neglected to state that the vessel had grounded at the rapids and could not be re-floated for three days. Her master, Captain Perry, named the river "Clarence". As a result of this expedition numerous settlers arrived and took up land. The first sheep reached the district in 1840, while great interest was shown in the rich tracts of cedar, and timber getters began to flock to the region. Most of the shipping to the river at this time, and for some years afterwards, was in the form of small ketches, schooners, brigs, cutters and other small sailing craft, though most of the few steamers went too.

By 1840 steamers had ceased to be the novelty that they had been, as more and more came onto the register. The "Victoria" was built that year at Raymond Terrace by one John Korff to the order of Edye Manning. The "Victoria" was built to take the engines of the "Ceres" which Korff had managed to salvage, and she was quite a greyhound at the time.

Three new steamers were on order that year for the Hunter River Steam Navigation Co., later to become the Australian S.N. Co. Founded in 1840, this firm became the colony's first legally constituted shipping company. The trio referred to became our first iron steamers: the "Rose" and "Thistle" of 1840 and the "Shamrock" built the following year.

The first two were built at Milwall on the Thames, and were 150 ft long with 20 ft beam, but only 6′ 6″ draft. They were also fast, 12 m.p.h. being recorded on trials. They were schooner rigged and like their predecessors, flush decked. The "Shamrock" was similar, but had 2 ft more beam, a raised quarter deck, and her rig; she was a 3-masted schooner built in Bristol, near the site where the famous "Great Britain" was then building. The "Victoria" held her own until these three settled in, when she was outclassed in every way.

Other steamers running at the time included the "Maitland", "Clonmel", "Sovereign", "Emu", "Kangaroo" and "Corsair" amongst several others.

By late 1845 the old "Sophia Jane" was past her prime and, when she touched a reef off Wollongong and suffered extensive bottom damage, her owner, now Edye Manning, decided to replace her as soon as he could and sold her in 1846. Accordingly the "Phoenix" was built in Sydney by Thomas Chowne, and the "Sophia Jane" 's machinery was transferred to the new hull. The "Phoenix" was rather smaller than her predecessor, but in light of previous experience had more power. She was placed in the Clarence River trade, under Captain Wiseman. In March, 1850, when less than four years old, she was driven ashore some 9 miles south of the entrance to the Clarence while on a passage to Sydney. The wreck was offered for sale, but no buyers came forward and as she was not covered by insurance her owners faced financial ruin. They determined on their own salvage operations and succeeded — but only after the engines had been removed and sent overland to Sydney. The hull was then refloated and sailed down the coast to Sydney where the machinery was re-installed.

The "Phoenix" resumed trading in 1851 after a thorough refit. She was now under the command of Captain J. Benaud, who had several years' experience in trading to the Clarence River in sailing vessels. He replaced Captain Wiseman who had gone to England in 1850 to superintend the building of a new vessel, the P.S. "Clarence" which he brought out from the builder in 1852. This ship never ran up the Clarence however, as she was sold to a Tasmanian company on her arrival in Sydney, bringing £29,950 — a profit of nearly £17,000 over her cost. But the "Phoenix" was destined to leave her bones somewhere on the North Coast for, in April 1852, while entering the Clarence River against the tide and with a strong fresh running out, she grounded on the bar and, damaging her machinery, was forced ashore on the north beach and soon became a total loss. Her rusted old engines are still there buried in sand and salt water, just north of Yamba.

The "William the Fourth" ("The Billy") continued in regular service to the river, making fortnightly trips until trade increased, warranting the use of a faster, bigger vessel. The "Billy" was never a fast ship and in December, 1854, she took thirteen days. She was, however, an excellent sea-boat, never missing a trip and Captain Wiseman, now in command of her, was very proud of this fact. However after 30 years of service under many owners, the latter ones since 1860 under the house flag of the Illawarra S.N. Co. she left our shores for the last time in 1863, being sent towards China seeking a buyer which she found there in 1864. She had been owned by the Grafton S.N. Co. from 1857 until her sale in February 1860 to the Illawarra Co.

According to the earliest records the Grafton Steamship Navigation Co. was formed on the 24th January, 1857, by a group of gentlemen whose interests lay in the Clarence River. This area had had up to that time inadequate service, owing to the lack of co-operation by the owners of the vessels then running. They ran their vessels to suit their own convenience, never bothering to arrange a timetable. Further, their ships could have been withdrawn at any time, and would have been had there been more money offered elsewhere. This was the main reason for forming the Grafton Steamship Navigation Co. The share capital of the company was £13,500 made up of £10 shares, and the first directors were Mr. Francis Mitchell, Mr. Clark Irving and Mr. Robert Waterson, while the first auditors were Mr. David Jones (founder of the Sydney retail Firm which bears his name) and Mr. Grant Tindall of Ramornie Station and Meatworks on the Clarence.

At this point another vessel enters our story: the iron paddler "Grafton" built by J. Laird of Birkenhead in 1854 under the supervision of Captain Wiseman who had again gone to that country for the purpose of bringing her out. She arrived in April, 1855, and carried 100 tons of cargo in addition to 30 passengers. Her first owners were R.S. Ross & Partners, but here is a puzzle: she was registered on arrival in Sydney as the property of Grafton S.N. Co. (R.S. Ross & Partners), but as we have seen this Company was not formed until January 1857. Possibly on the latter date the firm went public and offered shares for sale.

It is recorded that a single ticket from Sydney to Grafton on this vessel cost £7 which was a not inconsiderable sum, when it is remembered that fifty years later no less than three return journeys could be made by the "City of Grafton" for only £8 5s. 0d. ($16.50). Now, in 1977, economy class rail travel is $10.90 single to Grafton.

The "Grafton" was eventually sold in August, 1874, to J.E. Manning, the son of the founder of the Illawarra S.N. Co., Edye Manning, who converted her from paddles to twin screw in 1876/7 before selling her again to W.R. Williams of Auckland N.Z. She sailed for many years under the New Zealand Flag, being sold again to the Union Steam Ship Co. of N.Z. in 1885. Under their flag she was ultimately wrecked at Macquarie Harbour, Tasmania on the 12th June, 1898, on passage from Melbourne to Strahan. She sank the following day.

Owing to the expansion of trade resulting from the gold rush and the thousands of settlers who flocked to the country as a result, the company decided to expand the service to include the Richmond River which was first entered by His Majesty's ship "Rainbow" in command of the Hon. Captain Rous, (afterwards Admiral Rous, R.N.) in August, 1828, when he discovered this fine river. The first schooner to cross the bar was the "Sally" in 1842, which brought the first settlers to the lower part of the river. Only three years after the Grafton Steamship Navigation Co. was formed, the directors decided to increase the capital to £50,000 at the same time changing the name of the company to The Clarence & Richmond River Steam Navigation Co.

The new service to the Richmond River necessitated the acquisition of additional ships, and the "Duncan Hoyle" was acquired in a hurry, but proved unsuitable and was as quickly disposed of, probably to Hong Kong. In June, 1860, the firm bought the "Fenella" to replace her and took delivery of the new "Urara", an iron paddler of 382 tons, from Birkenhead. The "Fenella" was sold to Shanghai in 1862 when the new "Agnes Irving" arrived from Deptford Green (London). She was a fine, large, iron paddler of 439 tons, but both the "Urara" and the "Agnes Irving" were destined to come to grief, the former in May, 1866, in fine weather on the Clarence bar, the latter on the Macleay bar in 1879, but not before she had earned a reputation for being one of the finest and most successful vessels ever to work on the coast. Whilst crossing the Macleay River Bar on 27th December 1879 at low tide a big sea struck her without warning and drove her onto the South Spit, where she broke up. No lives were lost but the Master, J. Magee (no relation to the later Master of the same name), had his ticket suspended for three months.

In 1978 the wreck was re-discovered by skindivers 1 to 1½ miles off shore in a line from Grassy Heads in 30 feet to 50 feet of water. It had apparently moved during heavy flooding and inclement weather.

Another well liked boat was the "Ballina" also an iron paddler, this time one of 299 tons. She was built in 1865 for J. Alexander, but was bought the following year by the Clarence & Richmond River S.N. Co. and ran with great success until she was wrecked at Port Macquarie on 14th February, 1879. The wreck of this vessel was rediscovered in early 1978 when extensions to the northern breakwater caused the sand to shift and uncovered the wreck. She is lying in 25 feet of water and stands 15 feet above the bottom.

The Ballina is the first wreck to be proclaimed under the Historic Shipwrecks Act and may not be damaged. She is now (1979) under archaeological investigation by the Maritime Archaeological Association of N.S.W.

Other steamers built or bought second-hand in the eighteen sixties included the little "Ulmarra" in 1861, the "Rainbow" a small wood paddler in '63 — wrecked in Seal Rocks Bay in 1864, the "Platypus", an iron screw steamer from Queensland owners in 1868, plus droghers (shallow draft river boats) like the "Uloom", and others. The "Fire King", built on the Macleay River in 1866 by W. Marshall, was acquired in 1879, but she was lost when she went onto the north head at the Manning River bar on the 30th April, 1873, all hands being saved.

From the foregoing it can be seen that the firm did not allow the limitations implied in its title to prevent it from trading to the Manning and the Macleay Rivers as well as the Clarence and Richmond, and no doubt they also traded to such places as the Nambucca and Bellinger as well. It is certain that their steamers were seen at Port Macquarie as far back as the late fifties, and they seem to have been the North Coast Company in all but name even then.

In later years as the trade increased — and more farmers and graziers moved onto the land already cleared by the timber getters, and towns and villages sprang up—other lines of steamers were formed and made a bid for their share of the trade, but they were all eventually merged with, or taken over by, the parent company.

The development of these shipping companies rested solely on the fact that, in the last century, sea communications were the only link with the outside world. Railways were rare, and the very nature of the terrain, especially that immediately north of Sydney made the task of the builders of roads and railways doubly difficult and in any case sea transport was cheaper and, in most cases faster, even when the railways were open for business. Roads from one town to the next were little more than a pair of wheel ruts winding painfully through the bush, fording creeks and streams, and ending at river jetties or mountain ranges. Horses were the only source of motive power, and coaches offered local services between towns not served by navigable rivers and large enough to warrant a service being run. Mostly, however, one travelled on horseback, or failing that one walked. Cars (or horseless carriages) were unheard of in the bush, for years after the first ones chuffed and spluttered their precarious and improbable way down George Street. Indeed in the 1909 edition of the "North Coast Guide", a book published by the company by way of advertising their operations to the extent of 190 informative and well illustrated pages, only one motor car is seen in hundreds of illustrations of city and country life, although horses and sulkies, buggies, surreys, drays, waggons and coaches are to be seen in their dozens, and many are the advertisements singing the praises of so-and-so's line of coaches or livery stables with "Fresh feed always on hand", or "Good groom and large paddock".

The people living along the Clarence have many reasons to be

9

proud of their river, but like all the northern rivers, the "bar" or sand build-up at the entrance has always been awkward and many of its finest reaches are marred by shoals. These drawbacks in this and other rivers eventually played a big part in causing the coastal vessel to be superseded by the railways and road transport. The bar in particular was a big stumbling block, for very often the water was so shallow that even vessels drawing 10 feet or less would be caught inside the river, bar-bound for weeks at a time, or else they would have to stand off the beach for a similar period, unable to enter.

From the entrance of the Clarence to way above Iluka and around to Yamba, the most extensive series of harbour works and retaining walls, intended to improve and preserve the channel, were constructed by successive governments, until the north coast railway construction job made a good excuse for stopping the further improvement of these works in the early years of the present century. This applied to all the river entrances along the entire coastline, from Sydney to the Tweed.

The original plans for the Clarence Estuary were drawn up by Sir John Goode, who said that if carried out, the result would guarantee a minimum depth of 18 feet of water at low tide being maintained. However they were not carried out in their entirety, and the plans were altered over and over again as numerous engineers and experts tried out their ideas. As usually happens when government experts tamper with an original plan the end result was worse than useless, and hundreds of thousands of pounds were spent on this river alone, before the government finally suspended operations completely. Even then they still did not meet the requirements, in the opinion of the people who from bitter experience should know —the masters and crews of the vessels concerned. It may have been that, if Sir John's plan had been carried through to completion, unmarred, his guarantee would have been shown to be true, and thus, by avoiding many groundings and delays due to inadequate coverage of the bar, this story may have had a different ending.

In 1964 the N.S.W. Department of Works added to the breakwaters in a further attempt to improve this, and other entrances.

About this time the Manning and Macleay Rivers started to see accelerated development too. The Manning was the more developed, of course, having been settled rather earlier than the more northerly river. The Macleay was first settled about 1835 when Mr. Samuel Onions took a grant of land, later sold to Mr. Enoch Rudder, who named it Kempsey after the estate he had left in England. However progress was slow, as witnessed by the fact that in 1859 the population of the entire river was under 500. Indeed by 1904 it had only reached about 5,000 but the next four years saw a minor "population explosion". The total rose by some 3,000 to 8,336.

Mr. W. Marshall was responsible for the opening up of the Macleay with his vessel "Fire King" which was built on the Macleay in Marshall's own yard. He also built the "New Moon", lost on passage to Sydney, when she was wrecked off Port Stephens on the 1st October, 1864. In this disastrous wreck 10 persons lost their lives, while only two managed to swim ashore. He also built the "Rainbow" — mentioned previously, which had been lost almost four months earlier along with seven lives out of her complement of sixteen, under the Clarence & Richmond Steam Navigation Co. house flag.

CHAPTER TWO

Discovery and Settlement

The first official reference to Trial Bay and the entrance to the Macleay was the result of a search for a band of runaway convicts who had seized the brig "Trial" and headed north. When news filtered back to Sydney that a vessel had been wrecked north of Port Stephens the "Lady Nelson", Commander White, was sent to investigate. Wreckage was found on the beach just north of Smokey Cape, and this was identified as coming from the missing "Trial". The bay was later named Trial Bay.

Enquiries among the natives turned up only vague information as to the whereabouts of the escapees, but it was understood that some had put to sea on a raft and had disappeared. The remainder set off on foot in a southerly direction and were never found. The search party did discover the entrance of the Macleay River, which they reported to Governor Macquarie. Thus the credit for the discovery of this river goes to Cdr. White in February, 1817.

When the Surveyor-General, John Oxley, set out in the year 1818 to explore the area between Walcha and the coast, he intended to hit the coast at the Macleay, but came too far south and instead found the Hastings and the site of Port Macquarie, reaching the river on the 26th September when he named it in honour of the Governor-General of India, Warren Hastings. Later, on the 8th October, he crossed a large stream of fresh water, passed over excellent and rich country,

alternately thick bush and clear forest with small streams for nearly four miles, when "to our great joy and satisfaction we arrived on the sea shore about half a mile from the entrance of what we saw (with no small pleasure) formed a port to the river which we had been tracing from Mt. Sea View."

"I named this inlet Port Macquarie in honour of His Excellency the Governor, the original promoter of these expeditions". Following the report made by Oxley on his return, Governor Macquarie despatched a further expedition to survey and explore Port Macquarie and the Hastings River, with a view to the establishment of a convict settlement.

With Oxley again in charge, assisted by Lieutenant Phillip Parker King, they arrived on the "Lady Nelson" on the 11th May, 1819, and on this occasion made a thorough survey of the entrance, the river and the countryside as far as where Bain's bridge (north west of Wauchope) is now. After their investigations of the bar, the harbour and the position generally, Oxley reported to the Governor (12th June, 1819) "The port is perfectly capable to receive vessels of the class usually employed on the coast of this territory". He submitted a plan of the entrance to the port and a sketch of part of Hastings River. (A copy of an early plan by Oxley is to be seen in the Museum at Port Macquarie).

On receipt of this second report Governor Macquarie despatched to the Home Secretary an account of the fine country which had been added to the territory of the Colony. He was subsequently ordered by the Imperial Government to form a settlement at the place because, owing to various shortages, difficulty was experienced in fitting out a large expedition. A third visit to Port Macquarie was made by Oxley in 1820 when he was instructed by Macquarie to survey that part and fix an eligible place for the first public settlement.

There were three important reasons for wishing to form a settlement at Port Macquarie. They were the isolation of prisoners, the cultivation of tropical fruits and plants as suggested by Oxley, and the opening up of the road to New England from the Coast. Therefore on 18th March, 1821, the "Prince Regent", "Mermaid", and the "Lady Nelson" left Sydney with the pioneer party of soldiers and convicts to found the settlement.

This expedition arrived at Port Macquarie under Captain Francis Allman of the 48th Regiment who was appointed Commandant of the District, and comprised 2 Corporals, Lieutenant William Wilson (Engineer), A. Fentor (Surgeon), 1 Drummer, 3 Sergeants, and 33 private soldiers, Stephen Partridge (superintendent of the convicts), Cooke (a convict doctor) 60 selected convicts comprising 3 rough carpenters, 1 shingler, 2 pit sawyers, 1 blacksmith, 1 tailor, 2 shoemakers and 50 strong healthy labourers. The convicts were promised remission of their sentences for faithful service.

After anchoring in the Harbour, a suitable landing place was made on an outcrop of rock (now near a small concrete wall on the waterfront, north-west from the Royal Hotel) and the programme of works arranged by Governor Macquarie was proceeded with at once. On landing, the British flag was hoisted on the hill (near the present Public School) which became known as Allman's Hill.

A clearing was made and temporary bark huts were erected for the accommodation of troops and convicts. Work went on steadily and more substantial quarters for convicts and soldiers, plus a cottage for the Commandant, were erected with the stockade. Soon after the penal settlement was established at Port Macquarie, military officers began taking Land Grants in the district. By 1825 Major Innes had an out-station at Rowland Plains which was soon connected to the main settlement by road.

In addition to crops of vegetables grown in the garden near the town, suitable sites were selected for farms, Settlement Point being the first. Time was found to experiment with cotton, coffee, pineapples, and sugar. Not much success was had with the first two, although pineapples are still grown, but some small success was had with sugar, under the management of Mr. T.A. Scott who claimed that the local cane was equal to that of the West Indies. However the crops failed through frosts and Scott was dismissed by Governor Darling in 1828. Prior to 1830 there was only one treadmill to crush grain and this was attached to the commissariat store in Port Macquarie and used for grinding wheat and maize. On the hill beyond the flagstaff Major Innes erected a windmill to grind the corn for his contracts with the Government. George Halliday was the first miller.

Hearing reports of the excellent possibilities of the region, the first free settlers began to arrive, with Government approval, as early as 1830. This no doubt hastened the proper survey and laying out of the town, which was carried out under the supervision of the Government Surveyor in 1830. Until that time buildings had been erected along the rise which ran along the seashore, the centre of the town being a ti-tree swamp. This swamp was eventually filled in with earth carted from the hill by the chain gang, and the level of the ground was brought up to that of the camp.

Not much remains today of Macquarie's extensive building programme but St. Thomas's Church is amongst the oldest in Australia. The foundation stone was laid on the 8th December, 1824, and the Chaplain, Rev. Hassel, delivered an appropriate address. The building, completed in 1827, is a large one capable of accommodating nearly 700 people. The walls are solid, measuring almost 3 feet in thickness and are constructed with handmade bricks. These walls run true east, west, north and south. At the west end is a tower with apertures for a clock and it was hoped to install a peal of bells. In this sense the tower has never been completed. The roof was originally shingles and of a somewhat lower pitch than the present one, but the change came about owing to the church being severely damaged by gales on more than one occasion. To begin with, the floor was of red soil filled in to a height of 2 feet and well stamped down, but later bricks about 8 ins square were used and, being soft, became worn in time and were turned over. Large sections of this flooring still remain and show how the bricks became worn down a second time. Today most of the floor in general use is of concrete, finished with red cement.

On entering the building the visitor sees quaint old box pews. They are built of solid cedar, like the ceiling and wainscotting. To begin with there were only sufficient pews to accommodate the officials who controlled the settlement, but the time soon came when many others were added to seat the free settlers. The prisoners occupied the space at the back of the church and a file of armed soldiers kept guard over them, but there is no record of them ever being called upon to enforce order.

An officer making an inspection of the town in 1825 wrote, "The Government House stands nearly in the middle of the town, on a handsome esplanade open to the sea. On the right of the hill are two handsome cottages used as officers quarters".

The population of the town in 1833 was 550, there being 144 free settlers, including Government officers, and 436 convicts, but by 1836 the population of the County of Port Macquarie had risen to 1,500 persons, 936 of whom were convicts. These figures indicate the rapid growth of the town once it was thrown open to free settlement, and the increasing number of convicts who were being sent to the penal settlement.

When the prosperity of the town declined, a journalist wrote in 1868 "It was a town of great importance once upon a time, and though its glory has departed—or at any rate is in a very faded condition—its public buildings are big and ugly enough even for the metropolis itself...they wear such traces of broken down gentility, such badges of architectural conservatism, such painful evidence of having seen better days that there is something depressing in their aspect".

The first definite information about the existence of the Macleay as a river was reported in the Sydney "Gazette" published 1st December, 1825.

"Advices from Port Macquarie state that four prisoners, runaways from Moreton Bay, had arrived at the settlement after a journey of five weeks. As far as their capacities extend and allowing them credit for speaking the truth, they give a most pleasing account of the country over which they passed. They report that they crossed no less than sixty rivers or streams, and that about thirty miles northward of Trial Bay they fell in with a river as large as the Hastings. Plains of boundless extent are described as lying between Port Macquarie and Moreton Bay, and the country is said to be equal, if not superior to, any other part of the continent. If this statement should turn out to be correct, we shall be inclined to rejoice at, rather than regret, the absence of these men from the scene of their primitive sufferings."

The Commandant of Port Macquarie, after interviewing the

13

captured escapees apparently decided to prove the existence of this river to the north, for in the "Australian" of April 5, 1826, it was reported that a party guided by a native named Mooney, proceeded up the Maria River and, after carrying their boat about six miles overland, came upon the reported river. They immediately launched their boat and proceeded across the river which was 370 yards wide at this place and its depth 3 fathoms.

Next day they explored the river to the entrance into Trial Bay at what is now known as Grassy Head, recording that Oxley had made a very imperfect survey.

Returning to the point where they had first entered the river, the party rowed upstream "through a most fertile country" well endowed with "Large quantities of immense cedar trees". Further progress was prevented by the rapids at Belgrave Falls.

Following the report of this expedition to the authorities, the river was named Wright's River after the leader of the expedition, Captain Samuel Wright. Soon after his return Wright was appointed Commandant at Port Macquarie, where he remained until 1827 when he became Police Magistrate at Newcastle.

Because of the penal aspect at Port Macquarie, immediate settlement was restricted. Those restrictions were reviewed in 1830 and the authorities agreed to accept the applications which had been made for grants along the Macleay. Subsequently, in 1835 a surveyor was despatched to the area where he surveyed 812 acres for a Samuel Onions (ironmonger East King St Sydney), 1,306 acres for Captain E. L. Adams, 640 acres for Lieutenant Trappaud and 2,560 acres for John Verge (an architect of Upper Sussex St., Sydney). The two army officers, who were stationed at Port Macquarie were no doubt attracted by a desire to possess land rather than to pioneer this new country. The lot for Samuel Onions was on the present site of East Kempsey and was officially granted on June 6, 1836. Before this date however, Onions apparently had arranged to sell his grant to Enoch W. Rudder (a merchant of Spring St Sydney), for Rudder himself, in his memoirs, stated that he first went to the Macleay in March 1835, and that he, and his companions John Henry Sullivan and Benjamin Sullivan were the only three Europeans there.

Rudder and his party followed the same route taken by Wright in his expedition of 1826. Until a regular shipping service was commenced this was the main access route to the Macleay, the head of navigation of the Maria River becoming known as Boat Harbour.

J. H. Sullivan took up a selection on the southern side of the river a few miles above Kempsey. He called his property "Calatina". Captain Adam's grant was about two miles south of Kempsey on what was then the track to Boat Harbour.

On his first visit, Rudder also wrote that he commenced the construction of a hut and turned the first furrow in the area. He soon saw possibilities of the district and subdivided part of his grant into allotments, naming it the township of Kempsey.

The "Herald" of November 14, 1836 ran the following advertisement:- "Village of Kempsey, 35 allotments for sale by James & Co. on the 26th November. The highroad to New England and Liverpool Plains runs through the Village of Kempsey. A great many of the waterside allotments have been sold at £25 per acre by private contract."

Settlements had been made in New England as early as 1827, but Rudder's auctioneers certainly had a vivid imagination in referring to a high road through Kempsey in 1836—the first bullock team did not reach Armidale till 1855 the journey taking three months.

The name Kempsey was selected by Rudder in memory of the valley of Kempsey, in Worcestershire, England. Rudder brought his wife and nine children to Kempsey in January, 1837. Only two acres of ground had been cleared at this stage, but Rudder writes that they soon had "cleared and sown the first ten acres of land and had imported a few excellent cows at an average price of £10 per head, also a few sheep and pigs".

Assigned to Rudder were "ten or twelve convicts of the ordinary criminal type besides several others of a superior class called specials, literally gentlemen of education". These "specials" most likely included some poor unfortunates who had been transported for what today we would consider trifling political offences. They were employed (according to Rudder's son) in "fitting duties as overseer, storekeeper and family tutor".

Rudder carried out experiments with various crops, vegetables, fruit trees and grapevines. Quite a large area was cleared to sow the first crop of wheat on the Macleay, early crops yielding up to 60 bushels to the acre. "Rust" soon made its presence felt however, and became so bad that wheat growing had to be abandoned.

As the low-lying land across the river from Rudder's Kempsey was better adapted for a town and as a site for a wharf for shipping purposes, stores and buildings gradually began to appear on the Verge and Smith lands.

Among the first settlers in this area, now known as Central Kempsey, was Thomas Bradbury, who built and opened the first store, which he continued to run until his death in 1874. The first inn was built and opened in 1840 by James Thompson, a carpenter by trade, who built many of the original houses in Kempsey. In 1842 the settlements on either side of the river were linked by a ferry. This ferry was owned and operated by Enoch Rudder and for many years a charge of fourpence was made for each crossing.

In 1856 a Government surveyor laid out the township of West Kempsey, thus making three areas of settlement—the original site now became known as East Kempsey, despite the protests of Enoch Rudder. In 1859 the centre of law and administration was moved from Belgrave Falls to West Kempsey. Some schools and a post office had been established and there were regular visits from the clergy at Port Macquarie. The population of East Kempsey was recorded as being 150, West Kempsey 212 and the remainder of the river 1,001.

Central Kempsey is situated on subdivisions of part of what were William Smith's and John Verge's grants. One hundred and nine acres on the northern side of what now is Belgrave Street had been granted to Smith in 1850. Following his death in 1863, part of his estate was subdivided and sold by his wife. Verge's grant was along the southern side of Belgrave Street, Verge being instrumental in frustrating the progress of this section of Kempsey by refusing to sell any of his grant. Although he did grant leases, they were not of sufficient duration to encourage businessmen to erect buildings of a permanent nature. Mr W. T. Dangar, who arrived in Kempsey in 1858, commenced business as a saddler in a weatherboard shop which he erected on a block of land (fronting the southern side of Belgrave Street) which he was able to lease from John Verge for a period of fourteen years at a rental of £1 per acre per year. These conditions persisted until the early 20th century when the Supreme Court ordered the sale of the property.

Some of the older residents will still remember the evening in 1907 when a great fire destroyed most of the buildings on Barsby's side of Smith Street from Belgrave Street, to the Methodist Church (now the site of the A.N.Z. Bank). This fire, disastrous as it was, proved a blessing as it erased some of the very old and dilapidated buildings in the area and allowed their replacement with some of the buildings that still grace the street today. The village was proclaimed a municipality in 1886, incorporating East, West and Central Kempsey. The first mayor was P. C. Hill.

Shipping provided the only means of transport for goods in the early days and therefore played a vital part in the further settlement of the Macleay, as it was also for all the rivers along the coast. The most usual cargoes were timber, maize and livestock as well as passengers. Small schooners and ketches were the first on the river, and the usual charge was half the value of the cargo. These iniquitous freights caused John Verge to invest in the schooner "Rose of Eden", built near Frederickton by Chas. Lawson. This led to the establishment of quite a large shipbuilding industry in the 1840s. Yards were established by D. O'Callaghan, a Mr Bartly, and some Scotsmen, Messrs Newton, Ferrier & Malcolm. Another Scot, John Stuart, set up a shipyard at a spot just inside Grassy Head *circa* 1840.

Pit sawn timber was used by Stuart to build some particularly fine deep-sea barques, many of which roamed the seven seas. One particularly famous barque built by Stuart was the "Royal Tar" of 598 tons, built at Nambucca Heads of bloodwood and bluegum, fully coppered below the water, and copper-fastened throughout. The largest colonial built vessel up to the turn of the last century, she was owned by William Marshall and traded around the Pacific, going as far as Japan and North America. In 1893 she was registered in the name of William Lane, and conveyed the New Australia Association visionaries—including the future Dame Mary Gilmore—to Montevideo

to found their utopian settlement the same year. As history has shown, their dreams failed mainly because they were all equal: none was willing to do any work, but all were ready to give orders! The "Royal Tar" however, sailed on, being owned later by the famous Auckland shipowner, J. J. Craig.

W. Marshall has already been mentioned in connection with his small steamers, but he also was engaged in shipbuilding on the Macleay.

Kempsey is not of course the only settlement on the river, and Frederickton was named after Frederick Chapman who established a station at Yarrabandini in 1849. In 1852, he commissioned surveyor Darke to survey portion of his land at the junction of Christmas Creek and the Macleay River. Part of this was subdivided into the township known as Frederickton.

Jerseyville was named after the Earl of Jersey, who was Governor of N.S.W. at the time, while Gladstone perpetuates the maiden name of his wife, having been named in her honour.

Smithtown was originally part of Gladstone, being called West Gladstone until 1877 when the residents petitioned that the new post office there be named Smithtown. At that time Smithtown had two pubs, a smithy and a store.

The story of the Manning River follows pretty much the same line as the Macleay, but the first settlement began shortly before that just described. Oxley's 1818 journey of exploration brought him to the site of Harrington, then to the Farquhar Lake ("Old Bar"). On October 24 William Wynter received 2,560 acres (4 square miles) bounded on three sides by rivers, and he named the property "Taree" which means wild fig fruit. As on the Macleay, the locals turned to timber getting and, as the land was cleared, to farming, then shipbuilding to take their produce to market. The first schooners were owned by the cedar traders, and the "Taree", a 60-ton schooner, was built near the present town for the service to the Manning and also to Port Macquarie. She was registered in Sydney in 1834, and is probably the same "Taree" owned by Francis Girard, that was the second vessel to enter the Clarence, as already described.

The village of Taree came into being when Henry Flett, another landowner on the river, set aside one hundred acres to be subdivided for this purpose. The village became a reality on December 19, 1854, fully eighteen years after Kempsey was founded. Early homes followed the usual method of construction for the times, being made of red and white mahogany, tallow wood and stringybark trees. Later they were of split slabs, with bark roofs and bare earthen floors. Window glass was unknown and sacking did for curtain material. The usual arrangement was for these cabins to consist of only one room, and the essential fireplace and chimney was built of the least combustible material available, stone if possible, otherwise sun-dried brick. The interior of these cabins was spartan to say the least. The poorer settler, small farmer, labourer or convict, furnished his shack with homemade stools, table and bunk. Packing cases, if available, made chests, seats and all manner of useful furniture.

The slightly better-off settler, the trader, craftsman, doctor, etc., migrated to the colony with a wife and perhaps family, and brought with them some of their best furniture, maybe an iron tent-bed, and if possible a fuel stove for cooking. They would live in a two-roomed shack, but under the civilising influence of a woman, a stone or wooden floor and a ceiling of whitewashed hessian would lend a touch of "class". The wealthy, of course, lived much as they did in Sydney or anywhere else, in fine homes with rich furnishings, but there were not many such as these on the rivers at the time. The serious student of such matters can readily see these types of homes at several locations, but probably the best would be the "Australiana Village" at Wilberforce near Windsor, N.S.W.

As well as timber getting on the Manning there were large-scale vineyards, and sheep and cattle were grazed. A Mr McDonald and John See grew corn in the area for the Sydney Market.

In time of flood the river has been known to rise up to sixty feet. The great floods were in 1857, 1866 and 1929. The municipality of Taree was gazetted on 26th March, 1885. The last coach ran to the town on the 3rd February, 1923, and the following day the first steam train arrived.

Mr and Mrs Joe Dose of Croki on Jones Island in the Manning River remember the times when numerous vessels would lie at Croki awaiting a suitable bar, among them being the "Boambee", "Corra Lynn", the "Croki" which they remember as a long narrow-gutted four masted steamer, not to mention the "Maianbar". In those days local transportation on the river was by "Twenty Ton" open cutters —virtually open boats with a large hatchway and a mere gangway around the sides. These boats were sometimes pressed into service for picnic outings when everyone would go along; picnic hampers and children in the hold, adults around the sides and bunting everywhere. It must have been the aquatic equivalent of a hay ride.

The Nambucca river was probably discovered by a party searching for the vessel "William Caesar" which had been seized by convicts in July, 1817. In November, 1818, the "Nancy" ran about 70 miles north of Newcastle and sailed into a bay beyond Smoky Cape—Trial Bay of course. Two days later, sailing north, she hauled inshore and

17

sighted what was undoubtedly the entrance to a river, but apparently no effort was made to explore it.

The ubiquitous John Oxley, on his trip to survey Port Macquarie in 1820 was ordered to explore the Macleay and also the new river seen to the north thereof. Accordingly on the 2nd December he examined the entrance of the Nambucca from a small boat, but did not succeed in crossing the bar. On the 4th December Mr Kent, accompanying Oxley, did manage to enter the river and examine the country along its banks. It would seem that this was later forgotten, because in 1838 Lieutenant Henderson, who was visiting N.S.W., referred to the Nambucca as an unexplored river running parallel to and north of the Macleay.

Cedar getters began to work the Nambucca in 1842 but owing to the difficulty in getting the cedar out of the river, the industry was temporarily abandoned, and was recommenced later, continuing until as late as 1871. The site of the village of Nambucca was gazetted on 21st October, 1870. The village area was 420 acres in extent, with a further 469½ acres in the suburban area. The man who had the distinction of being the first white man to settle at the Heads was a fisherman named Lane. He squatted in a small but comfortable bark shack near the river and devoted his time to fishing and ferrying the odd traveller across the river. In 1867 when James Allan arrived on the river, Lane was already settled at the Heads, but how long he had been there no one seems to know. He had the place to himself and made a decent living as ferryman, charging 1 penny per trip. In 1867 there were about fifty people settled on the Nambucca (as it was then called) and the majority were in timber, both cedar and hardwood, though there was some spasmodic maize growing. The first general store was opened in 1884 by Mr and Mrs Robert Gordon, who also kept the hotel next door. Gordon was also responsible for the first church to be built, which was the Presbyterian, followed by the Catholic Church, built by a Mr Boulton. Some time in the 1890s the hotel and store were burnt down and their contents destroyed.

During 1898 arrivals and departures of shipping at the Heads totalled 277, aggregating 13,513 tons. Exports included 2,149,702 super feet of sawn hardwood, 29,000 cubic feet of girders, 8,000 spokes, 98,000 shingles, 25,000 feet of cedar, 40,014 sacks of maize, 1,800 pigs, 1,020 cases of eggs and 25 coops of poultry. These are good figures when we consider the state of the bar, which was never good. Local transport up and down the river was by drogher or small boat, from the Heads up to Macksville and the other settlements along the river.

The Davis family, originally from Davistown, Brisbane Water, were known far and wide as excellent shipwrights. A Nambucca Aboriginal, Lambert Waddy, became a fine shipwright following training by Mr Ned Davis. Much of the timber used was pit sawn at Nambucca Heads on the eastern slopes of what is now known as McClung's Hill but was formerly Billy Goat Hill.

But whatever did they do to amuse themselves in country districts? They could not switch on radios or television nor play records that continued for half an hour without being changed. Something that may tend to be forgotten is the fact that working hours were very much longer and wages, in many cases, were so low as to be meagre. Transport was slow and not readily available, as it is now, to the great majority of people. But in spite of all this people did not go without amusements and entertainment. Environment naturally influenced some of the activities and the Nambucca people made use of the river—surfing only became the vogue in the early years of this century. Regattas and sculling races were held at Macksville. The droghers, local small vessels which normally collected logs, pigs, produce, etc., were now and then put into use for moonlight

Drogher "Perseverance" near Copmanhurst.

excursions or to carry folk to Warrell Creek Crossing for picnics or to attend sports that were periodically held there. Great washing down of decks was done and flags were strung to make the old "punts" look as festive as possible.

Byron Bay and the Brunswick and Tweed Rivers were surveyed in 1828 by Captain Rous, but it was not until 1869 that the "Gneering", a stern wheel paddler, became the first steamer to enter the Tweed. Of this pioneer, the "Clarence and Richmond Examiner" wrote, at the time, "She is by no means the finest specimen of steam naval architecture and her trim on entering the river was anything but pleasing to the nautical eye. Her boilers and machinery are placed aft, close to the stern, and as she only had a couple of tons of goods on board, she was very much down by the stern, so much so indeed that her fore foot and part of her keel forward were thrown out of the water. Had she not had a smooth bar to deal with she would have been swamped before getting into the river. The greatest consolation about the matter is that when such a tub as the "Gneering" in such trim could cross our bar in safety, a suitable vessel could trade here with ease." The forecast of this early writer, of trading with ease, was never realised by vessels attempting to enter this river. It has remained to this day a difficult crossing.

A new era of progress dates from about 1880. The birth of butter-making on the northern rivers was practically concurrent with a reduction of sugar duties. Cane growers, fearing that the reduction of the tax on imported sugar would ultimately leave them without a market, turned their attention to other means of employing their land.

In the early days of settlement, before dairying was commenced in a commercial way the main north coast crop was maize, and at first the prices were good. Farmers succeeded timber getters on the Richmond and Tweed Rivers and maize appeared to be the most profitable crop. Later on however, increased production and large scale imports caused the bottom to fall out of the market, so many farmers tried other crops such as wheat, cotton, barley, potatoes, coffee, bananas, tobacco and sugar cane. But maize remained the staple crop and in 1869 the Clarence district exported no less than 762,123 bushels.

Early dairying attempts were only partially successful, and the obstacles were depressingly severe. The scrub was cut down and burned, but prolific crops of jungle weeds, including ink weed and wild tobacco, appeared to spring up almost from the hot ashes.

The first cows milked were rather scrubby animals from beef cattle stations and this type provided the first dairy herds of the Richmond-Tweed districts. Timber getters, sawyers and maize farmers, as well as a few other inhabitants, were glad of fresh milk and more and more cows were bred and brought in. Individual families probably made their own butter over a century ago, but it was many years before any thought was given to sending butter away for sale. Indeed, as late as the 1880s South Coast butter came via Sydney to the North Coast, salted in kegs.

In 1845 a sailing vessel arrived in Sydney with three kegs of butter from farms on the Clarence. In the early stages each farmer made his own butter even if it was to be sent by sea to Sydney, and the cream was obtained by placing milk in shallow dishes and allowing the cream to rise to the surface. It was a tedious process and at the mercy of the weather. In hot weather cheese was made.

The introduction of the separator revolutionised the process, but machines were costly and if a farmer bought one and wished to avoid much manual labour he had then to buy a steam engine to run it. Accordingly, groups of farmers banded together in a simple co-operative effort. They constructed a building, bought a separator, butter churn and steam plant, and brought their milk daily to this depot for conversion to butter, which was sent away, well salted, to Sydney. Refrigeration was way beyond the means of these groups and because of the climate the product arrived in varying conditions, to be sold at lower prices than South Coast butter. If not sold within a week it often went bad.

When clearings began to appear, rye grass, cocksfoot and couch covered a wide area from the Brunswick to Byron Bay, and inland towards the Richmond. These grasses were not satisfactory for butter production and in addition the English grasses which served well enough on the South Coast proved unsuitable to the hotter northern climate. The hot summer days dried them up in the red soil, and a weary search was made for a grass suitable to local conditions.

It was Mr Edwin Seccombe of Wollongbar, who discovered *paspalum* largely by accident, and the discovery came at a time when many farmers were despairing of ever finding a grass which would be suitable to that type of soil and climate, and would suit butter production.

Mr Seccombe came to the Richmond from Nowra about 1891, when the richest areas of the big scrub had been cut, and the farming community, many of whom had come from the South Coast, were seeking to develop dairying in the new area. He was an amateur botanist and when he came to Wollongbar he wasted no time in learning of the local conditions. He realised that English grasses were not suitable and carried out careful experiments with small quantities of seed he had sent to him from all parts of the world. Many experiments failed but he was watching a Japanese clover plant when an intruding plant caught his attention. It thrived, had lush leaves and a stalk of seed. This seed he planted in a new plot and it spread rapidly. He found that this was *paspalum* from the Melbourne Botanic

Gardens, but nobody had thought of it as a pasture grass in northern areas. Seccombe watched the milk production of some cows he grazed on the plot and was satisfied that he had found the answer to the problem. The cows gave a plentiful supply of rich creamy milk and the grass spread like wildfire. This would have been late 1892 and by the turn of the century there were tens of thousands of acres under *paspalum*. Edwin Seccombe died in 1915, but his discovery lives on.

After the first butter factory was opened in 1889 at Spring Hill (Wollongbar) there were similar moves in many small areas and by the time arrangements were under way to create a central co-operative Co. (Norco), following the historic meeting at Clunes at the end of 1892, there were small factories operating, none of which had modern refrigeration plant, and, as said earlier, the product was often of poor quality. The industry was neither profitable nor promising and the pioneers showed remarkable tenacity. It was this position that induced the farmers to discuss the idea of a large, modern, central butter factory, complete with the latest in refrigeration, to take the place of the smaller units, each of which had about 30 suppliers.

In November 1894, a contract was let for the construction of the factory for Norco which was completed the following June. The Co-operative was founded during the worst financial crisis in the country's history—the depression of the 1930s not withstanding. It was little wonder that it was hard to raise the money to float the company in 1893—the year that the banks crashed, ruining thousands; nor were financial troubles over when the factory was opened. The machinery had to be paid for. At one stage it had looked as if the factory would not be built, as the bank would not advance the money, but Mr George Reading, later Managing Director for many years, used his own credit and influence to ensure the necessary finance.

The first individual supplier to the new factory at Byron Bay on the day it received the first cream, 5th June, 1895, was Mr Thomas Armstrong of Cooper's Shoot. He brought in his cream in a cart. He had arrived in Ballina by the S.S. "Lismore" in September, 1882, and found a rugged land. He came from Kangaloon, near Bowral, with empty pockets, to seek his fortune. He had no friends, but he had health and the grit and determination to succeed.

For a time he worked at cane planting near Ballina, then, in 1886, he acquired a 472-acre selection at Cooper's Shoot, near Bangalow. There were no neighbours, times bad and money scarce, but the scrub was felled and burnt, and cows acquired. The opening of the butter factory at Byron Bay found Tom Armstrong the first and only individual supporter. For over 50 years he remained an active supporter of the co-operative method.

An amusing anecdote used to be told by Mr Fred Reading, a pioneer director of Norco, of the early days of the old Byron Creek (Bangalow) butter factory before the Babcock tester was introduced in the nineties. Suppliers were then paid simply so much per gallon for their milk and one farmer, who was suspected of "milking the iron cow" came along one day with milk in which the startled observers saw bullfrogs swimming! Explaining the phenomenon, the farmer said that it had been a hot night and to keep the milk cool, he had placed it in the little creek beside his farm. "That is all right this time", he was told, "but next time it would be better when you put the can in the creek to keep the lid on." The Norco Factory at Byron Bay would not have opened when and where it did had it not

21

been for the fact that the owners of the little ships then trading to the bay had promised to provide cold storage space for their modest shipments of butter.

Coraki is a quiet, beautiful spot where the north and south arms of the Richmond River meet. In fact, the Aborigines give the meaning of the name "Coraki" as "meeting of the water". It is difficult to envisage today the Coraki of yesteryear, when transport was almost entirely by water, and Coraki was the busiest inland port on the Richmond River.

In 1849, when Coraki was founded by William Yabsley, Lismore was a small cattle station, and Casino consisted of one store and an hotel. Even in the fifties, the gold rush years, Coraki grew, due to the extraordinary energy of William Yabsley and his sons. Cedar was the main industry on the river and attracted many newcomers. Working bullocks were in short supply, and Mr Yabsley designed and built a circular training ring for them and was soon able to supply well-broken teams to the cedar-cutters.

Orders were filled for small river boats, and also a contract for two Government bridges. A small trading store was opened at Coraki for the convenience of cedar-cutters, as supplies were difficult to obtain due to the dangers of crossing the shallow bar at the mouth of the river.

In 1856, the schooner "Coraki" was launched at Coraki and ran to Sydney for many years. The shipyard was growing and some of the sons of the pioneer settlers went to work there.

Probably the first sport on the river was horse racing. Races were held at Casino and Coraki in the early fifties. The first racecourse was located at the rear of the police station, where the old winning post—of prickly ti-tree, remained intact for about 70 years until destroyed by fire. Mr William Yabsley, one who assisted in erecting the post, frequently drew attention to the great durability of ti-tree. About 1878 a new track was cleared on the flat, south of Spring Hill and subsequent races were held there.

Mr Yabsley took great pride in keeping the racecourse, grandstand and the modern appointments he provided, in unsurpassable order, and his ceaseless efforts and expenditure in this respect greatly advanced racing and made Coraki Jockey Club famous.

The main races were held on New Year's day, and in the nineties there were regular attendances of upwards of 2,000 people. By 1933 when the grandstand at Coraki Racecourse was demolished, it seemed that a decline in racing outside the capital centres had taken place and prospects for country racing were dwindling.

In the fifties, too, a school was opened at Coraki House for the apprentices and the Yabsley boys and girls. These schoolboys built the next ship which was launched at Coraki named "The Schoolboy" for them—a barque which later sailed from Melbourne to the Richmond in the record time of four days. She was launched in the flood of 1864.

There were tremendous changes at Coraki during the 1860s due to the influx of new settlers who took up almost all the river bank land under the provisions of the Robertson Act. Many more ships arrived on the river and enormous amounts of cedar and pine were exported.

The plan of Coraki village was made in 1866 by surveyor Donaldson and the first land was sold at auction in Casino the following year. Joseph Edmondson opened the first general store on what is now known as Richmond Terrace and William Chalmers built the first hotel, "The Coraki Hotel", for Mr Kyran Nolan.

One of the much talked about events of the sixties was the arrival of steam-propelled vessels on the river. It was W. T. Yeager, who brought the first steam drogher, the "Keystone" to the Richmond in 1863. Mr Yeager gave a pleasure trip to the people of Coraki with this new stern-wheel steamer. The "Keystone" held her place on the river until she was scrapped in 1890.

The first resident Presbyterian minister on the Richmond, Rev. Thom, came to Coraki in the 1860s and it was he who in 1866 brought the first sugar cane cuttings from the Hunter River to the farmers at Coraki. It was his tragic death by drowning that led to the introduction of the first ferry punt soon afterwards.

The Rev. Holland from Port Macquarie visited Coraki in 1869 and conducted experiments in sugar-making. Soon afterwards a sugar mill was built by William Chalmers on James Hunter's property at Codrington. Other mills, including that of the MacKinnon Brothers, came into production quickly.

The sugar obtained, subject to Rev. Holland's directions, was produced under exceptionally crude conditions. A huge log was squared and made perfectly level on top. The cane was placed on this, then two rollers attached to another enormous log, weighted to about five tons, were placed on the cane and, passing over it, crushed out the juice, which was caught in vessels and subsequently boiled and allowed to crystallize in open boilers.

During the sixties and early seventies, the first regattas which were arranged by John Yabsley, brother to W. Yabsley senior, were held at Coraki. They became an annual event on 24th May. Rowing in those days was considered to be "the" sport, and settlers from all over the river competed in the two-oars, four-oars and double sculls, while huge crowds looked on from the banks. Skiffs were always used, no outriggers. These were all built by boatbuilders on the Richmond. John Yabsley built several of them. The principal rowers for the champion races were Steve Newby, F. Fredericks, Sam Cooke, John McDonnell, Denny Feathers and others. Later on, Fredericks obtained skiffs from Sydney which were faster than the local boats and won all the races.

In later years, Jim Paddon and his son, Evans Paddon, both world champions, Snowy Burns and Roy Dolby, Australian champions, defended their titles on many occasions on this fine stretch of water. Other big names in sculling at Coraki were Major Goodsell, Frank Scroope, J. McLaren and Fisher.

The Coraki Rowing Club was active for almost half a century. All classes of boats, butcher boats, single and double sculls, were housed in the boatshed which was situated in front of the present A. E. Kelly's butcher shop.

The great event of 1870 at Coraki was the launching of the steam barque "Examiner" from the Yabsley shipyard. Two years later she was ashore on a sandbank at the mouth of the Clarence River, but in five months the big vessel was refloated, and Captain Yabsley offered a free trip to Sydney on her to all the men who had helped in the amazing feat of refloating her. With the tremendous increase in river traffic, small wonder—for two of the Richmond's largest shipowners lived there—it was quite the usual sight at the Coraki wharves to see five or six oceangoing steamers, with river boats and droghers adding to the busy scene. Because the Upper Richmond was shallow, all passengers and freight to and from Casino were transshipped at Coraki. Australia's maritime history reveals few men as capable as William Yabsley, or with such business acumen as W. T. Yeager, but their success was also due to the fine type of early settler who assisted them.

In 1878 there was a second sale of town allotments for Coraki, and we note in William Yabsley's diary that he cut and cleared the main streets and had great difficulty in removing a huge fig tree. There was a Government grant for a telegraph line from Casino to Coraki and the ferry punt was subsidised by the Government. Mr Solling opened a branch of the Commercial Bank in the Yabsley home until an allotment was purchased and a bank building erected the following year with Mr Oakes as manager.

William Yabsley senior launched his last vessel "The Beagle" from the Coraki shipyard. This was later sold for the then enormous sum of £5,000. Already the Yabsley interests were being diverted to their grazing properties, and the sale of the now famous "Examiner" and the "Schoolboy" followed.

The year 1880 brought tragedy to Coraki with the death of William Yabsley senior, who was drowned on the river steamer "Vesta". It also saw the final conversion of the old shipyard into a sawmill.

In 1886 two outstanding men settled in the town—Captain John Storey and Louis F. Benaud. Captain Storey was district agent for the North Coast Steam Navigation Co., the local office of which was at Coraki for many years and its growth in the nineties owed much to him. He was a popular figure and several times mayor.

Louis F. Benaud selected Coraki as the most promising centre to establish his paper "The Richmond River Herald"—familiarly known as "The Pink'un" because it was printed on a pinkish type of paper. It is still considered to have been one of the best newspapers on the lower river and had a wide circulation.

In August, 1828, Captain Rous left Sydney to make hydrographic surveys of the North East Coast of Australia. On this trip he entered the Tweed River, which had already been discovered by surveyor Oxley. Not knowing the previous survey, he named this river the "Clarence", a name which was later transferred to the big river to the south. It was on this trip that Captain Rous crossed the bar of the Richmond River and dropped anchor in deep smooth water at a spot now known as Shaw's Bay. H.M.S. "Rainbow"'s boats were launched and soundings were taken in North Creek and up the main river as far as the Broadwater at the outlet of Tuckean Swamp, a distance of about 17 miles. On his return to Sydney, Captain Rous named the river the Richmond for the Duke of Richmond and Lennox, an ancient English title. Lighthouse Hill is marked Lennox Head on Rous's chart, a copy of which, with his published report, can be seen at the Richmond River Historical Society's Museum at Lismore.

In 1828 when Captain Rous first saw the river, its banks were thickly covered with mangrove swamps on one side and with jungle-like masses of cedar and other rare trees on the other, the "Big Scrub", as it was called, was so thick that it was impossible to walk or drive through it, and white settlers in later years told how they had to cut the overhanging foliage away from their ship's masts before they could pass up the river.

The "Big Scrub" extended from the north bank of the Richmond River to the McPherson Range in the north. The red soil was covered with an exceedingly rich mould from the thick vegetation. West of the "Big Scrub" there were open rolling plains and pine ridges more suitable for grazing. The main river, often called the South Arm, was navigable for vessels under two hundred tons as far as Irvington, which became the seaport of Casino and the launching place for timber cut in the ranges. The North Arm is winding and narrow but could accommodate large oceangoing vessels as far upstream as Lismore.

It was not until 1839 that the first white men came to settle in the wide Richmond Valley. They were two squatters, Clay and Stapleton, who drove their tired herds across the Richmond Range from the Broadwaters on the Clarence River to Tabulam and marked out the boundaries of a station which they named Casino.

A squatter is a pastoralist, or grazier, who occupies, but doesn't purchase, a portion of Crown Land and stocks it with sheep or cattle after procuring a licence from the Government. In 1839 the licence fee was £10 a year, plus a small charge for the number of stock carried. The land occupied was called a run, or station. Australian wool was selling for high prices in London and men from all walks of life came to N.S.W., after purchasing sheep or cattle and set out from Sydney to establish stations on unclaimed land.

It cost over a thousand pounds to start a sheep station, and most of that money had been borrowed by the N.S.W. squatters at a high rate of interest. Soon after they came to the Richmond River there was a great financial depression and many of the Sydney banks closed. So great was the panic that sheep sold for as little as 10 cents or 15 cents a head. To meet the emergency, a squatter from the Yass district, Henry O'Brien, introduced the Russian custom of boiling down his unsaleable sheep and cattle in large iron vats and extracting the fat, or tallow. This was packed in wooden casks, pressed down with a heavy weight and shipped to England where it was sold for about three pounds a hundredweight and was used for making soap and candles. The price of sheep soon rose to six shillings a head and a good bullock was woth £2 10s. 0d. The income from this new industry, plus the sale of hides, did much to save the colony

from total bankruptcy. In 1847, 99,847 hundredweight of tallow was exported from the Colony and earned over £11,181 for the squatters.

The first boiling-down plant on the Richmond River was built by F. C. Fawcett at Fairymount in 1846. Clark Irving soon built one on Tomki Station and an elaborate series of steam vats was built at Tatham by the owners of Wooroowoolgan Station across the river. Tunstall and Lismore Stations also boiled down their unsaleable stock. During the Crimean War, the price of tallow rose to £60 ($120) a ton, but boiling down was discontinued soon afterwards on the Richmond River, when better ways were found of selling surplus stock.

It was natural that Casino should be the main settlement on the Richmond River at first, and the meeting place of the land and police courts. Casino was the squatters' town and through it ran the only track from the Clarence to Limstone and Moreton Bay. Even before a survey had been made, or an allotment sold, a Clerk of Petty Sessions was appointed (1856). When Charles Moore became Clerk in 1854, his first job was to build a slab cottage which was used as a courthouse during many years and also served as a church or dance hall, depending on the occasion. Sometime in the 1850s a hotel, the "Durham Ox", was built near the river crossing, for journeys were long in those days and the tracks were very rough.

The squatters also guaranteed a living for a local doctor, Mr W. T. Barker, after whom Barker Street is named. Casino became a Municipality in 1880, following Lismore's lead. The timber trade was moving up the river and this became the town's main industry, until the breaking-up auction sales of the big squatting stations, and the quick development of dairying.

Ballina became the centre of the cedar industry, for it was there that the logs were loaded onto the vessels to go to Sydney. It was sometimes called Deptford, and there is some doubt about the origin of that name, but it seems clear that the name, Ballina, was derived from the Aboriginal word "Balluna" meaning "mouth of a river".

With the arrival of more sawyers and more timber schooners, a settlement was started at West Ballina in 1851, and saw-pits were built at the end of Martin and Norton Streets. Joe Eyles (owner of the schooners "Sancho Panza" and "Josephine") and Fred Bacon, built a small hotel on the river bank and called it the "Sawyer's Arms".

Soon, in 1855, Captain George Easton was appointed as Pilot and provided with five boatmen to help him in his dangerous work of guiding the flimsy little sailing ships across the bar and around the sand shoal in the river. His was a busy life as shipping increased. In 1869, 242 sailing vessels and 12 steamers voyaged from the Richmond River to Sydney in one year, carrying over three million super feet of cedar. The bar was very dangerous and thirty-nine vessels were detained, unable to cross the bar for as long as seventeen weeks.

Ballina grew with the shipping industry and became an important seaport. The breakwater, which was so badly needed to assist shipping, was begun in 1880 and resulted in bottling up Shaw's Bay and in the building of the Missingham Bridge.

A municipality was formed in 1883 and elected William Clement as first mayor. When the Colonial Sugar Refinery's Mill was built at Broadwater in 1881, the sugar punts travelled from Ballina by way of the new canal and Fisher Creek, where the Bagot Brothers had moved their timber mill. Breakwater and factory workers swarmed into town.

When William Wilson and his wife took up a station on the north arm of the river (1844/5) they were the first of the Richmond River squatters to come by sailing vessel. After that was wrecked on the bar at Ballina, it is said they floated up the river on a raft. They named their station "Lismore" for the picturesque island on Lock Linnhe in Scotland, which they had visited on their honeymoon.

The present city was only a cattle station for many years until Surveyor Perrcorne, in 1855, made a plan of a village there, in what was once Mr Wilson's house paddock. Timber workers and station hands bought allotments and many were sold to Mr Wilson himself. Henry Brown built an accommodation house near the creek which bears his name, also a small slab schoolhouse and he and Tom Foley and some others paid the expenses of some teachers from Sydney. But the young men did not like the little timber village and a public school was opened in 1862.

As more settlers arrived in the district, great changes occurred at Lismore. Churches and stores were built and a newspaper, the "Northern Star" was started by William Kelleway in 1876. Lismore was declared a municipality in 1879 and the chemist, James Stocks from Casino, was elected mayor. After a great deal of agitation, bridges were built over Wilson's and Leycester Creeks (1884/5), to replace the ferry punts. Larger steamers soon brought cargo and passengers to the Government Wharf, while the North Coast Steam Navigation Company built a wharf of its own near Fawcett's Bridge.

By the time the railway was opened in 1894, Lismore had become the main business centre on the river.

Land was first selected at Woodburn in 1866 when the Gollans and others landed on the Clarence and walked across to the Richmond. The village of Woodburn grew because it was the terminus for the coaches which ran between the Clarence and Richmond River ports.

North Coast Steam Navigation Co.'s vessel "Tomki" and drogher "Casino" viewed from Fawcett's Bridge. Government Wharf in background.

CHAPTER THREE

New Ships, Wrecks and Competition

In March, 1870, the Clarence & Richmond River Steam Navigation Co. purchased the "Diamantina" from the A.S.N. Co. and the following year added the "Waimea", which was the second screw steamer to be owned by the firm, the first being the "Platypus", bought in 1868. Both these vessels soon passed out of the C. & R. R. S.N. Co. service. The "Waimea" was wrecked at Richmond River Heads on 10th January, 1872, and the service had to be suspended until another vessel could replace her. The "Diamantina" was sold in 1875 as will be told later.

The first "Ramornie", a stern wheel paddle drogher, was built in 1869 for the company and she had a long life on the Clarence River, eventually rotting away. Another small vessel, only 64 feet long, was the 19-ton "Clarence"—bought in January 1873 from the Parramatta River Steam Co. She was eventually wrecked on the Clarence.

1870/1 also saw the wood paddler "Belmore" of 66 tons built for the Company by Stuart & Ferguson on the Macleay. She was eventually lost at Coffs Harbour in March 1893.

In the sixties the C. & R.R.S.N. Co. had a rival in the Clarence & New England S.N. Co., a modest concern which ran the steamer "Helen McGregor" built in 1866 and wrecked on the Clarence River Bar on 12th March, 1875, with the loss of eight lives. The "New England" of 1869 was sold in August, 1879, to the C. & R.R.S.N.

Co. after stranding on the Clarence Bar and she was later to be totally wrecked on 27th December, 1882, at the same bar with the loss of eleven lives including Captain Mann when the wreck broke up.

The drogher "Settler's Friend" of 1866, acquired in 1867, and the "Perseverence" (built in 1872), were both stern wheelers. At 95 tons and 120 feet "Perseverence" was large for a drogher but lasted for many years.

"The Clarence", an iron twin screw steamer of 603 tons, was another of their vessels but in March, 1883, she was sold to the A.S.N. Co. when the Clarence & New England Co. went into liquidation that year. Later she was renamed "Currajong" and was finally sunk by the "Wyreema" off Bradley's Head, Sydney, in 1910.

The little wooden paddler "Catherine" of 23 tons was sold by the C. & R.R.S.N. Co. in 1873 to a new concern, the Manning River Steam Navigation Co. The service to the Manning must have been lacking in efficiency for a group of dissatisfied settlers had formed the Company in opposition to the C. & R. Co. and in 1875 the "Diamantina" was sold to the young firm and with her sale, the C. & R. Co. retired from the Manning trade and left it to the locals. In 1878 the Manning Co. had the iron paddler "Manning" built at Darling Harbour, but on the 30th March, 1881, the "Diamantina" was stranded at the bar and wrecked.

This finished the Manning S.N. Co. and they went broke. The "Manning" was sold, going to John See & Co. and finally the N.C.S.N. Co., being scrapped in 1937. The "Catherine" was sold and broken up not long afterwards, but the cause of it all, the "Diamantina" was refloated and re-registered, finally being scrapped in Townsville as late as 1907.

The Clarence & Richmond River S.N. Co. was running the "Fire Queen" and in 1876 added the famous "City of Grafton", a magnificent sea boat and one that ran for many years.

In April, 1880, they bought the "Queen of the South" and took delivery of "Coraki", both iron screw steamers, and now had quite a respectable fleet of new modern steamers. In 1881, Captain Creer was sent to England to supervise the building of a new passenger vessel to be called "Nymbyn" but in March, 1882, the name was changed to "Tomki", and in May it was decided to improve her passenger accommodation at an extra cost of £1,280. Captain Creer was of course the Commodore of the line.

In the late 1870s another Sydney firm entered the Northern Rivers Trade. The firm was Nicoll Bros. and their fleet included some particularly fine and well-known vessels. The brothers Bruce and George Nicoll started with the "Bonnie Dundee", built at Dundee, Scotland, as were all of their passenger ships. They were all single screw steamers, iron hulled, and of distinctive appearance.

The second ship for Nicolls was the "Richmond" built in 1878 and the "Australian"–their largest so far–followed in 1879. On 10th March, the pretty little "Bonnie Dundee" was tragically lost when she was run down about eight miles south of Newcastle by Howard Smith's "Barrabool", taking the lives of five of her company with her. The "Truganini" was bought from Hobart owners the same year to replace her.

In 1880 the fine little "Lismore" was added to the fleet, and in 1882 the "Casino" followed. This vessel was sold while in Melbourne on her delivery run to the Belfast & Koroit S.N. Co. and thus never traded to the rivers. The same year saw the "Helen Nicoll" arrive but she, too, was sold on arrival in July, this time to John See & Co.

On 21st January, 1884, the "Richmond", when trying to get to sea in bad weather, was driven ashore at Port Macquarie, and was never refloated. She, too, had been sold in April, 1881, to John See and until 1970 her fo'c'sle head could be seen sticking out of the sand in the camping area at Port Macquarie.

The "Australian" was also sold to John See in November, 1880, and she ran until sold to Launceston Owners in 1902 by the N.C.S.N. Co. The "Helen Nicoll" was likewise sold in 1893 to Adelaide. This eliminated the entire first generation of the Nicoll Line as, about 1882, the partnership was dissolved. The two brothers continued in shipping, however, running separate lines under their own names.

In those days passenger accommodation was what was known as the open type, the dining table being in the centre of the saloon and the berths around the sides, screened by curtains. This type of accommodation was not very inviting, both from the point of view of the passenger who was in his berth feeling ill, and of the others who were at meals. It was not very pleasant to be taking a meal while another passenger was being audibly ill in the berth behind you, and it was equally upsetting to the sick passenger to have to put up with the smell of food. These berths were, as stated, around the side of the ship and all passengers laid with their heads forward, against the next one's feet. There is a story told that on one occasion a steward, careful for the cleanliness of the bed linen, asked a passenger who had just come from a stockyard who had gone to bed fully clothed, to take his boots off. This he did, and there was an immediate outcry from the man sleeping aft of him who insisted that he be made to put his boots on again!

It was the Illawarra Company which introduced cabins to coasters in the "Eden", built in 1900.

A Cabin on the S.S. "Orara".

In the eighties another line was formed under the style of Nipper & See. This firm extended its operations to include the Bellinger, Nambucca, and Hastings as well as the Manning Rivers and they found that business was brisk but, in 1884, this partnership too was dissolved and while the "Lubra" remained the property of Mr

Nipper, John See—later Sir John—ran a sizeable fleet. This included the "Fernmount" of 1884, the "Coorong"—an old vessel bought from Adelaide in 1884, the "Bortonious"—later renamed the "Lawrence", another second-hand vessel bought in 1885, the two droghers "Hastings" and "The Grand" both built the same year, the "Lorna" bought from J. T. McKittrick in 1889, and the "Wellington" which came from Lyttelton in 1887 and was to be wrecked in 1892 at Nambucca Heads. His last vessel was the "Burrawong" built new for him in 1890.

He was of course also running at this time the ex-Nicoll Bros. vessels "Australian" and "Helen Nicoll", having lost the "Richmond" at Port Macquarie as already related. He also lost the "Murray", an iron paddler, at the Manning 9th February, 1886. The "Rosedale", acquired from Melbourne in 1883, was another unit of his fleet.

John See nearly lost another vessel in a repeat performance of the "Bonnie Dundee"–"Barrabool" collision on the 7th December, 1886. In this case no less than forty-eight lives were lost when the "Helen Nicoll" cut down Howard Smith's passenger steamer "Kielawarra".

The "Helen Nicoll", under Captain Frazer, was cracking along, heading down the coast having sailed from Grafton earlier in the day. On clearing the bar, Captain Frazer handed over to Mr Knowles, the mate and went to his cabin to write up the log before turning in.

At the time the practice was for south-bound ships to proceed inshore, and north-bound traffic to lay their course further out, to seaward of the Solitaries. The wind was the usual nor'-easter, of about 15 knots, and the night was fine, but the wind was blowing the "Helen Nicoll"'s smoke ahead of her and laying it flat on the sea, as often happens with a following wind.

All unknown to the "Helen Nicoll", Messrs Howard Smith's 964-ton "Kielawarra" had left Sydney for Brisbane and northern ports the day previously, with seventy-one souls aboard, and she was now nearing the Solitaries heading north. Her Master, Nathan Buttray—a man recently returned from 20 years' blackbirding in the islands—intent on making a smart passage, was keeping well inshore and he was actually further inshore than was the "Helen Nicoll". Then the lookout on the "Kielawarra" sighted the "Helen Nicoll"'s lights in the distance and watched them approaching for some minutes. Suddenly they disappeared. The lookout's report brought Captain Buttray to the rail but he saw nothing as the "Helen Nicoll"'s smoke was in the way. Nevertheless, he ordered the helm over and shaped his course to the east. This normal turn to starboard was his undoing, for he was now crossing the "Helen Nicoll"'s bows. The "Kielawarra" was still swinging when the "Nicoll" tore into her side at full speed and ripped it open. The time was 8.20 p.m. and within seven minutes the "Kielawarra" had gone and with her forty-eight lives.

Knowles, on watch on the "Helen Nicoll", briefly saw the lights of another vessel approaching, but then lost them in the smoke. He was not concerned for he was on a south-west course and assumed the stranger would turn east. Apparently he did not realise that the other vessel was inside "Nicoll"'s bows. Moments before impact, Mr Knowles got another brief glimpse of the other steamer's lights, but too late to do more than desperately ring "full astern"!

All vessels built for Nicolls were responsive little greyhounds and the "Helen Nicoll" responded quickly. The commotion brought Captain Frazer from his bunk just in time to see the collision, as the "Kielawarra" was cut down just aft of 'midships. The sound of rending metal and the frightening jolt alerted everyone and they started tumbling out on deck as the "Helen Nicoll", with engines still going full astern, slowly dragged her bows clear of the awful hole. Instantly, tons of water roared in and the "Kielawarra" started to settle. On the deck panic ensued and rose until it reached fearful proportions. Men fought and cursed and trampled all over women and children in their rush for the boats. As the ship heeled further so did the panic. Some men trying to help the women and children were beaten up and shoved aside. When the boats were got away, they swamped, for some leaked and some were overloaded. Others, too hastily lowered, capsized and tossed the screaming mob into the water.

Many did not have lifebelts; those that did obtained them mainly by force. One of the "Helen Nicoll"'s passengers, the Rev. Maurice Grey, jumped from the "Nicoll" to the "Kielawarra" as the ships parted, to render aid, but his humane motive was unheeded by the mob and, worse, some of the other passengers on the "Nicoll", thinking he was abandoning her, followed suit. One missed and, falling into the water, was sucked into the "Kielawarra" and was not seen again.

The good Reverend, seeing assistance was futile in that mob, leaped into the sea with some other "Helen Nicoll" passengers and swam back to their ship. The "Helen Nicoll"'s boats were already in the water rendering aid.

The "Helen Nicoll" was also making water at a dangerous rate and as she backed further away from the doomed "Kielawarra", that ship was seen to raise her bows high, shudder and smoothly glide below the surface. Captain Buttray was last seen on the bridge and it is thought unlikely that he abandoned ship. He did not survive.

31

All survivors were taken aboard the "Helen Nicoll" and Captain Frazer had his crew jettison cargo from the forward hold. The pumps were then able to cope, and she started to limp towards Sydney escorted by the "City of Grafton" and the "Australian" which took the Nicoll's passengers.

The court of enquiry which ensued found the "Kielawarra" mainly to blame for reckless navigation, but Knowles was suspended for three months for not reducing speed earlier when he first saw the lights of the "Kielawarra". As a result of this collision vessels plying the N.S.W. coast were compelled to provide adequate life-boats and lifebelts for all on board.

The Clarence & Richmond River Steam Navigation Co. had not been resting on their laurels, but had been adding to their fleet. They looked primarily to quality rather than quantity, building, in 1887 the "Electra", the first vessel on the coast to be fitted with electric lights. They also acquired the drogher "Irvington" built in 1884 for F.G. Crouch, in April, 1887, while in 1884 they had acquired the "Woodburn" from B.B. Nicoll. Business had so improved by the late eighties that in December, 1888, another reconstruction of the Company became necessary to cover operations. Once again the name of the firm was changed, this time to the "Clarence, Richmond & Macleay Rivers Steam Navigation Co. Ltd." and the capital was increased to £150,000 in £1 shares. At the same time the Sussex Street offices and wharfage to the Company were enlarged and the whole establishment was generally improved. Meanwhile, only one new steamer was added to the fleet during the short period spent under this title. She was the "Kallatina" which came out in 1890, arriving during the great shipping strike in Australia that year and, owing to the fact that her English delivery crew continued to stand by her, she managed to sail on time on her maiden voyage on the coast, while the "Tomki" also managed to get away with a scratch crew. These two ships ran the blockade and maintained a service of sorts until the strike ended.

In the following year, on the 13th August, 1891, to be precise, the two rival concerns, John See & Co. and the Clarence, Richmond & Macleay Rivers S.N. Co. merged, and their respective fleets and interests came at last under the one flag and the one title. The name under this latest reorganisation, became "The North Coast Steam Navigation Co. Ltd" and the combined capital was increased to the sum of a quarter of a million pounds. ($500,000).

In the eighties, owing to the difficulty of making the Richmond and Tweed Rivers suitable for large steamers, the Government built a new jetty at Byron Bay to replace an earlier smaller one that was no longer satisfactory. When this jetty was built there was no railway (that came in 1894) and the country nearby was mostly undeveloped. It was G.W. Nicoll of Sydney who made a start when he sent his steamers there. First the small vessels "Tweed" and "Byron" then the "Excelcior". In the opening years of the new century he continued his trade with the "Cavanba" and the "Noorebar".

George Wallace Nicoll had been trading to the Tweed, Richmond, Coff's Harbour and Woolgoolga as well as Byron Bay with the steamers "Bellinger" built 1884 but sold the same year to Victoria, the "Janet Nicoll" also 1884, the "Tweed" (2), 1890, and "Byron", 1891, both wrecked in 1893 and 1896 respectively, "Chindera" 1895 wrecked at the Tweed the following year and the first "Orara" 1898 also wrecked at the Tweed in 1899.

Bruce Nicoll meanwhile was running a similar service with the "Wyrallah", 1887, "Woodburn" having been sold to the C. & R.R.S.N. Co. in 1884. The "Emma Pyers" was only owned for a short time,

The paddler "City of Grafton" rides serenely on the big flood at Grafton in 1890.
Acknowledgement: Clarence River Historical Society.

the "Bellinger", 1887, followed by the "Richmond" (yet another one!), 1885. He also had a "Tweed" (first) which was built in 1885 and wrecked at Tweed Heads in 1888. Another vessel was the "Tatham" sold in 1904 to Barney Corrigan. Bruce Nicoll seems to have faded from the scene before the turn of the century but G.W. Nicoll carried on until 1905 with the "Wollumbin" (1894) sold the following year to the N.C.S.N. Co. and the "Cavanba" and "Noorebar" early in the 20th century.

Upon the formation of the N.C.S.N. Co., John See became the Managing Director in conjunction with Mr T.R. Allt, who had been the Chairman of the Clarence, Richmond & Macleay Rivers S.N. Co., and who continued in this capacity.

The amalgamation of the two leading firms in the North Coast shipping field naturally resulted in considerable economies and the immediate effect was the lowering of freight and passenger fares, together with the elimination of duplication of effort, and the result was of great benefit to the settlers generally on the rivers that they served. However several firms still owned and operated small fleets, mainly to carry their own produce to Sydney. Among these firms were Messrs Allen Taylor & Co., Langley Bros, and W.G. Yeager, all in the timber trade. Also, of course, there were the two opposing lines of the brothers Nicoll, previously mentioned.

In the early nineties Bruce Nicoll's steamers "Wyarallah" and "Emma Pyers" were purchased by the N.C.S.N. Co. as an attempt to eliminate the opposition, but G.W. Nicoll continued to own ships for nearly 15 years longer. Meanwhile, W.G. Yeager, who owned the "Wyoming" and "Oakland" which were used to carry timber from his sawmill on the Richmond River down to Sydney – had in 1895 introduced the "St George", of 515 tons, into direct competition with the N.C.S.N. Co., in the Richmond Service. As a result he was soon in difficulties and within a few months he sold out to the larger concern.

In 1897 the little paddler "Euroka" of only 170 tons was specially built for the Nambucca River trade. She would most likely be amongst the last seagoing paddle steamers built – certainly for this trade at any rate. She only lasted for thirteen years as she was sold out of the service, to Messrs Valentine, Geary & Co. in 1910. Three years later she reached the end of the road when she piled up on Long Reef in 1913. The Nambucca and Bellinger Rivers in particular were always cursed with shallow, treacherous bars, and only small, specially built vessels were suitable for their service. Even then, several were lost.

On the 29th November, 1900, the famous and popular old "Coraki" was lost on the Macleay entrance, and I will quote direct from an eye-witness account of the event, a Mr O. Notley, now of Copacabana, N.S.W.:–

"I witnessed the wreck of the 'Coraki' in 1900. She was entering in a heavy swell and an easterly wind and on one swell, instead of answering her helm and enabling her course to be straightened up by the use of a 'Leg-o'-mutton' sail forward, she went with the wind and lay broadside on, wallowing in the trough between the swells. The second swell lifted her broadside onto the end of the southern breakwater. She was well and truly holed; the third swell lifted her off and on the incoming tide she drifted about 300 yards upstream

Grafton Wharf in Sussex St Sydney circa 1890.
Acknowledgement: Courtesy of Tyrell's Bookshop.

and sank in the channel. Her 'flying' deck, masts and funnel were above water, and as the days passed she became embedded. As she blocked the use of the port she was 'blown up'. Father's school had a half day holiday and the school children went down and witnessed the operation."

Prior to this, however, the "Coraki" had settled down into the sand so deeply that she had 14 feet of water over her poop and, according to a report in the Sydney "Daily Telegraph" at the time, the "Burrawong" in crossing into the river, had to pass over the poop of the wreck, giving all hands some nasty moments.

So far I have been writing of the years before the railway was constructed along the coastal route between Sydney and Brisbane. The completion of the railway connection throughout the Northern coastal area, the great advance in motor transport and the improvement of main highways out of all recognition, have brought country, only a short time ago referred to as "terra incognita" to a day's run under pleasant conditions from Sydney, thus linking the towns and settlements with each other. These changed conditions have increased the importance of the towns and added to their population. Lismore, for instance, at the head of navigation on the Richmond, seventy miles from the entrance, had a population in 1908 of 6,000 people. By 1935 this had risen to 12,000, and the town was complete with all the amenities of city life: electric light, sewerage, water, gas, and other less important features. Now, forty-odd years later, the population is over 20,000 and Lismore has most of the problems found in any modern city.

When the Richmond-Tweed railway was complete, G.W. Nicoll was running the "Wollumbin" and the "Cavanba" to Byron Bay, Woolgoolga and Coff's Harbour, and in 1904 he added the "Noorebar"

to the service. The "Noorebar" was built by Scott's of Kinghorn in Scotland and "G.W." sent his young son Angus to the old country with the captain to see her completed and to enjoy the delivery voyage out. What an adventure for a young lad — bringing his father's newest ship half around the world!

George Wallace Nicoll was by this time a very sick man, suffering from cataracts and nearly blind. He underwent an operation, but medical science was not as advanced then as it is now and the operation was only partly successful. Also, he had not fully recovered from the time when, returing to Australia on one of his steamers' delivery runs, the crew of runners mutinied and, as he rushed up on deck on hearing the sound of fighting, he was struck down from behind by a mutineer wielding a belaying pin at the companion way. He suffered a fractured skull and brain damage, and maybe this aggravated the cataracts — but in 1904/5 he was no longer able to continue the onerous job of running a shipping company. The N.C.S.N. Co. at once made an offer for the vessels, goodwill and connections, and this offer was accepted.

George Wallace Nicoll, shipowner, died on the 4th November, 1906, at his home at Canterbury, N.S.W. He had lifted the standard of our coasters from small, often slow tramps to a new high; fast, pretty little packets that were the envy of all. His death at the early age of 58 was a tragedy.

In 1904 the North Coast S.N. Co. acquired two small wooden steamers from Messrs Allen Taylor & Co. These were the "Pyrmont" and the drogher "Coopernook", and also the Allen Taylor services to the Manning and Bellinger rivers, although Taylor's retained their other ports.

In 1905 the "Duranbah" joined the fleet. This vessel was built for

T.S.S. "Coraki" passing Farm Cove and Fort Macquarie in the nineties.
Acknowledgement: From the copy in the Mitchell Library.

service to the Tweed, another tricky bar, and she was actually built for "G.W." but arrived after he had sold out. The "Brundah", an 883-ton passenger boat, came out in 1906, followed in 1907 by the "Orara" and the "Yulgilbar", and in 1908 by the "Tintenbar". When nearing completion a dockyard strike threatened to stop work on the "Orara" but the apprentices rallied and she was completed in time for her trials.

As new ships were built, so others were lost, some with tragic results. In 1903 the "Oakland" foundered off Cabbage Tree Island in a whole gale. The vessel, which left Newcastle for the Richmond and Clarence rivers shortly after midnight on Tuesday, foundered off Port Stephens at 4 o'clock on the morning of 26th May. Of those on board 11 persons, including Captain Slater, chief officer Lindgren, chief engineer Fischer, and second engineer Steel were drowned, while seven were saved including second mate J. Howes and Mr T. Gaites, monumental mason of Newcastle, the only passenger. The survivors were picked up by the steamer "Bellinger" on Wednesday morning and brought to Newcastle at 3 o'clock on Friday, 29th May.

Although there had been a heavy swell outside all day, the weather at Newcastle on Tuesday was not at all of a boisterous character. When the "Oakland" set out on her ill-fated voyage there was, therefore, nothing to warn Captain Slater of any special danger ahead, but as the steamer progressed northward the bad sea, which she met as soon as she got out beyond Nobby's increased in violence until it was frequently washing over the bulwarks and flooding the well decks. Soon after Port Stephens' lighthouse was passed, the steamer took a list to port and as this became worse Captain Slater decided to make for Port Stephens. He ran before the sea until abreast of the entrance of the port, and then brought the steamer round sharply, when she was heading a little to the south of west.

By now the "Oakland" had such a severe list that she would not steer in the cross seas, and she was at the mercy of the waves. Her bows canted round to the nor'-nor'-west and she was apparently going to run on to the beach at Cabbage Tree Island. That fate was averted by her taking a sudden plunge and going down head first in about 17 fathoms of water.

Before this, the ship's company had seen that she must inevitably be lost, and had got a life-boat out. Under the circumstances it was a terrible undertaking. The launching had to be done over the port side, with the decks at a very acute angle. In the struggle against these conditions, and the violence of the seas the boat got a couple of holes knocked in her sides by the belaying-pin of one of the davits. Before the job was finished, the men were able to walk on the upturned side of the vessel, and her funnel was just about touching water.

All hands got into the lifeboat, the lines were cut away, she dropped, and immediately capsized. Everyone was thrown out, and, while some succeeded in getting back to the craft again, five of the occupants were lost. The water-tight tanks of the lifeboat kept her afloat, and she was righted. The second engineer, Mr Steel, swam round and gathered up seven oars which had been thrown out, and brought them to the boat. Some of the men got into the boat, and tried to propel her with the oars while the others hung on to the lifelines with their hands, their bodies remaining in the water. It was a hopeless task, as the rowlocks were under water all the time, and no amount of bailing could free the boat sufficiently to permit them to rise above the surface.

S.S. "Oakland" lost off Cabbage Tree Island, 1903.
Acknowledgement: From the copy in the Mitchell Library.

As the boat touched the water the "Oakland" took her forward plunge, a shower of sparks shot out of the funnel showing that the water had got to the fires and the steamer disappeared from sight. That was only about 25 minutes after the list was first noticed.

The first objective of the castaways was Cabbage Tree Island, a mile and a half away. It was soon seen however, that it would be impossible to reach there, and the boat was kept before the seas in an endeavour to make Long or Broughton Island, to the north. The wind was icy cold and the exposure quickly commenced to have its effect.

An hour after the foundering, which occurred about 4 a.m. the cook, H. Bradberry, succumbed, and his body was cast overboard to relieve the weight on the boat. Very little time elapsed before the chief engineer Fischer, who had sat silent all the while, breathed his last sitting upright on the seat. Alick Cargill, the cabin boy, was the next to go. He made a remark to the second mate to the effect that it was grand, then swished his face in the water and died within ten minutes.

It was soon seen that the condition of Captain Slater was very serious and he was lifted into the boat. He only lasted a couple of hours until death came to relieve the awful strain. Before the body was cast overboard the second officer secured the Captain's watch, and retained it through all his subsequent experiences.

As the morning wore on, hope was revived by the sight of a steamer passing south, inside of Broughton Island. They signalled, but to their dismay the vessel passed on. This was the "Bellinger", heading towards Port Stephens. The time was now between 8 and 9 o'clock. Second engineer Steel had sat for some time upright in the bow of the boat. Then suddenly he said "Well, good-bye boys" and leaped overboard, instantly disappearing from view.

When the "Bellinger" made her appearance again, the seaman, John Willberg, who had stuck to one of the oars right through for the purpose of keeping the boat before the seas, if not to propel her in a given direction, hoisted a handkerchief as a signal for assistance. As the steamer drew close to them, the prospect of rescue was too much for the poor fellows, and in their excitement they forgot to steer the boat, and she took the last of her four capsizes. Save in the first instance no lives were lost by this overturning, and the whole of the six lost men who survived the first mishap died in the boat.

Of the skill and courage shown by Captain Tanglin of the "Bellinger" in effecting the rescue, too much cannot be made. She was not a powerful boat, and to manoeuvre her on the edge of the broken water, on a lee shore in the terrible sea which was running, so that it was not even necessary to launch a boat to secure each of the seven exhausted men struggling helplessly in the waves, was a performance as skillful as it was gallant. The men whose lives he saved spoke in warm terms of admiration of the seamanship and kindness of Captain Tanglin.

As to the initial cause of the terrible disaster, there is much that will probably remain for ever a mystery. Some of the seamen who lived through the awful experience formed the opinion that the "Oakland" sprang a leak, either under the main hatch or further forward. Nothing else, they said, could have caused the list which she took. There was a full cargo of coal in her holds, but the shifting of it, even if such did occur, would not account in their opinion for the events which followed. Another opinion is that a large quantity of the water, confined in the steamer's well deck after each succeeding overwhelming sea, must have gone down through the bunker hatch-ways.

Mr John Howes, the second mate of the steamer stated that at 1 o'clock on Wednesday morning it was his watch on deck, but as he had not had sleep for a long time, the captain told him to turn in, and he would call him when they were off Port Stephens. He accordingly went to his berth. Some hours afterwards he was awakened by a bag falling on him from a shelf above, and he saw that the steamer had a severe list. He rushed up on deck, and heard the captain ordering all hands up. There was then water up to the companion hatchway. Mr Howes ran back and scrambled into a few clothes, then went to the captain who suggested that they should now make for Port Stephens. The second mate seconded the proposal. She was kept on her course until abreast of the entrance, and then headed for the bar. By this time, however, the list to port was such that she would not answer her helm, and instead of keeping in the direction of the entrance, she veered round towards Cabbage Tree Island. Howes assisted to launch the lifeboat, as the "Oakland"'s funnel was dipping in the water. She then took her last plunge, and sparks shot up from her fires while her propeller continued its revolutions in mid-air. The experience in the boat was painful to recall for Mr Howes. He could not understand he said, how strong men could be overcome so suddenly. They would make some remark, and then, in a few minutes, become like wax figures. It was an appalling spectacle. After the Captain's death, he took command of affairs, and tried to cheer the men up. The wind was strong and chill, and rain fell at intervals. Their purpose all the time was to make land if they could, but hope was not strong in the hearts of any of them. The Captain had a lifebuoy around him until he died. This was one of the trophies of the wreck brought to Newcastle.

Names of the lost: Captain W. Slater; C. Lindgren, first mate; A. Fischer, chief engineer; R. Steel, second engineer; H. R. Bradberry, cook; A. Cargill, steward's boy; G. Wilcox, fireman; E. A. Brooks, donkeyman; T. Hadden, fireman; J. Johnson, A.B.; Albert Mattson, A.B.

Those saved were:- J. Howes, second mate; G. Gustavson, A.B.; Isaac Holm, A.B.; W. Jacobson, A.B.; J. E. Ohlsson, A.B.; T. Willberg, A.B.; T. Gaites, passenger.

Captain Slater, who was in command of the "Oakland" at the time of the wreck, was well known in the coastal trade. He was a man of middle age, who for many years was in the service of Messrs John See & Co. In this service he worked his way up from before the mast to a command. Altogether he was navigating the coast for a period of 16 years. His first command was that of the steamer "City of Grafton", in which he succeeded the late Captain Anthon. Subsequently he was in charge of the "Kallatina" for three months, then in temporary command of the "Oakland", pending the recommissioning, after refit, of the "City of Grafton". Before he left Sydney he applied for, and obtained, a week's leave of absence, to be taken on his return from the trip which had proved so disastrous. Captain Slater was of quiet and unassuming demeanour, and very popular. He left a widow, but no family.

On their arrival at Newcastle Mr W.S. Gardner, on behalf of Mr Frank Gardner, representative of the National Shipwreck Society, took the shipwrecked men in charge, provided clothing for them, and had their other wants attended to at the Sailors' Home. They went on to Sydney. The fireman, T. Hadden and E.A. Brooks, donkeyman, came from North Sydney. It is reported that they had been employed for some time on the North Shore ferry boats.

In addition to her coal cargo the "Oakland" took the following freight from Newcastle for the Richmond River:- 13 cases of stone, 4 bundles railing, 9 pieces of stone, 40 sacks of flour, 1 bundle of wooden rakes, 32 bags of chaff, and sundry other articles, and for the Clarence River, 50 sacks flour.

The little steamer "Bellinger" which was one of Messrs Allen Taylor & Co.'s line, met the full force of the gale on her run down the coast, and apart from the picking up of the shipwrecked men, her experiences were exciting enough. Captain H. Tanglin, her Master said, "We left Camden Haven on Tuesday night at 8 o'clock for Sydney. It was blowing hard from the southwest, with a heavy sea all the way. Seal Rocks were passed about 3 o'clock on Wednesday morning, and, as the weather was getting worse, I decided to make for Port Stephens. About halfway between Seal Rocks and Port Stephens, the state of affairs was very bad. We reached Long Island, one of the Broughton Group, about 8 o'clock, and Port Stephens about 10 o'clock. The sea was rolling in over the bar in tremendous breakers and we found it utterly impossible to go in. Therefore we decided to make for the shelter of Long Island.

"On the way south we had seen some wreckage, pieces of timber, and some awning stanchions. That was east-northeast of Cabbage Tree Island, which is about two miles north of Port Stephens. Having seen the wreckage, we kept a sharp lookout, and we had got very nearly abreast of the southernmost part of Long Island when the man at the wheel reported that he saw a boat with a lot of men in it, close to Esmeralda Cove on the eastward, or Port Stephens side, of the Island. I slewed the 'Bellinger' to the eastward and ranged her up until we were very nearly heading south again.

"There was a very heavy sea running, however, and the man whom I had sent aloft to keep his eyes on the boat told me that she was out of sight, although at the time we could not have been more than half a mile away from her. The sea was too bad to permit me to keep the steamer broadside on to it for any length of time, and just as I had got her round to the north once more, we got a view of the boat again. She was then nearly in the broken water along the shore of the island. I signalled to the men in her to pull out, so that I could get close to them and take them on board, but they did nothing. I now know that the boat was full of water, and the poor fellows were too exhausted to do anything with her. I manoeuvred about until I got the 'Bellinger' close up to the boat, on the weather side.

"When we were about three lengths off, the boat capsized. All the men clung on to the lifelines or to the boat itself however, and I brought the steamer close up, and we were able to lift them out of the water without launching a boat, although I had the lifeboat ready to put out if it had been wanted. Captain De Fraine, a passenger, took charge of the bridge while I got down and personally assisted to get the shipwrecked men on board. By standing on the broad sponsons of the 'Bellinger' we succeeded in reaching each man in turn.

"They could do little for themselves, and a couple of them were just seized in time. The seamen Holm and Gustavson were the worst off, the latter particularly so. We got some grog into them, rolled them about on deck to get the water out of them, then put dry clothes on them and put them to bed. In a couple of hours they were all right, and calling out that they were hungry. Mr Gaites, the passenger, was not too bad but at the same time pretty well done. The seaman Willberg appeared to have the most vitality left in him.

"It was about 11 o'clock when we effected the rescue, and I think we were at the time about nine miles nor'-nor'-east of Port Stephens lighthouse, and about a quarter of a mile from the shore, off Broughton Island. The men could never have made the land themselves in the condition in which they and the boat were. We left the boat in the water. She was still capsized, and appeared to have a couple of holes in her. From what I have been told, I think the 'Oakland' foundered off Cabbage Tree Island. After getting all the survivors safe on board, we steamed under the lee of Broughton Island and remained there until 6 o'clock. Some idea of the state of the sea will be gained from the fact that, although we had two anchors down, we had to keep the engines going the whole night, often at full speed ahead, to keep our position, and even so our anchors dragged. We were not, of course, in real danger but it was a very dirty night indeed. The morning brought us to Port Stephens again, to ascertain if the bar at Newcastle would permit us to get in. We had enough coal to bring us down, but not to take us back again, if it had been necessary for us to go back."

The "Oakland" had a record on the coast. She successfully negotiated the famous Maitland gale—in fact, passed that ill-fated steamer on her journey to Sydney. She was built for Mr W. T. Yeager, timber merchant, and for upwards of eight years was engaged in the timber trade between the Richmond, Newcastle and Sydney. She was subsequently sold to the North Coast Company. After the change in ownership, the vessel went on to the breakwater at the entrance to the Richmond, and was the first vessel to enter the Government dock at Riley's Hill on the Richmond. Her rescue from the breakwater was effected by Captain Bentley, who proceeded to the scene on behalf of the underwriters. The "Oakland" was a steel screw steamer of 398 tons, and 228 tons net. She was built at Dumbarton in 1890, by Messrs Murray Bros. The "Oakland" was propelled by triple expansion engines, with cylinders, 12 in, 19 in, and 32 in. in diameter, and a stroke of 24 in. The vessel was covered for £3,000, being insured by the South British Insurance Co. Reinsurances were effected in several local offices.

The "Oakland" was in splendid order, having only the previous trip been docked, and obtained a certificate from the Department of Navigation. She was well found in every respect, and had always proved herself a good seaboat. The company had recently spent a considerable sum of money on her in fitting her with tanks for the carriage of molasses in bulk form from the northern rivers. These tanks, the manager explained, were empty at the time she left Newcastle, and they would add considerably to her seaworthiness in heavy weather. The company, Mr Bell stated, had communicated with their agents at Newcastle, and had arranged for them to meet the survivors on arrival, and afford all manner of relief possible.

In 1907 the "Tomki", no longer the crack vessel she had been, but still popular none-the-less, came to grief at Ballina while attempting to cross into the river. It was the 14th September. Apparently her steering failed just as she was about to reach the breakwater; she sheered northwards, hit the end of the wall, and drove on to the north beach.

Since the publication of a previous book I have received many kind letters from people I did not then know. Several have since become good friends and have given me much interesting background information. Among these friends was Mr Phil Bailey, who described so well life on the Macleay River from the turn of the century. He wrote:-

"I spent my early boyhood at Kempsey, where my Dad was a P.W.D. Engineer in charge of harbour and river works from Camden Haven to Coff's Harbour. This was the heyday of the wall and river construction. It was my delight to go with him on school holidays during his tours of inspection and believe you me there was plenty to thrill a young boy. The unique droghers such as the stern wheeler 'Cornstalk' and the very up-to-date 'Coopernook' were favourites. Captains Beech and Ellery were frequent visitors to our home and I had the run of the North Coast ships and would take a run down to Jerseyville with them and come back on the 'Olga'.

"The 'Coopernook', a nice type of boat with day cabin accommodation would meet the 'Yulgilbar' at Jerseyville, and take the passengers and mails on up to Kempsey while the 'Yulgilbar' worked up river discharging at wharves on the way. The 'Olga' ran a day-service between Kempsey and Jerseyville. Her owner-skipper was an American shipwright named Jack Baldwin who also built her." She used to leave Kempsey at 11 p.m. on Saturday nights and Phil recalls that there was much frivolity until she sailed.

"In those days there was little or no social activity centred around clubs because they didn't exist. Consequently there was a good deal of home entertainment, dances, garden parties, etc., Wirth's Circus being a special treat. Ships' arrival days also caused interest. The ships usually stayed about 48 hours and their Captains would invite the towns' leading men, doctors, lawyers, businessmen, auctioneers and newsmen aboard in the evenings for a quiet game of cards. The bar would, of course, be open and it was not unusual for bets to be made on the card game."

Shopping: "How many remember the days when butter came in kegs and was served by the grocer using wooden pats? When cheeses were round, and when grocers' shops smelt like grocers' shops?

"Christmas Eve has never been the same: 200 people and as many dogs—the whole town used to turn out."

Beaches: "Then as now, the main resorts were South West Rocks and Crescent Head. Not much swimming was done in those days, but it was known to occur."

Phil Bailey also told me of at least one occasion when the old "City of Grafton" was dressed overall with flags because she had as passengers a pair of honeymooners. Imagine that happening today.

There is an island in the lower Macleay, known as Pelican Island, and a steamer (the "Bellinger" (3) owned by J. Doepel of Bellingen) was wrecked on the Macleay Bar in 1918. She was carrying a cargo of beer and this found itself in the river, still in its kegs, of course, finally drifting upsteam to Pelican Island, which was the Aboriginal settlement. The natives had quite a party over the next few days.

Another shipping company, Nicholas Cain's Coastal Co-operative Steamship Co., was operating about this time. It had its beginnings in 1904 when Cain dissolved his partnership in the timber trade with Allen Taylor, taking with him the "Hastings", a small wooden vessel of 193 tons. The partnership had begun about 1900. Nicholas Cain concentrated on the Hastings River trade and also Camden Haven, carrying at first timber but finding a demand existed for a passenger service and he soon expanded into this field as well.

In 1905 he had the "Wauchope" of 269 tons built by D. Sullivan at Coopernook. This pretty little vessel, similar in appearance to Langley's later "Boambee", had limited accommodation for passengers and, by giving good service, he soon attracted the lions' share of trade to Port Macquarie. The "Wauchope" was an excellent sea-boat, much favoured by her many passengers.

Apparently the N.C.S.N. Co. failed to react vigorously enough, because they soon found themselves with severe competition. Cain, heartened by his success, decided to expand into the Macleay River, and ordered a fine steel passenger vessel—the "Kempsey"—to inaugurate this service. She arrived in 1907 and Captain Greer was placed in command. Built by Scotts of Kinghorn, she was a pretty model of a vessel, but decidedly narrow-gutted at only 27 ft beam.

Her maiden voyage to Kempsey was a real event. A holiday was declared for many and she ran an excursion from Kempsey down to the entrance. This was a disaster for Cain as the ship proved to be excessively tender and on the return, when berthing at Jerseyville, she heeled over and actually lay on the wharf. All sorts of stories went the rounds and on her next trip from Sydney she was carrying a good deal of permanent ballast.

Where rivalry and competition exists between the respective owners, vessels often race each other "unofficially" and on one outward journey the "Kempsey" crossed the Macleay Bar only about ten minutes astern of the old "Burrawong"—at the time the N.C.S.N. Company's regular trader to the river—and the race was on. It was said at the time that the "Kempsey" blacked out her lights that night and was not sighted by the "Burrawong", which went up Sydney Harbour just after daylight—whistle tooting—the whole shipping world knew that the race was on, wondering how far back the "Kempsey" was, and

there at the wharf was the "Kempsey" unloading and looking for all the world as if she had been there a week!

Within a couple of weeks the "Burrawong" was taken off the run for overhaul, and the "Electra" did her run. The "Burrawong" returned in due course with an addition to the length of her funnel; Indeed it was practically mast-high. This was done to get extra

S.S. "Kempsey". Fast, pretty, but lacking stability.
Courtesy R. Dufty.

draught for the boiler fires and consequently more speed. However the "Kempsey" was still too fast for her. Captain Taplin, on being queried about the extention to the funnel, is reported to have said that he had had enough of waves coming aboard and going down the funnel, putting her fires out; now he could cross in at any time without fear. He held an extra-master's ticket and was acknowledged as outstanding in his command. He would enter the Macleay in any weather, against the "stand-off" signal from the pilot station, and was at times obliterated from sight by huge seas and flying spray, but he never failed to make it. He certainly had no fear in handling a boat.

The "Kempsey" proved absolutely unsuitable for river trading, and Cain started to look for a way out. He held consultations with the N.C.S.N. Co., which had by now replaced the old "Burrawong" with their brand new "Yulgilbar", which proved far superior to the "Kempsey" in every way, and an agreement was reached. Cain would relinquish the Macleay, and the N.C.S.N. Company would withdraw from the Hastings River. This new arrangement lasted until 1929. Cain sold the "Kempsey" to the Illawarra & South Coast S.N. Company in 1908 and they re-named her "Tathra". They traded with her for some time but she proved too cranky for open jetty work. After some soul searching, they chartered her to a firm of Island traders, late in 1911. On the 4th January, 1912, when near Ambrym Island in the New Hebrides, she took a lot of water aboard in heavy weather, became unmanageable and was swamped or capsized. It is not known which as there were apparently no survivors. Twenty-four lives were lost.

Having sold the "Kempsey" Cain's replaced her with the "Macquarie" without, however, duplicating her shortcomings. The new vessel, built in 1909, proved an outstanding success in the Hastings River trade under Captain Merritt, and remained extremely popular until her ultimate sale in 1929. Cain's service prospered and in 1911 he added the "Ballengarra" to the fleet. Two years later he sold the "Wauchope" as the "Macquarie" was adequately managing the passenger trade, and the little vessel went to Messrs King Island Steamers Ltd, managed by Holyman's of Melbourne.

Nicholas Cain's last ship was the "Pappinbarra", a steel cargo vessel very like the "Urana" of the N.C.S.N. Company and built in 1925. She was wrecked at the base of the cliff under the lighthouse at Port Stephens, in September 1929. This loss forced the company into liquidation. The North Coast S.N. Company took over the service, goodwill and last remaining vessel the "Macquarie", trading to Port Macquarie from then on. The "Macquarie" was sold immediately to New Zealand.

In 1909, on 27th March, the "Burrawong", by now 20 years old came to the end of her days in a manner typical of many of the coasters: The end came while she was attempting to enter the Manning River at Harrington (whence she had gone after she left the Macleay) when she touched the bar and then hit the breakwater. Obviously badly holed, she settled deeply by the head until her fo'c'sle was awash, and she was found upon inspection to be beyond salvage. The wreck was sold and the buyer broke her up for scrap. An interesting feature is her bell—it is now the bell of St Andrew's Presbyterian Church at Harrington, where it may still be seen, as, on receiving a request by the congregation, the company presented it to them. The wreck was finally blown up.

One steamer for the N.C.S.N. Company never reached Australia. She was the "Ourimbah", a 750-ton cargo vessel which was wrecked on the coast of South Africa in fog, while on her delivery voyage from the builder's in 1909, the date being the 26th November.

The "Canonbar" ordered soon after, would seem to be her replacement.

T.S.S. "Burrawong" soon after becoming wrecked at Harrington.
Acknowledgement: Ken Wheeler.

The North Coast Company's steamer "Minimbah", while attempting to cross the Manning bar at 10 o'clock on 13th April, 1910, struck on the extreme outer end of the northern training-wall in exactly the same spot as the ill-fated "Kincumber" did in November of 1908, and lay a total wreck, being full of water, with her back broken. She had a large number of passengers on board, all of whom, with her crew, were safely landed by the aid of the lifeline under the capable control of Pilot Kerkin and his crew. The vessel carried a large and valuable cargo consisting of general merchandise and railway material. There were also two racehorses and some pigs, which were drowned. The whole of the passengers' luggage was saved but the cargo washed out of the ship's holds into the river. The "Minimbah" was on only her fourth trip to the Manning, and was under the command of Captain Aitken. She was designed and built expressly for the Manning River trade, being of combined cargo and passenger type. She was built to replace the company's steamer "Burrawong", lost the previous year at the river. This wreck afforded another strong argument as to the construction of the southern training-wall recommended by Mr deBurgh, and for which the people of the district had long been agitating. The wall was never built.

The "Minimbah", which left Sydney on Monday, 11th, called at Newcastle, and left there on Tuesday morning for the trip to the Manning.

T.S.S. "Minimbah", still brand new, a total wreck on the Manning River breakwater at Harrington, 1910.
Courtesy of Tuncurry Historical Society.

The scene of the wreck was looked upon as one of the most dangerous spots on the North Coast. The entrance is narrow and the channel constantly shifting. A training-wall runs out from the shore but, looking at the area from the sea, the visitor for the first time is surprised to find that there is any entrance at all. Several accidents occurred at the entrance to the Manning River, including the wreck of the "Kincumber", and not long before the steamer "Electra" struck the bar, and lost her rudder.

The disaster to the "Minimbah" was the third loss sustained by the company in connection with the Manning trade within twelve months. The "Burrawong" was first; the new steamer "Ourimbah", specially built for this trade, was wrecked off the South African coast on her maiden trip to Sydney; and now the "Minimbah" had come to grief. The news of the disaster was received with feelings of deep regret, and expressions of sympathy for the owners were heard on all sides. During the day Mr R. A. Bell, the general manager, received many telegrams and letters expressing sympathy in connection with the disaster. One message came from M. W. Basham, the Mayor of Taree, on behalf of the citizens of that town.

The first news of the disaster came from Pilot Kerkin at the Manning River. He telegraphed:- "The vessel struck on the end of the wall while crossing in. As a result of the impact the vessel was badly damaged, and she now lies on the wall full of water. The passengers have been landed safely. They were rescued with the aid of a lifeline apparently none the worse for their adventure." Later in the day the pilot reported the vessel a hopeless wreck.

The "Minimbah" was covered by insurance through Lloyd's London and was running under a 12 months' policy, which included the run out from Glasgow to Australia and also on the coast. The cargo was covered in various local offices, the amounts ranging from £200 to £1,000.

The directors of the North Coast S.N. Company, with their customary enterprise, took steps to replace the "Minimbah". At a meeting the same day it was decided to cable to Glasgow for a new steamer to take the place of the wrecked vessel, and this became the "Maianbar".

The drogher "Manning" arrived at Taree at 8 p.m. bringing the passengers' luggage and parcels from the wreck. The wharf was thronged with anxious friends, eager to gain details of the disaster.

From the various accounts of passengers and others it appeared that the sea outside was moderate, but there was a heavy break on the bar. When entering, the "Minimbah" struck the south spit, and slewed towards the end of the breakwater. The two following rollers lifted her onto the end of the breakwater, where she was hung up.

A boy and girl who were fishing from the breakwater, and watching the boat come in, saw her strike and ran towards her. Those aboard flung a heaving line over and the children managed to get the hawser attached ashore, enabling some of the crew to get on the wall. Spectators from the shore hurried to assist, and tackle and a breeches buoy was soon rigged, landing the passengers safely. Seas kept continually breaking over the steamer. The racehorse Seismo, winner of the Manning Jockey Club's Handicap at the last Taree meeting and engaged in the Wingham races the next Saturday, was thrown overboard and drowned; also a mare and foal. The racehorse Saucepan and three other horses were still on board. When the drogher left the crew were making efforts to rig derricks to sling them to the breakwater. Captain Aitken directed the various operations. The passengers and crew showed exemplary coolness and discipline. Two men were washed overboard and, sadly, one was drowned. He was Burns, a Scot, who came out with the ship.

The continuous break of the heavy waves bumped the hull against the stones, the ship breaking her back. The water rushed in through the broken plates and, as the tide fell, the bow was left high and dry, and the crew set to work saving the passengers' luggage and parcels of freight from the parcel room. As much as could be placed in the drogher was brought to Taree. Captain Aitken's wife had gone from Taree in the drogher to meet her husband, and witnessed the disaster. One of the "Minimbah"'s firemen had his leg badly injured. He was brought up to the hospital by ambulance. On arrival of the crew of the drogher every effort was made to save all the cargo and fittings possible before the tide rose. The sea was then calming down.

Messrs Smith, Timms & Co., contractors for the North Coast Railway, had 100 tons of rails and five four-ton waggons on the ship. Local storekeepers had large consignments of goods and, as they were mostly uninsured, lost considerably. Exhibits and fruit for the Wingham Show were also aboard. The vessel's chief officer, L. M. Gordon, was largely responsible for the fact that it proved possible to salvage the engines and boiler, and these were shipped back to Scotland to be installed in the replacement vessel. The boiler proved most difficult to salvage and was eventually floated into the river for recovery, but the problems that it caused, and their solution by the mate so impressed the management that he was selected to command the "Gunbar" when she was built, as will be told later.

Those steamers which were more lucky, were fine little vessels indeed, smartly run and smartly fitted out, and the "Yulgilbar" and "Orara" are good examples. One ran to the Macleay while the latter was specially built for the Byron Bay express service and had a speed of 15 knots. The standard of accommodation was, for those days, most comfortable (these days it would be considered rather austere). The passenger steamers had a large, tastefully decorated dining saloon, and even a music room. Sometimes there was a smoke room as well. All these vessels were especially constructed with a particular river destination in mind, and everything about them—size, draught, speed, accommodation, special features such as molasses tanks, etc.— were carefully planned for that run. Not that they were not versatile; indeed, many times a ship was called upon to do another run, and she would do it too, with no fuss or bother at all.

One of the great Test Cricketers, Frank B. Johnson, who played for Australia in the English test series of 1909, was a marine engineer by trade, and he returned to Australia after the series in the "Burringbar" as one of her engineers for the delivery voyage. He stayed with the N.C.S.N. Company and later rose to become chief engineer in the "Orara" and the second "Wollongbar".

From June to November it was normal for the "Wollongbar"(2) to be laid up and the Byron Bay service was then run by the "Orara" and "Pulganbar". During this lay-up period the "Wollongbar" was sometimes chartered to relieve the "Nairana" on the Bass Strait service and when Messrs Huddart Parker's "Riverina" was wrecked near Gabo in April, 1927, the "Wollongbar" ran for some weeks from Sydney to Hobart.

During these periods when the flagship was off, the "Pulganbar" earned her nickname—S.S. "Plungingbar" and I have been told of one south-bound trip when, after a particularly rough night, daylight showed her in new colours—her funnel was snow white from top to

The Dining Saloon on a North Coast S.N. Co.'s Express Passenger Steamer.

bottom with caked salt, and glistening as only salt crystals can in the morning light.

Talking of rough weather brings to mind various tales of mal de mer. Of course coastal vessels do not have an exclusive claim to causing seasickness in passengers — that can happen in any ship, but an old north coaster named Jack Simpson, claimed an unusual variation on the theme. On sailing he was all right, likewise at sea, but every time his vessel entered port and reached smooth water he was sick! This happened with monotonous regularity and eventually he transferred to ferries on Sydney Harbour. It was apparently not the smooth water that caused his seasickness but rather the entering of smooth water after some days at sea.

The "Orara" when built was the largest and finest vessel that the Company had owned up to that time. Of 1297 tons she was a magnificent sea boat, and was employed in the express service to Byron Bay for which she was designed. She established a reputation for reliability and speed which was not equalled until the fabulous "Wollongbar" arrived in 1911, when the two vessels ran the service together, "Orara" sailing from Sydney at 9 a.m. on Saturdays, and from Byron Bay at 7 p.m. on Tuesdays while the "Wollongbar" sailed from Sydney at 11 p.m. on Tuesdays, returning from the 'Bay at 7 p.m. on Saturdays. If the weather was fine, the "Orara" would stop off the Manning and allow the passengers to do some fishing on the Sunday afternoon. The service was well patronised, especially by commercial travellers as the early Monday arrival suited them.

Later, the two ships exchanged sailing days, as this allowed the "Orara" to run Sunday excursions—between normal trips—to Cronulla and Port Hacking. Many Sydneysiders had their first taste of sea travel on these short excursions, which were very popular.

On one occasion the "Orara"'s electric generating set failed on her way north and the trip had to be completed using oil lamps and candles to provide illumination at night, and the ship's old oil-burning navigation lights had to be dug out and pressed into service.

"Pulganbar" coming alongside Byron Bay jetty on a bad day.
Acknowledgement: Photo H. Young (Purser).

The North Coast S.N. Company's Express Steamer "Orara".

"Orara" entering the Hunter against the Black Ball. *Acknowledgement: Photo W. Goodfellow.*

At Byron Bay a local electrician managed to perform temporary repairs, and the ship got back to Sydney with her lighting plant giving only ½ power. Messrs Warburton Franki then took the set away for overhaul and repair, but it was not ready in time for Saturday's sailing time. Her departure was put back until Monday by which time a screaming southerly gale had blown up. Sailing time came round and she got away all right, but approaching the Heads to turn seawards she nearly ran down a Manly Ferry which had been hidden behind a large swell. "Orara" went full astern and avoided a collision but lost steerage way in the process. In the huge sea that was running, with her propeller out of the water much of the time she could not regain forward way and drifted rapidly down onto North

Head, out of control. When one anchor failed to hold her a second was let go which fortunately bit in and held her within feet of the rocks. She had a lengthy battle before she managed to claw her way offshore, but she eventually succeeded and proceeded to Watson's Bay where she spent the night. The next day she returned to the Sussex Street wharf. In forty years on the Coast it was about the only time she failed to get to sea.

On another occasion about 1928 she entered Newcastle in extremely bad weather, crossing the bar safely although the port was closed at the time, with 'standoff' signals flying as the bar was considered too dangerous. The Captain's excuse — "It was too uncomfortable out there". This was Captain James Hunter, the mate being Mr Gilmore.

In August 1908, when "Teddy" Roosevelt's American "great white fleet" arrived in Sydney on its world cruise, the older "City of Grafton" was among the hundreds of craft, large and small, which met the warships outside the heads and followed them into the harbour. The "City of Grafton" alone had no less than 600 sightseers crowded aboard for the occasion which must have been one of the most colourful sights ever seen in Sydney.

By this time, too, the trade to the Clarence which, it will be remembered, had been inaugurated with the "Phoenix" so long ago, needed no less than three modern saloon steamers: the "Kyogle" of 702 tons, the "Kallatina" of 646 tons, and the "Nymboida" of 563 tons to maintain the passenger service, while the "Macleay" of 398 tons and the new "Tintenbar" of 667 tons, also were used in this service, handling that cargo which could not be accommodated in the three saloon (passenger) boats.

Most of the steamers had, by this time, been fitted with refrigerated holds and/or a large freezer for butter and meat, which occupied part of a hold, and special cargo trades assumed greater importance. This applied especially as Byron Bay (Norco) butter assumed a commanding share of the export trade, and the North Coast Company made arrangements (which lasted for many years) for the coasters to proceed alongside the overseas mail steamers in Sydney and there discharge the refrigerated cargoes direct into the foreign-going vessels' own refrigerated spaces.

This meant, of course, that North Coast butter and meat could be safely stowed and on its way overseas almost within 24 hours of leaving the factory, 350 miles away, saving at least two handlings and the attendant risk of partial thawing and consequent deterioration.

Similarly, the opening up of the Dorrigo Country behind Coff's Harbour, and the phenomenal land boom which followed, led to special attention being given to the Coff's Harbour run so that this harbour, which only a short time before was nothing more than a timber exporting centre, became one of the best served minor seaports on the whole coast of Australia.

Early in 1910, the N.C.S.N. Board offered to buy out the "Pig & Whistle Company" (Illawarra & South Coast Steam Navigation Co. So called because of its penchant for whistle blowing whilst pigs formed a prominent part of its deck cargoes.) The offer was accepted, but disagreement arose on terms and details, and after much haggling, the N.C. Company withdrew its offer in disgust.

A go-ahead policy was always a feature of the Company throughout its long history, and one other effect of this was the bringing of all the North Coast Centres to within little more than a day's journey of Sydney. For example, one could have luncheon in Lismore, on the Richmond River on Saturday and, travelling via Byron Bay and

T.S.S. "Coramba" at Newcastle Shipway and Engineering, 8th March, 1921.
Acknowledgement: Photo Newcastle City Library.

In 1911, three ships came out. These were the "Coolebar", "Coramba" and the first "Wollongbar". The "Coolebar" and "Coramba" were average small cargo vessels of 479 and 531 tons respectively, whilst the "Wollongbar" was a beautiful little liner of 2,005 tons named after a small town in northern N.S.W. as was the Company's usual policy. Ordered in 1910, she was to be both larger and faster than the "Orara", up to that time the Company's largest vessel. As her portrait shows, she was a beautifully proportioned little ship, and in building her, the Ailsa Shipbuilding Co. of Troon really outdid itself. The "Wollongbar" improved her builder's reputation for creating fine vessels, and they later built several similar ships for South American trade as a result. One of the fastest vessels ever to run on the coast, she was capable of a little over 20 knots, and she immediately proceeded to shatter speed records wherever she went. After being admired at every port of call on the way out from Scotland, she arrived in Sydney on 27th November, 1911, forty-four days out, having taken only 2½ hours to do the run from Wollongong to the Hornby light at South Head. Shortly after she was to take only four hours, from Sydney to passing Nobby's and she quickly built herself a reputation which has endured to this day. Her timetable was as regular as clockwork and it was not unusual for her to berth in

by the S.S. "Orara", could be settled in Sydney on Sunday evening.

The "Canonbar" — sister of the "Tintenbar" — was built in 1910. She had a very long life, surviving until 1967 when she was sunk in the Meikong River as the "Valiente". Of the fleet in 1910, nearly 25 per cent were twin screw and this enabled these ships to be more readily manoeuvred in narrow and tricky bars.

Sydney regularly within five minutes of the advertised time of arrival. Surfers at Collaroy beach got quite used to saying "here comes the 'Wollongbar' it must be 10 past 4". (This occurred every Sunday afternoon.)

On Tuesday 19th September, 1911, the "Sydney Morning Herald" broke the news to its readers that the "Rosedale" was seriously overdue, and that no reports had been received since the previous Friday. In a small paragraph on page 9 it reported:

The North Coast Company's steamer "Rosedale", 274 tons, which left the Nambucca River on Friday with passengers and cargo for Sydney, is seriously overdue. In ordinary circumstances she should have made Port Jackson on Saturday, or Sunday at the latest. The last heard of her was when she was reported passing Smoky Cape on Friday afternoon.

The secretary of the company, Mr Allen, is of the opinion that the vessel put in somewhere for shelter during the southerly gale, which blew late on Friday night, and all day Saturday. He admits it is strange that she has not been seen anywhere along the coast since the weather moderated, but is quite hopeful that she will be heard of to-day.

The report went on to say that the "Rosedale" had ridden out storms of the worst kind in her time, and had been re-floated on many occasions when in an apparently hopeless position ashore. She had previously been employed in the Manning River trade where she used to carry 25 to 30 passengers in the saloon and steerage, but since entering the Bellinger/Nambucca to Sydney trade the passenger accommodation was reduced to a maximum of 14, and she was then principally a cargo-boat.

The "Rosedale" sailed from the Nambucca on

The first "Wollongbar": A magnificent vessel.
Acknowledgement: Photo R. Dufty.

Friday, 15th September, 1911, and was seen passing Smoky Cape southbound at 2.45 p.m. the same day. No one knows for certain what fate befell her, but it seems pretty certain that she foundered before passing Korogoro Point or soon after. Of her complement of 18 crew and ten or twelve passengers no soul survived, and the steamer herself simply disappeared. In a small way the loss of the "Rosedale" was like the disappearance of the magnificent ten thousand ton liner "Waratah" of Lund's Blue Anchor Line on the 27th July, 1909. (The "Waratah" disappeared between Durban and Cape Town in bad weather with 200 lives. The mystery remains unsolved.) This tragedy must have seemed very fresh in the minds of those who wondered as to the fate of the little coaster, only two years later.

Over the next few days concern for the safety of the vessel and her company grew, and while the hope was expressed that she might have stood out to sea, there was proof that she had run into a whole gale shortly after putting to sea, and the general opinion in shipping circles was now that she had gone down with all hands. In answer to a request from the Navigation Department to the lighthouse keepers on the coast to keep a lookout for the missing ship came negative reports; only Smoky Cape had seen her, and not since Friday.

In view of these reports, the N.C.S.N. Company engaged the tug "Irresistible" to search north from Newcastle, and on a different course to that of the "Yulgilbar" which also left there to search on her way north. In addition, the masters of all Company vessels were ordered to search at varying distances offshore, at five mile intervals.

On Thursday, 21st September the "Herald" published a report that the steamer "Cape Finisterre" (Captain McDonald) had passed through a lot of wreckage at 3 p.m. the previous Tuesday, about 20 miles north of Smoky Cape, and this caused the gravest anxiety as to the fate of the missing steamer. In his report, Captain McDonald stated that the wreckage consisted of doors and panels painted in white enamel, with brass electric light fittings attached, and all had the appearance of having been in the water two or three days at most. The "Cape Finisterre" was unaware that a ship was missing — not being fitted with wireless — and unfortunately did not stop to lower a boat to recover any of the wreck, although she passed through it closely enough to observe it in detail.

In the meantime the tug "Irresistible" and the "Yulgilbar" had both failed to sight anything at all. None of the other coasters then keeping a lookout for wreckage had had any luck either. Any doubts remaining as to the fate of the "Rosedale" were removed the next day, Friday the 22nd, with the report of more wreckage, some of which was identified as belonging to the vessel.

Captain Farrell of the "Burringbar" reported on arrival from the Clarence River that he had found a bridge box and a wooden bucket belonging to the equipment of the "Rosedale" off Smoky Cape. Another similar bucket was found on the beach at Trial Bay that morning, a ship's fire bucket not long in the water. The steamer "Yulgilbar" reported seeing two dead pigs, also a red painted stage 18 feet long and 4 feet wide off Smoky. From Kempsey came the report from Mr Henderson the agent:

"Discovered yesterday piece deckhouse painted white, with old fashioned brass port; floated in over bar; also wooden bucket, rope handle, no name; tin engine oil, Trial Bay today. Inspector of police instructed his men to search. Pilot and men scouring beach. Will keep you fully posted of any further news."

The "Kyogle" reported: "Cruised 25 miles off shore, saw nothing."

The "Orara" stated: "Steamed 30 miles off the land without results".

The A.U.S.N. Company liner "Wyreema" reported on arrival at Brisbane, however, that she had sighted a large life raft painted teak colour on Wednesday afternoon, and that it, too, had not been long in the water. Captain Grahl also mentioned a deck chair, and these relics were found in the same area as those seen by "Cape Finisterre" —20½ miles north of Smoky and about 14 miles east of Bellinger Peak. "Wyreema" steamed around the raft, but when she was sure that it was unoccupied, resumed her course.

Captain Edward Farrell stated that taking into consideration the way the wind and sea had been since the 15th, he felt that the "Rosedale" would not have been far off the land, as the "Burring-bar" had been set inshore when going North that trip. The log also showed a one-knot set to the north. He set a mast-head lookout at South Solitary, and kept away to signal Smoky Cape. While still four miles north of Smoky, they saw some pieces of fruit cases, also a whole fruit case, and later a large painted box which they picked up. With a fresh wind and sea, the white caps were very misleading. They continued to cruise about, everyone on the alert, and the chief mate and a sailor at the mast-head. His report goes on:

"When one mile north of Smoky Cape one of the stewards drew my attention to a small white object. We steamed...out to it and picked up a teak bucket. Continued searching about, but saw nothing more. At 5 p.m. a heavy thunderstorm came up, and obscured everything. Wind, rain, and sea fierce all night, so proceeded towards Sydney."

One of the crew of the "Rosedale", Charles Yansen, the winch driver, had been in the ship for eleven years, and had been in coasters for 30 years. His opinion of the ship was that she was a very fine sea boat and "could do everything but talk". He liked her so much that he had more than once declined to join new vessels when they came out from the builders. He also had the distinction of having been stranded six times in the ship and his wife refused to believe that he was not all right this time. But she was wrong—he was dead.

The stewardess, Miss Mary Rafferty, had come to Sydney from her home in Perth on a 12-month working holiday, and intended returning home by Christmas. Twenty-two years of age, and a tailoress normally, she took the position on the "Rosedale" for a change.

Captain Einerson was about 33 years of age. He came to Australia when he was about fifteen, and eventually won his master's ticket. His first command was the "Nerong" at twenty-nine, and three years later was posted to the "Rosedale" in command. He was a married man with one child.

It is easy to be wise after the event and say that so small a steamer should never have sailed in the face of the weather that was brewing, but Captain Einerson no doubt wanted to avoid being bar-bound, and the vessel had a reputation for being a good sea boat. She had often weathered worse. She was a regular trader to the Manning, Hastings, Bellinger and Nambucca rivers, and in her long career had been commanded by Captains Pawlson, J. Nicholson, J. O. Anderson, and finally Earling Einerson. There were many others.

The most poignant feature of this terrible disaster was that three of the passengers need not have been aboard. At this time the McKay family were living out of Bowraville and a Mackay family living at Valla. Mrs McKay had gone to Sydney for medical treatment and

Mrs Mackay was also in Sydney in indifferent health. On the day the "Rosedale" was to sail a telegram arrived at Bowraville stating that mother was dangerously ill. The telegram was meant for the Mackay family at Valla but the Post Office, knowing that Mrs McKay had gone to Sydney for medical treatment naturally assumed that the telegram referred to her family and delivered it accordingly. Mr and Mrs Jack McKay and a daughter, Mrs Murphy, immediately packed and took passage for Sydney in the first steamer—the "Rosedale". She sailed, into obscurity, until in 1995 the wreck was located near Port Macquarie.

Twenty-six days later, distaster struck again! The "Macleay" was lost in circumstances which unfortunately occurred all too frequently, and showed that the utmost care and attention are needed at sea, even when sailing in familiar water. The old steamer sailed from Newcastle on the afternoon of 11th October bound for the Richmond. The weather was fine and clear, but there was a strong southerly blowing, so she hoisted her trysail to help her along as her engines were only sixty horsepower.

The story is best continued in the words of Charles Peterson, a seaman and one of the only two to survive. He was at the helm at the time, and gives a graphic description of the events to follow:

"After passing Port Stephens' light at 7 p.m.

when I was at the wheel, the ship's course was altered and the captain left the bridge. Soon afterwards I remarked to the officer of the watch that I could see something white ahead. The officer replied:-

"Rosedale" "on the beach" near Urunga—an earlier mishap.
Photograph by courtesy of R. Dufty.

"It's only a school of fish."

I looked again and shouted:-

"No! It's a school of rocks."

"The ship, running at nine knots, then struck heavily, opening up the port side. As she commenced to fill the Captain rushed up onto the bridge, swung the helm over, and demanded to know why the course had been altered without his permission. By this time the ship had slid sideways off the rocks and was drifting towards the open sea with a heavy list to port.

"The crew in night attire assembled on deck, and realising that the vessel was lost, prepared to abandon her, but owing to the list could not launch the boats. Within ten minutes our "Macleay" sank under us.

"A number of horses carried on deck plunged into the water along side the men and added to the confusion in the pitch darkness as man and beast struggled together for their lives. I saw the steward clinging on to the tail of one animal. With two others, I clung all night to a horse box, and after thirteen hours in the cold water, I was washed ashore with another man next morning. Neither of us had seen any others of the crew throughout that long night."

The other survivor was W. Swanney, A.B., a Scot.

When the news of the disaster reached Nelson's Bay, several launches, together with the Pilot Tender "Ajax" and tug "Irresistible" from Newcastle put to sea and made a search for more survivors, but only bodies were found. However the tug did locate the wreck which was lying south-east of Boondelbah Island. Fortunately the "Macleay" had not been carrying passengers as the accommodation had been removed shortly before and the ship converted to carry cargo only.

Captain Keith had been in the North Coast Company's employ for three or four years, serving first as chief officer and then as master. He was one time in the "Kallatina". The chief officer, Mr Goldsmith, was on his first voyage to the Macleay, though he had been seven or eight years in the company's employ. The second officer, Mr J. N. McLean, was new to the company. He was formerly in the steam collier "Undola". Mr A. T. Tarleton, the chief engineer, was a son of Mr Harry Tarleton, the chief wharf manager at the North Coast S.N. Company's wharf.

The "Macleay" was one of the regular traders of the North Coast fleet and all the officers and crew shipped at Sydney, many of them married men with families. At the time of the disaster she was proceeding from Sydney and Newcastle to the Clarence River. She had called at Newcastle to take in coal, which comprised the principal portion of her cargo and was consigned to the Colonial Sugar Refining Company, Clarence River. Well manned and apparently in the best of trim, the steamer cleared Nobby's about 4 o'clock Wednesday afternoon and she appears to have struck about 8 o'clock in the evening.

The news of the disaster following so close on the loss of the "Rosedale", caused a profound sensation, and the company's office was besieged by relatives and friends of the crew seeking the latest information. The telegrams received by the company were confirmatory of the news from the Newcastle correspondents and instructions were given by the managing director, Mr R. A. Bell, to see that the welfare of the survivors was attended to.

The company took prompt action when the news of the disaster was received. Within ten minutes the Newcastle agent, Mr Hough, had Messrs J. & A. Brown's tug "Irresistible" despatched to the scene. The company's steamer "Kallatina" was also signalled and instructed to proceed to the locality to search for survivors. The Navigation Department also hurried the Newcastle Pilot Steamer "Ajax" to the locality, and she continued the search.

By a strange coincidence another steamer was lost the day before —10th October—she was the "Wyoming", which had come to the North Coast Company from W. G. Yeager in the mid 1890s and had been resold in 1908. She piled up on Kiola Beach, having been driven ashore by the same southerly.

There were lighter moments too; on the far North Coast the nor'-easterly sea breeze is much stronger than that seen farther south, and the smaller, lower powered, vessels used to follow the indentations of the coast to gain some shelter from the violence of the wind (which often caused them considerable delay) behind the headlands.

One anecdote which comes to mind concerned the little paddler "Euroka" which was steaming north, keeping well inshore to avoid the worst of a typical nor'-easter. The skipper, old Jimmy Langlands, who had a well-earned reputation for having one of the saltiest vocabularies on the coast, when handing over the watch to the mate, who was new and comparatively inexperienced, told him to:-

"Keep her close inshore"

and went below to turn in. Sometime later he was awakened by a change in the vessel's motion, and going on deck to ascertain the reason for this phenomenon, found her "close inshore" all right— she was almost in the breakers! She was, however, still steaming north, and the mate appeared to be quite unconcerned.

The skipper at once crustily demanded to know what the young fool of a mate was playing at, and was told:

"...But Sir, you told me yourself to hug the beaches."

To which came old Jimmy's dry rejoinder:

"Yes I did, you bloody fool, but I didn't mean you to run our paddle-wheel along the sand!"

In 1912 no less than four new vessels were built. They were the "Pulganbar", a lovely 1,160 tons passenger boat of similar size to the "Orara", but of shallower draught, and otherwise improved; the "Gunbar", a sister for the "Coolebar"; the "Tambar", slightly smaller than the "Maianbar"; and the "Coombar" which was a sister for the "Coramba". The "Gunbar" and the "Tambar" appear to have been intended more or less as replacements for the ill-fated "Rosedale" and "Macleay", although the new pair were considerably larger than were the lost ships.

When the "Gunbar" arrived in Sydney in April, 1912, it was the end of a most eventful voyage. She left Ardrossan on the 1st February, deeply loaded with coal, and almost immediately ran into bad weather in the Channel. Although faced with strong gales and the short, steep seas common to those parts, she made good progress and by the time she had reached the Bay of Biscay the weather had moderated. Through the Mediterranean and Suez Canal and down the Red Sea to Aden then on to Colombo, the weather was fair and she averaged 8½ knots. The conditions remained favourable across the Indian Ocean to Fremantle, but shortly before her arrival at that Port it was discovered that she was making water.

The leak was tracked down to the starboard bow where a seam had opened up, but it was soon plugged and she made her Australian landfall without ado. The "Gunbar" left Fremantle on the 10th April and had a good run across the "Bight" to the vicinity of Cape Howe, where she ran into a gale on Easter Saturday. The next day the wind freshened and by the time she was off Jervis Bay it was very strong, accompanied by high seas, lightning, and heavy cloud. Although these conditions moderated slightly they persisted until she reached Port Jackson, which she entered without a pilot, proceeding straight up the harbour to her berth.

The "Gunbar"'s skipper on the delivery voyage was Captain Linton Matheson Gordon who, at only twenty-five years of age, was one of the youngest skippers on the coast. He will come into our story again later on.

The "Gunbar" was intended for use in the Bellinger River trade but by the time she arrived in Sydney that bar had shoaled down to 4 feet 2 inches, so the Company had to find temporary employment for her elsewhere. Even the "Nerong", a far smaller vessel than the "Gunbar", had been unable to cross in for over three weeks, and a little government tug, due to go to Sydney for overhaul, was bar-bound and unable to get out.

Only one new vessel was added to the fleet in 1913—the "Poonbar", a remarkable vessel; she was at least a quarter of a century ahead of her time. So much so that she had not altogether merited criticism as a result. Very like the earlier "Coramba" and "Coombar", she was much larger, and sported such innovations as goal-post masts and steam cargo handling cranes. These last two features were never repeated on any of the Company's later ships, but they

became common on all types of ships in the years since the Second World War. She was also fitted with twin screws, and, at 909 tons, was the largest cargo ship that the N.C.S.N. Company had owned up

"Poonbar" in the North Arm of the Richmond River—a cramped place for an ocean-going ship.
Photograph by courtesy of W. R. Duggan.

to that time. She was placed in the Richmond River trade where her greatest drawback soon made itself evident. Her length of 200 feet, together with her twin screws, caused many anxious moments as she picked her way up the narrow, tortuous North Arm to Lismore. The Richmond is particularly narrow and winding along this section, and the "Poonbar" several times had damage caused to her propellers when she came too near the banks.

Only one master managed to navigate the "Poonbar" successfully in the North Arm of the Richmond, and he never lost a propeller, but by then she had her reputation as a hard ship, and the damage was done. In places the river is so narrow and overhung with foliage that the ships using it "acquired" branches, leaves and other foliage as they swept past, and green tree-snakes were also known to drop onto the decks of the steamers. Later vessels built for service on this river —which was the scene of numerous minor strandings—were fitted with single screws as a result of her experience.

She ran on the Australian coast for many years after her sale to S. H. Hammond of Tasmania in 1927, being later purchased by Messrs Nelson and Robertson (who still have her model) and was not finally scrapped until 1951, in Hong Kong, after serving her last owner, John Manners since 1947. At the least she was a notable experiment but, as I have said, too far ahead of her time.

The navigators of the steamers which pioneered the trade to the northern rivers had to be men of resource, as modern aids to navigation were not there to assist. The later vessels making their way up any one of these winding rivers at night were assisted by high-powered electric search lights, fitted on the foremast, but the skipper of the early days had to depend on his knowledge for the locality. One captain was credited with finding his way at night by his sense of smell from the various farms along the banks. The warning at one particularly dangerous bend was a smell of goats, but the goats were disposed of at short notice and, with the captain's sense of location gone, the ship got stuck temporarily. The farmer of course came in for a lot of abuse as a result.

The early mistake made with the "Poonbar" was that she was sent fully loaded with railway and gas coal for discharge at Lismore only. The Sydney Traffic Department (against the advice of practical shipmasters) was anxious to demonstrate to Lismore clients the large carrying capacity of the vessel and, at the same time to complete the coal orders lagging at the time. It had always been the practice in the past to lighten a vessel by discharging partly at Ballina and at the C.S.R. Company at Broadwater before proceeding into the narrow north arm to Lismore. To alter the safe procedure to a "one port of discharge" at Lismore, and with the largest carrying river vessel the company had ever owned up to that time, is beyond all understanding.

A famous master, Captain Benjamin Alley (before the "Poonbar"'s time) could take the "Brundah" up and down the Lismore arm of the river at almost full speed and the story of willow trees and snakes also applies to this vessel. There were many excellent masters in the Richmond River Trade and some of the best that come to mind are Captain Peter Anderson, Captain Adams, Captain T. Nicholson, Captain Charles Benson (Master of the "Wollongbar" when torpedoed in 1943), Captain Soderbohm, Captain Lucey, Captain Purdie and Captain Buckingham. Only the best were successful in the Richmond River trade but, with all respect, I do not think any of the latter-day masters ever surpassed Captain Ben Alley.

He was remarkable in keeping his timetable, fog not withstanding. Under him the "Brundah" would leave Sydney at 8 p.m. on Saturday night with eighty or a hundred passengers and a full cargo, and cross into the river on the Monday morning tide. After proceeding up the river to Lismore she would cross out on the first tide on Wednesday, and be back in Sydney on Thursday.

Ben Alley was no youngster: at the time he was in command of the "Brundah" he was said to have been over 80, and he hardly ever left his ship to go ashore—certainly never in Sydney anyway. His wife lived on the lower Richmond and old Ben would stop the ship off his farm on the way upstream and send his washing ashore by boat for laundering, repeating the performance on the return trip to pick it up again.

Captain Alley, however, was not infallible, and on one occasion when he left Lismore in the dusk there were patches of fog down river near Coraki. The Captain took up his position on the bridge, one hand on the rail, the other on a stanchion and, with his feet apart in a characteristic pose, sailed his "Brundah" downstream in his usual manner, on the way passing a sand barge tied up to the bank for the night.

Now Ben had a marvellous lamp trimmer (bo'sun) who knew the river as well as he knew his own face, but this time he made an error of judgement and ran into the bank while in a patch of fog and the ship stopped. She was, however, soon afloat again and they set off for Sydney. Shortly afterward they sighted a sand barge tied up for the night!

"Brundah" stuck fast on the bank of the Richmond, near Foywell's Bend, as the crew watch anxiously for signs of movement.
Acknowledgement: H. Young.

As they passed her there came a hail—
"Ahoy, 'Brundah' were are you going?"
"To Sydney," from the ship.
"No you're not, you're going to Lismore!"

Consternation: It was the same barge that they had passed earlier. What had happened was that in refloating the ship earlier they had allowed her stern to swing in the current until she had turned around completely, but no one realised it, and they set off back the way they had come. They again turned around and finally reached Ballina and the open sea.

At this juncture it is fitting to pay tribute to the bo'suns, or "Lamp trimmers", as they were then known. These leading seamen would take the wheel when approaching the bar entrance and do all the steering until the vessel crossed out again. They were fine men, experienced and very capable. Masters seldom had to give an order as it was usually anticipated. There is no doubt that masters had to thank their helmsmen for a lot of their success in the rivers. One or two masters did their own steering—Captain Simonsen was one—but he had risen from the fo'c'sle and had been a bo'sun himself.

1913 saw the end of the road for two of the old stagers. The "City of Grafton" was laid up, while the old "Nymboida" ex "Otway" was cut down and turned into a coal hulk. Both these once proud vessels ended their usefulness in this manner, and in 1919 were sold to W. Waugh for continued service as harbour hulks. The "Nymboida" was eventually scuttled off Sydney Heads in August, 1920, loaded with unclaimed customs goods, and in October, 1930, the "City of Grafton" went the same way.

With the beginning of the Great War in 1914 the introduction of new coasters was drastically curtailed, as the British shipbuilding industry became preoccupied with the building of warships to increase the already formidable power of the Grand Fleet of the Royal Navy. Nevertheless two steamers were built locally for the North Coast service, the "Narani" by Wrights at Tuncurry for Allen Taylor & Co. and the other, the "Tamban", in Sydney for the Macleay River Co-operative Society which had been formed to compete with the North Coast Company on this river. In June, 1922, she was bought from this organisation by the N.C.S.N. Company and was renamed "Kinchela" to avoid confusion with the "Tambar".

"Narani" under construction at Wright's Yard, Tuncurry.
Acknowledgement: Mrs E. Wright.

No book about ships and the sea would be complete without mention of buried treasure, and even the north coast of N.S.W. has its tales and legends. One such legend—I won't claim it to be authentic, though it may well be—concerns the "Seydlitz" treasure. The story, for what it is worth, is this:

The sudden outbreak of war with Germany in 1914 was responsible for a German captain burying a quantity of gold and valuables on the north coast of N.S.W. On board the German steamer "Seydlitz" of the Nord-Deutscher Lloyd, was a large quantity of jewellery, diamonds and gold, worth many thousands of pounds. It was being taken to Germany on behalf of wealthy Germans residing in New South Wales. The Captain considered that he would not be able to get to Germany with his valuable cargo, so he pulled in somewhere in the vicinity of Ballina and buried the treasure. There is no record of it ever being reclaimed.

A natural hindrance to river navigation—especially on the Richmond River, although other rivers were also affected—was caused on occasions by a rather attractive little flower, the water hyacinth, which at times completely blocked the Richmond from Broadwater up. It could not survive in salt water, but thrived in fresh, especially from Woodburn to Coraki. It was so bad at times that even the big ships like "Poonbar" could not force the passage and became trapped. Booms were placed across the river to arrest the passage of the weed, which was then pulled on to the banks to rot. Vessels were often held up and forced to anchor, waiting for the tide to turn and the boom to be let go, before they could proceed upstream.

The weed presented a pretty sight, but caused a lot of worry on the Richmond. It was not so bad on the Clarence River, however, as the salt water went well upstream.

"Burringbar" in the hyacinth, Richmond River. *By courtesy H. Young.*

CHAPTER FOUR

Well-known Personnel (Sydney)

No story of the North Coast would ever be complete without mentioning one of the truly great men of the time, who was the Company's manager. I refer, of course, to Mr Robert Aitken Bell.

Mr Bell was a product of the Union S.S. Company of New Zealand, Ltd. and came to the N.C.S.N. Company at a time when it needed a vast reorganization to meet the looming opposition from the coastal railway which was then being constructed.

He was a most able and experienced shipping man who did not spare himself in his efforts for the Company, and he expected the same of his employees. He was responsible for transforming the fleet from a collection of small, mostly old, tramp coasters to a modern one of combined passenger and cargo vessels, running to a fast, regular timetable.

Whether one liked or disliked him personally, it must be generally admitted that his period of office from the turn of the century, first as manager, and later as managing director, was the most progressive in the Company's history. He was a hard driver, and could be rather intolerant, and therefore must have been under considerable strain when he had to contend with the first militant onslaught of the wharf labourers led by the then secretary of their union, the fiery William Morris Hughes, who later became our famous war-time Prime Minister. The following anecdote serves to illustrate the type

Robert Aitken Bell.

of man that the Company had in Robert Bell, for Billy Hughes still thought highly of him thirty years after Bell's death.

Not long before his own death, Mr Hughes was being driven home from a function at Sydney University. Before he turned out of Sussex Street for the approach to the Harbour Bridge, he stopped his car at the company's wharf offices and said that as he was passing he thought that he would like to look over his old stamping ground (the wharf labourers' office had once been opposite the N.C.S.N. Company's offices) to renew his memories of many bitter fights with his old antagonist "Bob" Bell.

With a fleet of 27 vessels, each making short regular voyages, the Company was probably the largest employer of casual waterside labour and therefore well worthy of the attention of William Morris Hughes. Any visitor to the board room of the N.C.S.N. Company, however interested he may have been in the many fine models and photographs could not have missed the array of nicely framed "Bulletin" cartoons of Billy Hughes. Robert A. Bell did not amass wealth, an impression that unions so often try to impute to the "Grasping Shipowners"; there was nothing self-seeking in his drive to make the Company an efficient transport organisation to the "Garden of Eden" of New South Wales.

His great pride was the first "Wollongbar", which in 1911 was probably the fastest vessel owned in Australian waters. When she was doing her trials in Scotland the workmen called her the "Pride of the Clyde". She was exceedingly popular also with the large passenger traffic comprising both North Coast residents and tourists to Brisbane, who were met at Byron Bay by modern motor coaches specially built for the traffic by the New England Motor Company. In 1915 she was selected to be the flagship for the Anniversary Day regatta, an honour only given to outstanding vessels.

During Robert A. Bell's term of office the Company also had as its Chairman of Directors well-known and able men in Mr T. R. Allt, followed by Mr Walter C. Watt; and Robert Bell enjoyed the utmost confidence and support of these gentlemen.

In 1915 the two old steamers "Rocklily" and "St George" were sold out of the service, the former going in October to Nick Johnson & Co., while the latter in December went to On Chong & Co. In the following year the "Coorong", which had been hulked in 1911, was broken up in Sydney for scrap.

In 1917 Allen Taylor's had the "Wallamba" [sic] built by Wright's at Tuncurry and she was typical of the vessels turned out by this yard. The old "Nerong" which had been built at Balmain back in 1903 foundered off Norah Head on the 19th September in very heavy weather and, although all hands managed to get into the boats, the chief engineer, together with a passenger and a sailor, died from the effects of immersion and exposure. The survivors were picked up by the "Coombar".

Nothing untoward happened in 1918, and the Company continued normal trading. The first World War was drawing to a close after four bitter years of bloody conflict, and it looked as if peace was at long last in sight. Not that the war had seriously affected trade to the rivers, as the Company's business was mainly the carriage of essential requirements for people living between Newcastle and the Queensland border, and returning south with the produce of the area which consisted of sugar, maize, potatoes, timber and livestock. It was not a luxury trade therefore, and it had to continue, war or no war. The only effects of any consequence were the suspension of the overseas building programme and natural management difficulties that are associated with the threat of surface raiders, etc., a threat which was daily expected to materialise.

The strain of the last few years had taken their toll of Robert Bell, however, and he was no longer a well man. In 1919, after a long illness he passed away, and his passing left a void that would have normally been very hard to fill but, fortunately, there was a man at hand to take over, in the form of the Hon. Sir Allen Taylor, M.L.C.

An important part of Robert Bell's policy for the development of the Company was the introduction of some very able men, who came mostly from the efficient and well known Union Steamship Company of New Zealand, Ltd, and these men were to play a most significant part in the success story of the North Coast Company.

Bell's introduction of foreign-going ships' personnel and the transformation of the country branches by the appointment, from this source, of selected branch managers after they had gained experience of the trades and vessels concerned, will be told later, but here I am going to tell of some of the Sydney-based Head Office personnel who also came to the Company in this manner.

It is not difficult to understand why it was sometimes thought that the N.C.S.N. Company was a subsidiary of the famous Union S.S. Company of New Zealand; the general managers for nearly fifty years were ex-Union Company officials, and key executive positions were also held by officers from the same source. Other supporting factors to this idea were the similarity of vessels' funnel colours in both fleets and adjacent wharf premises. However, there was never any shareholding in the N.C.S.N. Company by the Union S.S. Company; rather it was just good fortune and good selective judgement that the Company was able to interest able young men from such an efficient source.

Up to the turn of the century, information available does not show up any outstanding business executive, but it is possible that there may have been men overshadowed by the able and prominent personalities who controlled the Company as its managing directors. There is no doubt of the ability of these leaders of the early period of the story, but they nevertheless had other interests and were probably unable to devote themselves entirely to their shipping interests and its staff troubles.

Wherever the difficulty lay, it appears quite evident that all was not "shipshape and Bristol-fashion" in the Sydney head office when Robert Bell was brought in as manager. Staff records show the names of many near relatives of influential gentlemen and ex-employees, as well as old retainers of amalgamated and absorbed shipping concerns. Discipline, too, left much to be desired.

One may only conjecture at the thoughts of the new manager, coming as he did from such an efficient concern as the Union Company, but as the subsequent record clearly showed, Bell was undaunted and lost no time in getting the house in order.

Mr Charles McAllister was appointed as superintendent engineer, which took care of a very important department, and the Company's comprehensive marine workshop. This officer was a highly qualified engineer from the Union S.S. Company who, in the early stages, also took over the duties of Marine Superintendent. This gave him full control of both the engineering and deck departments of the vessels.

Later, Mr McAllister was appointed (with the Company's approval of course) engineer surveyor of the London-based "British Corporation Society", a body similar to Lloyd's Register of Shipping but a little more elastic in some constructional requirements of shipbuilding—not vital ones of course, but of value to ships where every inch of draft counted. Years later, the British Corporation amalgamated with Lloyd's who, it must be said, were mindful of the very real advantages of the Corporation's requirements.

Austere on the surface, he seldom showed any light humour but he had a kindly side to his nature and, notwithstanding his Scots' caution, he was ever generous when the hat was being passed round for a worthwhile cause. Frugal with words, he wasted them neither verbally nor in his reports, and avoided both if possible, but when circumstances made it necessary, he could be caustic in both the spoken and the written word. He was averse to high pressure salesmen endeavouring to sell the many things that go with ships. The quiet, efficient representative fared well with him, but the long-winded salesman did not return to see him again.

There is a story told of a voluble young man who would not take "no" for an answer, nor realise the fact that his prospective buyer, deep in plans and specifications for a new vessel, was not in the right mood for interviewing salesmen. He insisted on saying his piece according to the book, and erecting on the desk a small heating apparatus and a metal plate to illustrate the absence of any injurious residue in his brand of lubricating oil, which he was anxious to introduce. McAllister, amazed at his persistence, relaxed in his chair and listened silently to a long dissertation on elementary facts. The salesman finished, gathered his equipment, placed his suitcase, and looked at his buyer for favourable comment. All McAllister said was:

"Quite a good act my boy, but you didn't bring the rabbit out of the hat!" Needless to add, he was not bothered by that salesman again.

Charles McAllister was a tower of strength in the Company for many years, both in the building of vessels and their maintenance to the high standard required. With the addition of motor vessels to the fleet, he was most ably assisted by very experienced, hand-picked "guarantee engineers" who came out from Denmark in the first two diesel vessels, "Nimbin" and "Melinga". The Company also sent a young engineer to Copenhagen for a long period to gain experience while the "Nimbin" was building. The builders naturally realised that future business depended on the success of these early vessels in the departure from steam to diesel and exercised the utmost care in the selection of guarantee engineers. With the guidance of the guarantee chiefs of the "Nimbin" and "Melinga", Mr McAllister quickly adjusted himself to the diesel engine.

While the "Nimbin"'s engineer returned to Denmark after training personnel for the Company, meanwhile establishing the vessel as a great success, the Company was fortunate that the guarantee chief of "Melinga" (which arrived two years after the "Nimbin") decided to remain in Australia. This officer, Mr D. R. MacFarlane, was experienced in both steam and diesel engines and proved invaluable during his long service from 1927 until the Company closed down. Mr MacFarlane was later Engineer Superintendent for several years and carried out his administrative duties in the same highly efficient manner as he carried out his sea going service. He was very highly thought of by the American Army during World War II when he served under them as chief engineer of the "Comara".

Mr McAllister retired after the "Nimbin" and "Melinga" were both firmly established as desirable types for further tonnage and there appears no doubt that he played a major part in building up the modern fleet of the North Coast Company that operated during his 30 years of service. He was also responsible for the highly efficient workshop which occupied three floors of a building in Napoleon Street, Sydney, opposite the Company's wharves. It housed all necessary skilled workers and apprentices and was the envy of many waterside workshops. All running repairs were carried out promptly without interfering with vessels' schedules and practically all periodical overhaul work, other than docking, was also effected by the workshop. During World War II, although the Company's fleet was sorely depleted, the workshop worked to capacity on Navy and American Army requirements. Many compliments were received by the Company from these organizations and more work was available than could be efficiently handled. The Company was always reluctant to lower the standards of their workshop by "diluting" labour, although it must be admitted that practically all the skilled men were potential foremen.

The next arrival from the Union S.S. Company was R. S. Hulme, a very able young man with both general office and wharf office experience. He settled down quietly in the accounts department and soon gained an insight into the Company's financial business and in particular into the financial matters relating to the country branches such as they were at that time. He was then sent to Grafton to act as an assistant to Mr Samuel See (a brother of Sir John See) who needed more assistance with the additional work and changed conditions at Grafton following the amalgamation of his brother's shipping interest with the now North Coast's S.N. Company Ltd.

Mr See welcomed R. S. Hulme who soon lightened the office duties by installing what was to become the model system of accounts and head office returns at all branches. Hulme also reorganised all other matters at the branch and Mr See had no further worries. The agency ran like clockwork. However it was not the intention for R. S. Hulme to remain permanently at Grafton and he was transferred to take charge at Byron Bay and to reorganise that agency to cope with the changed conditions that evolved from the take-over of G. W. Nicoll in the Byron Bay and Tweed trades. Mr Hulme managed to gather round him some excellent support in the outside practical work of the Agency, including a few Shetland Islanders; wonderful men in any capacity, whom Captain Hunter had brought out as seamen on his visits to Scotland to deliver steamers for the Byron Bay trade. (Captain Hunter was proud of his homeland, the Shetland Islands, and disliked very much to be referred to as a Scotsman.)

Mr Hulme was very successful at Byron Bay but, as at Grafton, he was not destined to remain for long.

In 1915 Mr Bell, now firmly in the saddle as General Manager, was having serious personnel trouble in the accounts department and R. S. Hulme was brought to Sydney as Chief Accountant. From then on vast changes took place, which culminated in the building of more modern offices and the installation of up-to-date office equipment with Mr Hulme in complete control, not only of the accounts branch, but of all other head office clerical staff. He was a wonderful organiser and a beautiful penman; his books and financial statements were a delight, much admired by the directors and auditors. Sir Allen Taylor also had a very high opinion of Hulme and spent much time with him. It is of interest to note that the late Bishop Hulme-Moir was a nephew of R. S. Hulme.

A little after R. S. Hulme joined the Company another addition came from the Union Company, Captain Alexander Hird, master of the Union Company's S. S. "Karitane". It was intended that Captain Hird was to take over the position of Marine Superintendent and to relieve Mr McAllister of these duties as, with the continual building of new vessels and the increase in fleet numbers, it was too onerous for one man, however willing and capable, to carry on as both Superintendent Engineer and Marine Superintendent.

To enable Captain Hird to have practical knowledge of the trades and the vessels before his shore appointment was announced he went to sea in the vessels for about two years as mate and at the time he was officially appointed marine superintendent he was master of the "Ramornie" in the Richmond River Trade. This may seem rapid promotion, but Captain Hird had had a lot of experience in small vessels and shallow bar harbours on the New Zealand coast.

Captain Hird, a quiet and very likeable personality, soon gained the respect of the masters and the dockyard officials with whom he came in contact and also worked very harmoniously with the

Engineer Superintendent and his staff, which speaks highly of Captain Hird's aptitude for the position, as those who know life on the waterfront will know.

In 1906 the first of the modern passenger and cargo vessels arrived from overseas; this was the S.S. "Brundah" which proved not only popular with the passengers but also was a profitable success in the Richmond River cargo trade. She carried nearly one hundred passengers, saloon and steerage, and it was decided to do the new flagship justice by appointing a topline steward from the Union Company to take charge of the vessel's passenger department as chief steward. This officer was a remarkable asset to the Company for many years. It could be said that Chief Steward F. C. Ward was the man mainly responsible for the Company achieving the reputation of having the best fed vessels out of Sydney. Special lunches for prominent businessmen and other leading citizens became quite a feature on the vessels in which he served, and Mr R. A. Bell, and later Sir Allen Taylor, proudly led their guests aboard knowing full well the lunch would be enjoyed by all.

Ward served in the "Brundah" and "Burringbar" until the "Wollongbar" No. 1 was built and he became her first chief steward. After she was lost he was sent to Scotland to superintend his department's affairs in the second "Wollongbar" and, returning with her, remained in her until he retired.

Soon after Steward Ward joined the Company there was a reorganization of the Victualling and Marine Store Department which was originally in a building in Margaret Street, away from the wharf. An additional wharf was leased and the Stores and Victualling Department was transferred from Margaret Street.

When the Providore, a fine old gentleman named Mr Johnson, retired at this time he was replaced by Mr Gray, another of the bright personnel from the Union Company's stewarding staff. He was appointed as Superintendent of Victualling and Marine Stores Department. Gray was a tall fine looking man with rather a dark complexion and seemed widely known as "Maori" Gray. Whether this was because of his complexion or his service in a crack vessel of the Union Company history does not enlighten us, but he was always referred to as Maori Gray. He was a disciplinarian, intolerant of anything less than perfection, never popular but always respected and certainly showed results in his handling of his Department and seagoing personnel. Unfortunately he only stayed with the Company for a few years as he was offered a more lucrative position as manager of a large fashionable sea-side hotel in Manly, but he certainly proved an asset to the Company at the time the new passenger vessels were establishing themselves.

However, the Stores Department did not lose any of its new efficiency as the Company was fortunate in obtaining the services of Mr Samuel Livingston, a Scot with world-wide sea experience and experience of Australian conditions in interstate passenger vessels as well.

Sam Livingston became quite a personality on the waterfront, widely known and respected. He was very capable and demanded similar efficiency from his employees. Service to passengers continued to improve for he and F. C. Ward made an excellent team, and the Company had good reason to be proud of the reputation its passenger vessels held, until this side of the business was lost forever when World War II disrupted the service.

Captain Eric Livingston, formerly Sydney Harbour Master and later a Commissioner of the Maritime Services Board, was a son of the late Sam Livingston. Captain Livingston also had a link with the Company during World War II as he was commander of the M.V. "Wyrallah" for the Navy during the period of her most successful work. He later went on to command H.M.A.S. "Westralia". Readers will now begin to appreciate the wonderful work carried out by former Union S.S. Company officials from the turn of the century to 1920 under the guidance of Robert A. Bell. They welded and continued welding, a mass of small shipping companies or shipping ventures, either taken over (never harshly), or by way of amalgamation, into one organization, a Company with at one period a fleet of nearly thirty vessels and many more smaller steam vessels on the rivers used as droghers to the ocean going ships.

The N.C.S.N. Company then had a monopoly of transport to the whole North Coast as far as the Queensland border. The term monopoly—if it indicates any slackening in efficiency—is a misnomer because to the lasting credit of the firm, its policy was always to give satisfactory service and woe betide any employee who overlooked this first and foremost duty. It was ever a case of "the customer is always right" and more than a few employees found themselves in trouble as a result of overlooking this rigid requirement.

The Company was never extortionate in its freight rates or passenger fares; these were always under review and any representations from clients for variation were given careful consideration and agreed to if possible. The Company was regarded as a gilt-edged security, not spectacular in the distribution of dividends but a safe investment with a steady, assured return, and therefore regarded more or less as a trust investment. It retained this reputation up to the time it went into voluntary liquidation when shareholders were paid in the vicinity of 42s.6d. for each pound share.

PASSENGER FARES

.. OF THE ..

North Coast Steam Navigation Co. Ltd.

3 Sussex Street, Sydney.   March 1st, 1912, until further notice.

	SALOON. Single.	SALOON. Return.	2nd SALOON. Each Way.	STEERAGE Each Way.
	£ s. d.	£ s. d.	£ s. d.	£ s. d.
Byron Bay	1 17 6	3 5 0	1 10 0	1 0 0
Tweed River	1 10 0	2 10 0		
Richmond River—Ballina	1 15 0	2 17 6		0 17 6
„ „ Coraki	1 17 6	3 0 0		1 0 0
„ „ Lismore	1 17 6	3 5 0		1 2 6
Clarence River—Maclean	1 15 0	2 17 6	1 5 0	0 17 6
„ „ Grafton	1 17 6	3 0 0	1 7 6	1 0 0
Macleay River	1 12 6	2 15 0		0 17 6
Trial Bay	1 12 6	2 15 0		0 17 6
Manning River	1 2 6	2 5 0		0 17 6
Bellinger River	1 12 6	2 10 0		0 17 6
Nambucca River	1 12 6	2 10 0		
Coff's Harbour	1 15 0	3 0 0		1 0 0

INTERMEDIATE FARES.

	SALOON. Return.	SALOON. Single.
	£ s. d.	£ s. d.
Trial Bay to Coff's or Woolgoolga	1 5 0	0 12 6
Trial Bay to Richmond or Clarence Rivers	2 10 0	1 12 6
Trial Bay to Byron Bay	2 15 0	1 12 6
Coff's Harbour to Woolgoolga	0 15 0	0 7 6
Coff's or Woolgoolga to Byron Bay	1 15 0	1 2 6

The treatment of the staff was always considerate and there was never any difficulty in obtaining suitable young men; salary rates were generally in excess of other shipping companies (until in latter years they became more or less uniform) and service under the various able executives, officers from the Union Company and their successors who wisely followed their methods, provided excellent training, not only for future positions in the Company, but in other industries as well. Many young men who received their grounding in the North Coast Company have had successful careers. It was pleasing to note when the North Coast Company went into liquidation its employees had little or no difficulty in obtaining suitable employment, either in the shipping industry itself, or elsewhere.

One of the most picturesque masters in the North Coast service between 1863 and 1908 was Captain George Ricketts whose commanding presence, burly form and hearty manner were the epitome of the true British sailor of the great days of sail. His racy style was always forceful but never unkind. Born at Folkstone, Kent, in July 1833, he was apprenticed to the celebrated Richard Green, whose Blackwall Frigates made history in the days prior to the opening of the Suez Canal, and the introduction of ocean liners. In these ships he voyaged to India, China and other fabled places.

He completed his indentures in 1851 at Sydney while in the "Malacca" and returned to England, but Australia lured him back in the following year. He sailed to Victorian, Tasmanian, South Australian and New South Wales ports till he gained his Master's ticket in 1859. In 1863 he came to the Manning River as skipper of the schooner "William and Mary" and in 1868 joined the C. & R.R.S.N. Co. where he was appointed to command the P.S. "Belmore" about 1870, when he became the first to cross the Bellinger bar after the severe flood of that year, taking provisions for the relief of the flood-bound settlers. Then he did the same for the Nambucca settlers, thus inaugurating the direct service to these rivers.

In 1873 Captain Ricketts was appointed local manager on the Manning for the company, but three years later, as told elsewhere, they sold their interests, with the "Diamantina", to a local firm and the Captain joined them until 1879. By 1881 he was local agent for Nipper & See, later John See & Co. in 1883, remaining with them until the 1891 merger which created the N.C.S.N. Co., in whose service he remained until his retirement in 1906.

In 1885 the "Bortonius" was wrecked on the bar whilst crossing out of the Manning and was abandoned to the underwriters. John See bought the wreck and Captain Ricketts succeeded in refloating it, arriving in Sydney only 16 days after the purchase. For this John See & Co. presented him with a beautiful gold watch and chain valued at £50. The "Bortonius" was renamed "Lawrence" and traded on.

In 1903 Captain Ricketts was "running" the ex-Watson's Bay ferry "Oceana" to the Manning for the butter factory at Purfleet, but as she was crossing-in a heavy sea struck her, she broached to, and was totally wrecked on the breakwater. All hands were saved by the tug "John Gollan" but the gold watch was, sadly, among the effects lost by the veteran skipper. On his retirement from the N.C.S.N. Co. the directors voted him 12 months leave on full pay. He took a prominent part in most facets of public life over many years yet found time to father no less than 13 children. He died in 1908, aged 77.

75

CHAPTER FIVE

Country Branches and Seagoing Staff

One of the more important sides of Robert Bell's management was the organisation of the Outports and their management. In common with his policy of building up a modern fleet of vessels, he sought to improve the standard of management in the branches and in doing this appointed experienced shipmasters with a flair for business to manage the offices in the larger towns. How well he succeeded made shipping history and made Sir Allen's future task very much easier.

Some of the deep sea foreign-going officers who came to the North Coast did not stay long. These men — the snobs and the nervous or lazy types soon went back to their big liners and their luxury. Coastal and river navigation is very different to their type of sailing with the long periods between ports and days out of sight of land. Indeed, when the water hyacinth was bad, you could in a Coaster be out of sight of water!

Some men, the lazy ones, could not abide calling at six or more wharves in one day; the nervous ones grew even more nervous when the ship was in the smaller or trickier rivers—"Gutter Sailing"—they called it, and they were petrified when the ship was bumping her way over a bar or a shoal in a river. The snobs simply missed the gay life of big liners. The foregoing types could all, however, be perfectly certain on one fact. Not one of them was missed for a moment by the Company or the ships.

"Coolebar" off Bennelong Point, Sydney Harbour prior to 1914.
Acknowledgement: R. Dufty.

Those deep-sea men who did stay—the fearless, bold, skilled, the real men—were all worth their weight in gold.

Two bright young men who came early to Bell's notice were Captains W.G. Rippon and L.M. Gordon. While that fine shipmaster Captain James Hunter was sent to the U.K. for the S.S. "Orara" and the first "Wollongbar", this wasn't the practice with delivery of cargo vessels, but the always progressive Managing Director R.A. Bell decided to send two of his young chief officers with Foreign Going Masters Certificates to Scotland to take delivery of "Coolebar" and "Gunbar" which were building at the same time. Rippon and Gordon were selected for these vessels. Captain Rippon, who was the older man had spent some time as chief officer with Captain Hunter and the latter did not part with him very gracefully as he had a very high opinion of the man.

Captain Rippon was a very successful master in the small ship trade, especially on the Tweed River where bar navigation was always a hazard. He had plenty of daring, tempered with common sense and a true seaman's ability. In later years, he suffered from a severe arthritic leg condition, and was brought ashore to be appointed marine superintendent. Under his control not just one ship had to be spick and span; the whole fleet had to follow suit. The paint bills may have increased, but the improvement in the general condition and appearance of the vessels more than compensated for any extra expense.

Captain Rippon was forced to retire on account of ill-health and he spent the evening of his life at Tweed Heads. He was quite a personality at coastal ports, especially the Tweed.

Captain Gordon, selected to bring the "Gunbar" out from the builders, was more fortunate in his officers than Captain Rippon, as the "Gunbar" had a young company engineer as Chief, Mr Finlay Lawson, an excellent engineer who later became chief of many of the Company's vessels, and a young Scot as second mate who was anxious to remain on the coast after the vessel was delivered. This young second mate, Mr W. Taylor, proved a fine coastal officer but he later transferred to the South Coast Company and ultimately became their wharf superintendent.

With three driving forces like Gordon, Lawson and Taylor it was no wonder that the "Gunbar" looked like a yacht on arrival and it was remarked that "one could eat a meal on any part of the engine-room," while the same could be said of the deck department. It was also said that the crew of "runners" (men signed on for a delivery voyage only) could not get over the side quickly enough!

Captain Gordon was probably the youngest master the Company ever employed. Certainly, he was the most youthful ever to bring a vessel from overseas on her delivery voyage. Fortunately for him he appeared older than his years. He later became quite a personality in the Company and also in the far north coast territory of Byron Bay and the Richmond; always the most important and profitable trading centres.

Linton Matheson Gordon went to sea while still very young and spent several years as an apprentice, and later as an officer in sailing vessels. When he obtained his Foreign Going Masters ticket he joined the North Coast Company as chief officer of the "Minimbah" on her delivery voyage, staying on as the vessel's first mate. He came prominently under the notice of the management through his efforts in salvaging the engines and boilers from the "Minimbah" when she was wrecked so early in her career.

Gordon was then rapidly transferred from vessel to vessel as chief officer, to obtain all harbour and river pilot exemptions.

Towards the end of 1911, Gordon, then only 25 years of age, was sent to Scotland to bring the "Gunbar" out. He was later master of several other vessels and gained a very comprehensive knowledge of trades and vessels. The Company's policy at the time whenever possible, was to appoint suitable shipmasters as local managers at country centres, and in 1915 Captain Gordon, at the age of 29 years was selected by R. A. Bell to take over the then very important district of Byron Bay and the Tweed River.

He found no difficulty in making the change from a vessel's bridge to an office desk and he proved beyond doubt a most able local manager. In 1920 the Richmond River was showing rapid development and Sir Allen Taylor, then chairman of the Company, impressed by Gordon's ability, appointed him district manager of the Tweed, Byron Bay and Richmond River Districts, with headquarters at Lismore, where the Company purchased a very nice residence for the use of the manager.

His success in the post was phenomenal and the Company's business developed to its highest peak during his tenure of office. The district was progressing and he took great care that the Company's affairs matched this progression. He was so highly thought of by the directors, who visited him frequently, that no important business or change of masters in the Richmond River trade was ever finalised without being first submitted to the Lismore Office.

Captain Gordon would have gone much further in the service of the Company but for his untimely death in 1938 at the age of 52 years. Many tributes were paid to him in the Far North Coast press and the Northern Star (Lismore) in a leading article said, "as a citizen he filled an unique position in Lismore; people went to him when they had a scheme to benefit the town; he was a man who got things done".

Other seafaring personnel who proved to be successful local managers were as follows. The first and probably the foremost that comes to mind was Captain James Cockle, who represented the company at Coffs Harbour for many years. While this was not one of the more prosperous trades in itself, because of the fact that timber was its main export cargo, nevertheless, it was a very important port to the company.

Vessels going north to the Richmond, Clarence, or even the Macleay Rivers when the river bars were not carrying the necessary water, could still leave Sydney with capacity cargoes, which would include the Coff's Harbour cargo, the discharge of which then lightened the vessels of the required draft for entering the bar harbours. Of more importance still, Coff's always had plenty of timber loadings, the accumulation of which at times became a source of extreme worry to the local manager. He could never get the tonnage (cargo capacity in the vessel) he required and had to depend mainly on steamers coming from the north which had not obtained sufficient loading in the rivers, or were restricted because the bar did not permit maximum draft loading.

The standing instructions to the local managers and the masters of the vessels were — "If draft will not permit full loading of vessel, she is to call at Coff's to complete". This always left Coff's Harbour rather "up in the air" and with only short notice to load the timber trucks for the haul down the long jetty by railway.

These difficulties, together with the handling of interstate and New Zealand vessels all loading timber at the port and for whom the Company acted as agents, made Coff's a seven-day-a-week job including night work, and no doubt the most onerous of all the coastal ports. I venture to say very few men could have handled this port efficiently in the heyday of coastal shipping and remained sane. Nevertheless there was one, and he was Captain James Cockle. There was not much of him, but what there was, was all 24 carat and he was absolutely tireless. One could not keep up with him when visiting Coff's Harbour; he was like quicksilver — turn your back on him for a few moments and you would probably find him down on the jetty having jumped on a passing locomotive when he had perceived some hitch in the loading or discharging.

It was commonly said, (when some matter arose that caused a tricky situation to arise at Coff's) "leave it to Cockle, he will know how to handle it." Within the company the port was not often called Coff's Harbour, it was more commonly referred to as Cockle's Harbour. With all his onerous duties and long working hours he had a fine sense of humour and very seldom lost it. This must have been a great assistance to him.

With regard to the name of the port, it would appear that it was originally known as Korff's Harbour and the following extract from the "Daily Telegraph" of 19th May, 1914, is perhaps worthy of reproduction:—

The name of Coff's Harbour which has appeared for many years past on the maps of the Eastern Coast is a corruption of the proper name, Korff's Harbour, which it was called after the discoverer, Captain John Korff, a well-known ship-builder and marine surveyor during the 1840s. The Under Secretary for Lands was recently approached with the object of restoring the proper name on the official maps of his Department but, finding that this would be attended by official complications, he adopted a suggestion to have the name 'Korff's'

placed in brackets under that of Coff's." This was of course the same Captain John Korff mentioned in Chapter One.

The earliest continuous records of shipping date from about the year 1906, when it was reported that 417 vessels of a tonnage of 97,072 tons entered. The following is an extract from the Third Edition of the "North Coast Guide" published in 1920, and it will be seen that at that time a healthy future was forecast for the port. Time has proved that forecast to be correct:—

Coff's Harbour has during the past fifteen years come out of obscurity into much prominence. Originally merely a timber shipping port, it is now the outlet for a vast and rapidly growing district stretching northward to the Orara River, south to the Bellinger River and inland to the Dorrigo."

Mutton Bird Island, situated at the northern extremity of the harbour is half a mile long and one-third of a mile wide. Its highest point is 148 feet above sea level and the lee provides good shelter for vessels in southerly weather. The Island was connected to the mainland by the northern breakwater, about 1912/16. It derives its name from the large number of mutton birds which migrate there about November of each year. The birds tunnel into the ground to make their nests and leave the Island when the young can fly.

Due to circumstances such as the depression of 1930/34 and the war period, when practically all coastal shipping was requisitioned for war purposes, the number of vessels which entered Coff's Harbour varied between 412 in 1915 and 87 in 1943/44, but it is pointed out that the size of vessels had increased during that time. Since the demise of the N.C.S.N. Company shipping trade has progressively come to a halt.

The main types of timber shipped from Coff's Harbour comprised

Coff's Harbour prior to the building of the breakwater in 1916. S.S. "Orara" leaving for Sydney.
Acknowledgement: From the copy in the Mitchell Library.

all classes of Australian hard and soft woods, and were generally exported in the form of sawn and hewn logs, while piles have, on occasions, been shipped in 110 feet lengths for special work.

Logs were generally cut to weigh not more than 6 tons in order to facilitate handling, but turpentine piles up to 9 tons in weight have been shipped to Sydney for transshipment to Britain.

A timber jetty on piles, 1,740 feet long and 20 feet wide was built at the Port about 1886, and approval was given in 1941 for the structure to be extended by 300 feet. This work was completed by 1947 and it is possible to berth three vessels at the jetty at once, one of a tonnage of 5,000 gross on the south side and two coastal vessels at the northern berth. The jetty was strengthened over a length of 15 spans from the shore end in 1930 and four new fender dolphins were fitted at the south berth in 1933/34.

Captain W. Anderson, local manager of the N.C.S.N. Company Ltd at Grafton on the Clarence River was a fine example of the older generation of shipmasters. Not always tactful, he stood no nonsense from anyone, client or employee, but was very likeable in spite of his rather gruff manner. He was a very efficient local manager and highly respected by the Clarence River people with whom he came in contact. Captain Anderson was a former master in the Byron Bay trade for some years before going to Grafton where he remained for many years until his retirement from active duties. It was perhaps fortunate he did not see the days of industrial anarchy in the shipping industry, for he would never have tolerated the changing conditions.

Captain A. S. Ellery, local manager at Kempsey, was another of the able young foreign going ships' officers brought into the Company by Robert A. Bell to strengthen his seagoing personnel for the modern passenger and cargo fleet he was building to replace the more or less old-fashioned coastal vessels. This importation of deep-sea officers also built up a pool from which he could draw suitable local managers at key outports and marine and wharf superintendents at Sydney. Captain Ellery was an officer in the England-Australia mail liners and came under the notice of Mr Charles McAllister on one of his many trips to Scotland when new vessels were building. As Ellery showed interest in the coastal shipping and had ideas of settling in Australia, Charles McAllister must have thought "Well, here is another bright deep-sea boy for Mr Bell". Captain Ellery quickly adapted himself to the vastly different conditions in small ships in the coastal trade and became master of the fine steamer "Yulgilbar" running in the Macleay River Trade.

When the Macleay developed considerably due to the huge factory built by Nestlés at Smithtown and other natural progress in the district generally, the Agency personnel needed strengthening and history repeated itself as Captain Ellery was appointed local manager for the Macleay River with his headquarters at Kempsey. Ellery was successful in his new sphere and never quite lost his mail boat style and early training. He went right to the point, no beating about the bush and was intolerant of others with less vision. He entered into local shire and council business for the betterment of the district. His ideas were quite refreshing, and somewhat revolutionary by comparison with the more staid country outlook. However, when he became better known he was respected for his down to earth and rather salty criticisms. When news got round that "the Skipper" was getting on the box at any meeting there was always a good attendance. He was missed when he retired on account of ill health and advancing years. He was a good family man and would have been proud of his eldest son who has since become a prominent figure in the field of banking.

Robert Bell's plan of completely reorganising and improving the quality of both the ships and the staff of the Company had reached a further milepost when he had the key outports — the Richmond/Tweed districts, Clarence River, Coff's Harbour, and Macleay River — in the hands of vigorous and competent shipmaster-managers. In the early years of the century contact with the country centres was difficult, as there were no long distance telephones, mails were slow and telegrams were subject to long delays. Shipmasters in those days were their own traffic managers at the outports and little was heard of their activities after they left Sydney until telegrams arrived or lighthouse sightings advised, saying that they were on their return passage to Sydney.

Ship's officers carried out all stevedoring work with their crew and a sprinkling of local labour, paid wages and victualling accounts at outports from the master's cash advances, and collected passage money paid en route. Country agencies comprised mostly local men acting as delivery clerks for the cargo, with no authority or ability to control the shipmasters.

Although the masters in the early days did wonderful work at the outports without all the present day aids and other amenities it was hardly to be expected that they would, or could, give consideration to the overall obligations of a shipowner, most important of which is to make every endeavour to consider and give satisfaction to his clients. Masters naturally considered their ships first and had a tendency to choose from accumulations of cargo at outports the back loading most suited for trimming their vessels for the passage south to Sydney.

Most masters endeavoured to avoid the loading of large quantities of empty casks, drums, cases, etc., which filled their holds without giving any draft; this was always a source of complaint from the consignees in the country and the merchants in Sydney. Other masters, with an eye to not only their own comfort on the passage south, but also to having more time off in Sydney, tried to avoid cargo that would necessitate a shift while in Sydney to more than one discharging berth.

There were naturally many disadvantages in this system, where there was no firm control, and some masters were a law unto themselves; but all these defects were tidied up with the advent of shipmasters as local managers. As mailing facilities improved copies of ships' manifests reached outports prior to the vessels' arrival and local managers were able to work out a prompt discharging and loading programme. On the Richmond for instance, while the Office at Lismore was only 20 miles by road from the entrance on the river at Ballina, vessels had nevertheless to steam 70 miles with several wharves at which to discharge before arriving at Lismore.

Under the improved methods of ship control the master, on arrival at the wharf in Ballina, received his working instructions for discharging up the river and loading for the return passage to Sydney. Estimated times of arrival and departure were worked out by local managers who knew the river conditions and who had personal experience in working the rivers. This relieved the seagoing masters of a lot of worry, considerably improved their turn around and also did away with the disadvantages of the old "different ships different tallies" methods. Naturally there was a lot of passive resistance and dislike to what some masters referred to as "being treated like a lot of schoolboys" but after a time they appreciated the improved conditions and it became common to hear them remarking amongst themselves "give me the Richmond River Trade—you know exactly where you are there, and there is no humbugging about".

Another great advantage was that as Lismore became a large discharging port, considerable shore labour was employed and it was essential to have the time of arrival at Lismore to enable wharf labour to be ordered in without incurring long waiting time periods. Forward planning also assisted with the ordering in of cargo for shipment to Sydney, and this was appreciated by intending shippers and carriers. Similar programme methods were soon adopted at other rivers and most of the outport worries were things of the past for the Sydney Head Office.

Before closing the story of the country branches, mention should be made of a family highly respected in the district even before the turn of the century who looked after the affairs of the Company in the River for many years; the Storey family, father Captain John Storey and two sons John Jr. and Frank. No information appears available of the time Captain Storey joined the Company or of his early background, but it is understood he came from sailing vessels, although it doesn't appear that he had any seafaring experience with the Company. He was a man of fine physique, well over 6 feet with a long white beard. He was seldom seen by the vessels trading to the river as he left all cargo matters to his sons and mainly occupied himself looking after the large fleet of river droghers and punts. When Captain Storey paid occasional visits to the river towns and called on the storekeepers he travelled on the drogher "Irvington" (commonly referred to as "Captain Storey's yacht") or by horse and buggy.

In those far off days an important person's wearing apparel included a high stiff collar, stiff-fronted white shirt with 4 in to 5 in stiff white cuffs and Captain Storey thought fit to dress himself accordingly when on his periodic visits to clients. It is common knowledge that the most irritating and contentious matter that crops up when shipowners meet clients is the matter of cargo claims; the shipowner quotes his bill of lading exemptions and the client retorts that "if you are going to shelter behind your mumbo jumbo on the bill of lading it seems you accept no responsibility for anything". The result is either a compromise or an unfriendly parting with the client.

Storekeepers used to recount that Captain Storey was different in his method of dealing with claims and other complaints; he shot out his large stiff shirt cuff and painstakingly noted thereon all complaints and claims, invited the clients to partake of liberal refreshment and parted the best of friends. The story ended, however, on the Captain's return home, when he changed and bathed, the stiff shirt with the day's notes on it went into the washtub!

Mr R. G. Piggott, of Raleigh, remembers that the "Euroka" was the last vessel to navigate the Bellinger River as far as Fernmount and she only proceeded as far because she was carrying an 8-ton boiler for a Dorrigo client, and any other wharf would have meant a river crossing by punt. This would be early in this century. As a boy, he says, he was very interested in the "Euroka"'s engines, which he remembers were of the oscillating cylinder type.

The "Rosedale" used to go up the river as far as Fernmount, and the "Avon" before her got as far as Government Wharf at Bellingen, but in late years only droghers and log punts used the river beyond, say, Repton.

Mr Piggott also says that Allen Taylor's "Wootton" only got as far as Raleigh on her maiden trip, and there she grounded. The

SANDY CREEK
R.R

IRVINGTON

droghers on the river in those days included Allen Taylor's "Dawn", the "Bull Rout", the "Our Harry" (Doepel's) and the "Eric"—a round-bilge vessel with the engines from the "Bull Rout", which had been wrecked on the wall at Urunga. The "Sudden Jerk" was a stern wheeler.

The river also had four saw-mills, each with its own log punt so traffic must have been pretty busy at the turn of the century.

The Bellinger has also seen a few strandings in its time. The "Petrel", "Harrington", and "Fernmount" all went ashore north of the entrance, and one was hauled over the sand-hills by bullock team and was launched into the river. The "Rosedale" went on to the South Beach another time and the "Coolebar" also went on to the beach. They were refloated. The tug "Repton" went on to the end of the wall and had to be blown up.

The Schooner "Alma Doepel" (still afloat in Hobart) stove in some planks on the wall, but got off; her Captain, George Petersen, was a law unto himself, repeatedly entering against the "Black Ball".

Mr Piggott also points out that there is a controversy about the introduction of *paspalum*

as described in Chapter Two. Some people still say that one Hudson Bird deserves the credit, the story being that his brother, a Naval

Bar Tug "Repton", removed from this inelegant position with dynamite.
Acknowledgement: K. Wilson.

Drogher "Irvington"—Captain Storey's "Yacht"—in the water hyacinth—Richmond River.
Acknowledgement: D. Wilkinson

officer, sent him some seed from the islands. An acquaintance of his, a lady then in her 99th year, remembers that her people bought some seed in 1892 from a Bellingen storekeeper. Certainly by 1901 Raleigh farmers were using it for hay, and roots were being sent to Kempsey.

Mr Piggott travelled in the "Rosedale", the "Yulgilbar" to the Macleay River, the "Tambar" in 1914 to enlist, and also the "Cavanba" to Coff's, and several times in "Fitzroy" under James Colvin.

Years ago, it was not necessary for skippers of droghers and small river craft to have a master's ticket, and when this requirement came in old skippers with more than so many years' experience were granted one without examination. This type of ticket was called a "Certificate of Servitude", and merely recognised a man's ability to skipper a boat because of long experience in the game. Younger men sat for the new examination, being awarded the usual certificate as is the case today. There would be very few, if any, of the old "Ticket of Servitude" men still living.

The story is told of the old days on the Bellinger, when the pub at Urunga used to front right on the wharf and in the evenings all the river droghers and launches—maybe a dozen or more—would tie up for the night and the crews would go over to the pub for a drink and yarn. One of the drogher skippers was a young fellow who had just been granted a ticket, having passed his examination, and he was very proud of all his knowledge of matters nautical. Seeing an old veteran—a Swede by birth—nearby, he went over to him and, airing his knowledge, said:- "Oh Hans, I passed you on the river the other day and blew a short blast on my whistle to tell you I was turning to starboard and you didn't acknowledge it. Why?" The old Swede looked up from his beer, squinted at the young

fellow, scratched his head, and said: "Vistle? Vistle?—Damn der Vistle! If you vant to signal choost vave der hand!"

A very large number of seamen, including the officers, were of Scandinavian origin, and their homeland's loss became this country's very great gain. Many have already been mentioned in these pages, and others will appear later, but their skill as seamen deserves some special mention. Dane, Swede, Finn or Norwegian, they had a history of seafaring going back to the dawn of recorded history— to the Vikings and their wonderful longships. The sea is in the blood of these men to a degree at least as strong as the Anglo-Saxon, or the Scot and the Welshman. Other races also played an important role, amongst them the German, Estonian, Pole, the Dutch, and some Russians. Their daring and skill was matched by their dry humour, and at times an imperfect command of the English language added further to this reputation as a band of comics. They worked hard, drank hard and played hard, and their loyalty was legendary. They stayed with their ships for years, often performing voluntarily additional jobs to make their particular vessel a bit more "tiddley". One, an Estonian named Martin Pool, broke his foot when a girder fell on it on the "Nimbin" but refused to leave the ship for treatment. Another, a seaman known as "Charlie", once fell down an open hatchway. "I put my foot on noddings and then I knew I was going somewheres", was the way he explained the event later. With so many Andersens, Carlsens, Petersens, Jansens, Hansens, etc., it was natural that many should acquire distinctive nicknames and thus there were "O.T. Joe", "Cooee", "Gunner" and many many more.

River droghers played a very important part in the early days before road motor transport. The droghers, often towing punts, brought various farm produce and timber, etc., from the river banks of the farms and the small timber mills on the smaller arms and creeks, and also on the main river itself where berthing facilities did not exist for ocean-going vessels. Often the farmers were late in getting their produce to the river bank and the droghermen assisted in sewing up the bags of maize, potatoes, etc., and drove the pigs and calves down the paddocks to the droghers.

The foregoing serves to illustrate the kind of men that the Company had along the coast, and who were responsible in large measure for the success the firm enjoyed for so many years. It also pays tribute to the man who was responsible for managing this success—Robert Aitken Bell.

T.S.S. "Yulgilbar" at Jerseyville Wharf. Thought to be departure of enlisted men, 1914.
Acknowledgement: Photo late H. M. Sullivan, courtesy J. M. Sullivan.

CHAPTER SIX

Allen Taylor & Co.

Sir Allen Taylor, M.L.C., was probably the leader in the field of the N.S.W. hardwood timber industry at the time he joined the North Coast Company and became the most prominent personality in North Coast shipping from 1920 until his death. While he had a solid foundation on which to build as a result of the untiring efforts of Robert A. Bell before him, nevertheless the North Coast Company had to thank him for the fast diesel vessels which he had ordered from the leading builders of this class of vessel—Messrs Burmeister and Wain in Copenhagen; coastal vessels which were admitted by shipping people of the time to be unequalled anywhere in the world.

Sir Allen's previous experience of ships had been confined mainly to Ernest Wright's locally built wooden vessels, all of which had been specially built with the carriage of turpentine piles in mind, but with his far seeing record in the municipal, political and commercial fields, he was naturally quick to readjust his ideas and realize the needs of the general cargo and passenger trades on the coast, although he insisted that the new "Wollongbar" (then building) have deck space large enough to carry turpentine piles.

Sir Allen was also a tireless worker and was considerably more than a mere chairman. He was also a managing director and spent a lot of his time practically every day at the Company's wharves in Sussex Street, where he visited all the heads of departments, the superintendent engineer, marine superintendent, draftsman, accountant, and so on, commencing with the practical branches before 8 a.m. Ships' plans and accountancy figures and graphs were meat and drink to him. He had a wonderful memory for figures and it was most unwise to quote figures without being certain of accuracy, as one could be faced with the same question months or years hence, probably for comparison purposes and one was not in a very comfortable position if the answers did not agree.

Not content with the many long hours that he put in at the North Coast Company offices, Sir Allen found time to run his own firm which is still in existence, and also served as a member of the Legislative Council, not to mention several terms of office in Sydney Municipal Council where he was Lord Mayor on more than one occasion. He was born in 1864 and died in 1941.

Sir Allen Taylor became closely connected with the North Coast Company in the following manner. Under an agreement dated 16th May, 1919, the Company took over the shipping interest of Allen Taylor & Co., including in the transaction the transfer of the wooden steamers "Glenreagh", "Narani", "Our Jack" and "Wallamba". Shares were issued to Sir Allen's Company, and it is possible that there was a cash consideration also. Under this agreement, Taylors had the right to nominate a director to the North Coast Board who did not have to present himself for periodic re-election by the shareholders. Sir Allen himself appears to have been the nominee in the first place but, in 1920, he became a director in his own right and was therefore available later in the same year to become Chairman of Directors when Mr Walter C. Watt died. Walter Watt was well known in Sydney business circles as the "Watt" of Messrs Gilchrist, Watt & Sanderson.

Upon Sir Allen's appointment to his office, Allen Taylor & Co.'s nominee became Mr F. A. Sargeant. After the 1919 agreement, the North Coast Company did not compete against Allen Taylor & Co. in the small timber ports, nor did Allan Taylor's offer any competi-

S.S. "Hastings"—cargo and PASSENGER! vessel, built on the Manning River 1901.
Acknowledgement: R. Dufty.

tion to the larger company in the principal trading centres on the coast. Allen Taylor & Co. dates back to 1893 when its founder acquired timber on the North Coast and elsewhere, subsequently building mills and a fleet of ships to carry the timber to Sydney and other ports.

At first small schooners and ketches were engaged in the trade, plying from various coastal ports to Sydney; then in 1900, their first steamer was built. This was the "Wootton", a single screw wooden vessel of 151 tons, built by Mr J. Miles at Forster. Fitted to carry passengers, the ship plied from the north coast to Sydney for some years and was then sold to the Kaiapoi Shipping & Trading Co. Ltd., operating on the New Zealand coast until converted to a hulk in 1927.

About this time Mr Taylor (as he then was) joined forces with Nicholas Cain of Wauchope and they traded as Cain & Taylor in the timber business until the partnership was dissolved about 1904.

The next steamer was the "Hastings" of 193 tons, also of wood, built in 1901 by D. Sullivan at Coopernook on the Manning River. Mr Sullivan built a number of vessels in the early part of this century which became well known in the coastal trade. "Hastings" was only a few years in the Taylor service, for she was sold in 1904 to Mr N. Cain for the Port Macquarie passenger and cargo trade and ultimately ended her days in Tasmanian waters.

In 1902, two wooden vessels were built—the steamer "Pyrmont" of 213 tons by Sullivan at Coopernook, and the ketch "Ladysmith" of 111 tons by Miles at Forster, which ran for many years until wrecked on the North Coast.

Further expansion took place in 1903, three steamers being added to the fleet. The steel steamer "Croki" of 303 tons was built by the Montrose S.B. Co. Ltd at Montrose, Scotland. Having a length of 135.5 feet the "Croki" was propelled by triple expansion engines installed aft, could carry 240 tons of cargo and had accommodation for 24 passengers in deck cabins. The vessel, named after a township on the Manning River, arrived in Sydney in July, 1903. However her career in the coastal trade as very short as, on 13th September of the same year the "Croki" was totally wrecked on Little Seal Rock while en route from the Manning River to Sydney, fortunately without loss of life.

The second ship was the "Narooma", a single screw wooden vessel of 105 tons built at Narooma on the south coast. Later sold to J. T. Evans, she was wrecked at Boat Harbour north of Broken Bay on 4th February, 1909, due to heavy weather.

The third vessel to be built in 1903 was the "Tuncurry", also a wooden ship of 162 tons, 113.5 feet long and propelled by compound engines; she was built by J. Wright at Tuncurry. Later the vessel was sold to the Resident Commissioner, Gilbert and Ellice Islands and renamed "Tokelau". Subsequently she was bought by Mel-

bourne owners, given back her old name and she traded on the Victorian coast. Her name disappeared from the register in 1919.

In September, 1903, we find that regular services were being maintained by the Allen Taylor line to the Manning and Bellinger Rivers, Tuncurry, Camden Haven and Port Macquarie with the steamers "Croki", "Pyrmont", "Hastings", "Commonwealth" and "Bellinger", the two last named being under charter.

S.S. "Pyrmont" passing the suburb for which she was named.
Acknowledgement: R. Dufty.

By 1905 the fleet had been reduced by the sale of the "Hastings" to Nicholas Cain, and river steamer "Coopernook" to the North Coast S.N. Company who employed her for some years as a drogher on the Macleay River. The "Pyrmont" was sold to the North Coast S.N. Company also in 1904 and they ran her mainly to the Hastings River. On 6th August, 1909, after the Company had abandoned that trade to Nicholas Cain, the "Pyrmont" suffered great damage when, inward bound from Sydney, she crashed on to the training-wall at the entrance to the Manning River. The ship was subsequently re-floated and brought to Sydney for repair. Sold in 1910 to Burns Philp & Co. for the Island trade, she was renamed "Mindoro" and was finally wrecked in New Guinea in 1913.

In between the years 1906 and 1909 four wooden twin screw steamers were added to the fleet and, being specially built for the North Coast River bars, were shallow drafted. The first was the "Ellerslie" launched in 1906 and wrecked at the entrance to the Bellinger River on 29th May, 1913. Her engine and boiler were salvaged and put into the hull of the "Wallamba".

The next to be built was the smallest of the fleet, the "Wandra" of 164 tons, launched in 1907. Running to both the North and South Coast for timber, "Wandra" was wrecked on the Drum and Drumsticks Rocks, near Jervis Bay on 15th December, 1915.

The "Uralla" of 200 tons was built in 1908 and like the earlier vessels she was also fitted with compound engines. This vessel ran for only three years in the Allen Taylor interests, carrying timber mainly from the Bellinger and Nambucca Rivers and Camden Haven to Sydney. Sold in 1911 to the Illawarra & South Coast S.N. Company she was renamed "Tilba" but was destined to have the shortest career of them all, being totally wrecked on 18th November, 1912, at Wreck Bay, whilst bound from Narooma to Wollongong with a cargo of timber. The engines and boiler were recovered and later installed in the "Belmore".

The last to be built was a second "Tuncurry", also a wooden vessel but twin screw propelled by compound engines, of 236 tons. She was built by John Wright at Tuncurry. The vessel, which was fitted with passenger accommodation, was a regular trader between Sydney and Tuncurry for many years, for the most part making two round trips per week. Departing from Sydney on Monday and Thursday evenings, she began the return trips from northern ports on Wednesday and Saturdays, the journey each way lasting about 14 hours. In the early 1920s "Tuncurry" was lengthened by 20 feet.

With the onset of the depression there was not enough trade for both the "Tuncurry" and the larger "Allenwood", so the former was laid up in Sydney, being sold in 1932 to H. R. Pountney of Cook's Hill, to carry coal from the Belmont Mine, Lake Macquarie, to Sydney. In 1935 Cam & Sons, the well-known trawler owners of Sydney, bought her and after overhaul re-employed the vessel in the Lake Macquarie coal trade. The "Tuncurry" also ran to Shell-harbour for blue metal and to Port Macquarie for timber. She was dismantled in Sydney soon after the 1939/45 war.

Wright of Tuncurry built yet another wooden ship for the Company, "Comboyne" of 281 tons, launched in 1911. The vessel traded to North and South Coast ports for timber and whilst so engaged was lost off Bass Point, in September, 1921.

In 1912 the "Blaxland", a steel twin screw steamer of 399 tons gross, was launched by Mackie & Thomson Ltd. of Glasgow. Very similar to the Illawarra Company's steamer "Bermagui", she was propelled by two sets of compound engines installed aft. After

T.S.S. "Our Jack" stuck on the Nambucca Bar with a big deck cargo of timber.
Acknowledgement: Tuncurry Historical Society.

running mainly to Camden Haven the "Blaxland" was sold in 1915 to William Holyman & Sons, who in turn sold her the following year to Australian Steamships Pty. Ltd. They renamed the vessel "Innisfail" and employed her in the Townsville to outports trade for many years. Requisitioned by the Navy at the outbreak of war, she was for a time stationed in Sydney. After the war "Innisfail" was returned to owners who sold her to Chinese buyers two years later. Her name disappeared from Lloyd's register in 1959/60.

Then, in 1914, the "Narani" was built by E. Wright of Tuncurry. Somewhat larger than "Comboyne", she was of 381 tons and ran in the North Coast timber trade for about five years when, along with "Wallamba", she was bought by the N.C.S.N. Company Ltd., who ran her mainly to the Nambucca and Richmond Rivers and Byron Bay. In February, 1924, she was bought by the Illawarra & South Coast S.N. Company Ltd., to replace the "Bodalla" which had been wrecked at Narooma.

The "Wallamba" was somewhat similar to the "Narani" but of 331 tons, having a stovepipe on the top of her otherwise conventional funnel; the vessel was also built by Wrights in 1917 and registered as jointly owned by Allen Taylor & Co. Ltd. and E. Wright & Co. Ltd., but had only a short career in the Allen Taylor interests as she passed into the hands of the N.C.S.N. Company Ltd. in 1919. Her deadweight capacity was 280 tons and her compound engines had, as mentioned earlier, been salvaged from the "Ellerslie".

"Glenreagh" of 498 tons, again from Wrights at Tuncurry, was built in 1919 but soon after was transferred to the N.C.S.N. Company. A twin screw wooden steamer, "Glenreagh" was propelled by triple expansion engines and was fitted with two boilers placed side by side with her two funnels placed athwartship. Although the engines and boilers were placed aft there was a small hold between the engines and her stern. Under the North Coast flag this unusual vessel ran to Coff's Harbour, the Clarence and Richmond rivers. For some time during 1924 and 1925 "Glenreagh" was engaged in the timber trade to Melbourne, being under charter to Allen Taylor & Co. Ltd. In any case she did not see a great deal of service when owned by the North Coast Company, spending much of her time laid up in Sydney. Sold to Penguin Ltd. of Sydney in 1934, she was dismantled and converted to a lighter shortly afterwards.

Incidentally the Company had an interest in the wooden steamer "Our Jack" of 272 tons built by John Wright at Tuncurry in 1907. Although registered in the name of the latter, the vessel frequently ran in the Allen Taylor interests before passing into the hands of the North Coast S.N. Company Ltd.

T.S.S. "Glenreagh" off Rose Bay—note unusual funnel arrangement.
Acknowledgement: R. Dufty.

The last ship specially built for the Company was the "Allenwood", a wooden twin screw vessel of 398 tons, built by Wrights and launched in 1920. The engines, which were installed aft, were notable in that they were not identical sets and she had a distinctive profile with two funnels placed closely one behind the other. At first her trade was mainly to Camden Haven but from 1932 when "Tuncurry" was sold, she was the only ship in the fleet and her trading included Tuncurry as well. She also made frequent trips to Port Stephens and on occasions visited Port Macquarie and the Manning River on the North Coast and Narooma and Eden on the South Coast. The "Allenwood" was totally wrecked on Wybung beach about 5 miles north of Norah Head early on the morning of 14th September, 1951. Bound for Port Macquarie in ballast she was enveloped by heavy fog and, losing her way, ran ashore. This left the company with no ships and it appeared as though its days as a shipowner had ended, but, in 1952, they acquired the "Bermagui" (402 tons), "Bergalia" (548 tons) and "Cobargo" (860 tons), all ex Illawarra Co.

Their colour scheme differed greatly from the traditional Allen Taylor light grey hull and yellow funnel with black top, as their hulls were black with a white band and red boot topping, whilst the upperworks were white, the funnels deep scarlet with black tops and broad white bands. Thus with the exception that deep scarlet had been substituted for chocolate on the funnels the ships still looked like Illawarra boats.

The Company's main ports on the North Coast were Port Macquarie, Camden Haven and Port Stephens with occasional visits to the Macleay and Clarence Rivers. They have owned no ships since October, 1957, and it does not seem that they will again enter into shipowning. For many years the Allen Taylor ships operated from a wharf in Black Wattle Bay near where the freighter "Burwah" now discharges cement. The wharf was known as Taylor's wharf, Pyrmont. Their ships brought timber and passengers, returning with back-loadings of general cargo to the North Coast. The ships were advertised to sail from Sydney for Cape Hawke, Forster, Tuncurry, Nabiac, Krambach, Failford and Coolongoolook, also for Camden Haven, Laurieton, Kew and Kendall. In the days before the railways and sealed roads they were also advertised to carry passengers and cargo for Gloucester and the Comboyne. The Company moved to Commercial Road, Rozelle, in 1941.

Perhaps a brief word about Wright's of Tuncurry would not go amiss at this juncture. John Wright Snr. was the founder of both Tuncurry itself, and also the shipbuilding industry for which it was well known. In 1890 he built a small sailing vessel, "The Stanley" and used her to carry timber to Sydney, returning with general cargo. She was replaced in 1903 by the steamer "Tuncurry" which was owned jointly by John Wright and Allen Taylor. The screw steamer "Bellinger" at 350 tons, the same size as the "Tuncurry", was built soon afterwards. She was lost in dramatic circumstances at Nambucca Heads in April 1912. In 1907 "Our Jack", 281 tons, was built, also for the same owners. The year 1910 saw the laying of the keel for a vessel of 400 tons, the "Comboyne" but only the keel had been laid when John Wright died.

His son, Ernest, completed this ship in 1911, and followed her with the "Narani", 1914, "Wallamba", 1917, "Glenreagh", 1919, "Allenwood", 1920, "Nambucca" 1, 1922, "Nambucca" 2, 1936, and the "Uralba", 1942, in the meantime building many small tugs, lighters, yachts, lifeboats, and launches, etc. During the Second

World War no less than thirty vessels were built for the war effort between 1942 and 1945. They were in two classes, 45 feet and 85 feet respectively, and were numbered not named.

In 1946, on 23rd January, Ernest Wright died. He had, in 1942, formed the company of E. Wright & Son, and this son, John Jnr., built the 350 ton "Santa Cruz" in 1948. She was sold on the stocks to W. Coach of Sydney, then to S. G. White & Co. The yard then closed down owing to lack of work.

Shipping in N.S.W. was closely allied with the timber industry and a great deal of the loading was composed of timber of all kinds. The names of many timber merchants have already been mentioned but the best known was Allen Taylor & Co. Ltd. This Company was responsible for the opening up of large areas of timber country. The timber was mostly hardwood and comprised ironbark, blackbutt and spotted gum, amongst others.

Forestry in N.S.W. is under State control and country of 6,000,000 acres or more has been reserved or dedicated for the conservation of timber supply. The Forest Laws are embodied in a code of regula-tions, under which all workers in Crown Forests are required to register or license themselves.

The hardwoods of N.S.W. have achieved a world-wide reputation. A considerable export trade is done in these timbers. Railway sleepers of the highest grade are cut from these woods and turpentine piles for wharves and piers have been found in sound condition after long years of service.

Sailing ships used to trade to open roadsteads and when there were no loading facilities, the logs were drawn to the beach by bullock teams and hauled through the surf by lengthy gear from the ship. A lifelong friendship was formed during such work by a ship's officer who afterwards became master of the "Wollongbar" and one of the bullock drivers who later became one of the most prominent businessmen of the North Coast, in fact, a leading figure throughout Australia in primary industry, with which he was connected. The ship's officer concerned was, of course, Captain Hunter, the bullock driver was Mr W. Clifford, later manager of the Norco Co-operative Co.

The Author wishes to thank G. A. Hardwick Esq. of Sydney for information contained in this chapter. "The Log", Vol. 4 No. 3, gives more detail.

95

CHAPTER SEVEN

The Roaring Twenties

By 1920, several of the older steamers were no longer up to the exacting standards demanded by the company for work out of the various bar harbours involved in the North Coast service, and they consequently became redundant. Indeed, they had only remained this long in service because of the Great War.

That wonderful old paddler, the "City of Grafton"—laid up in 1913—was hulked but even in this form she was to render another ten years of faithful service, while the "Cavanba" and the "Noorebar"—both acquired from G. W. Nicoll in 1904—were sold to serve on other coasts; the "Cavanba" in China and the "Noorebar" in Sumatra.

During the course of the year the "Maianbar" grounded at the entrance to the Macleay River and she defied efforts to refloat her for more than a month. Eventually, after the most strenuous efforts by all concerned she was refloated somewhat the worse for wear and moved to Sydney for a major overhaul. It was, I believe, at this time that she underwent her "operation" at Mort's Dock, whereby her length was increased by some 17 feet. This was accomplished by the simple expedient of cutting the ship in halves just forward of the bridge structure, dragging the two parts the required distance apart, and plating in the gap. The job was not as simple as it sounds above, of course, but it was done, and in a most satisfactory manner too.

She ran for 20 years after this "operation" until her sad loss in 1940.

Mort's Dock was something straight out of Charles Dickens, with the office staff in frock coats and toppers. Even the payroll was collected from the bank by the cashier wearing a frock coat, riding in an old Brougham drawn by a pair of greys, the driver in full livery, and lobsterback cap.

Old turners used the same lathe for over thirty years, and if anyone else touched it, or leaned on it, there was the very hell to pay. Several of my correspondents have written about their apprenticeships at Mort's and all say that it was an enjoyable part of their lives. Some were there when "Bill" McKell was a boilermaker's apprentice; later he was Premier of N.S.W. and finally Governor-General of the Commonwealth, Sir William McKell. Two sons of Captain Colvin of the "Fitzroy" also served their time with Mort's. Alas, this Firm is another of this country's institutions that is no longer with us.

The famous old "Electra" which, it will be remembered, was the pioneer of electric light and refrigeration in coastal vessels, was sold in 1919 to W. Waugh & Co. and was, in November of that year, cut down and hulked. She was later sold to The Broken Hill Pty. Co. Ltd. and became a tar store. She was not finally broken up until 1930.

Another of the old ships, the "Ramornie", which had been built in Glasgow in 1902 was sold to Western Australia, also in 1919. She had spent her life trading to the Richmond, the Clarence and the Macleay Rivers and in 1916 her passenger accommodation was removed and her cargo hatches lengthened. In common with many of these coasters livestock was carried on the forward deck and the passenger accommodation had been situated under the poop and also in a house on the upper deck near the stern. This house was moved further aft when the hatches were lengthened. After her sale in 1919 she was used for a time as a lighthouse tender on the western coast of the continent before being sold again, this time to New Zealand. She was renamed "Opua" and was wrecked at Tora, near Pallister Bay on 22nd October, 1926. Her wreck may still be seen.

The little "Wauchope"—a wooden steamer of only 120 tons—was built in Sydney for the Allen Taylor fleet and she and the "Allenwood" were the only boats to be built for the combined fleet at all during 1920. However, trade was beginning to return to normal—that is as "normal" as it would ever be again after the Great War. Everything had changed. The motor car was now becoming more popular than the horse, a trend that was to continue until it developed into something of a transport revolution, while shortly aeroplanes would be built which would make scheduled air transport a practical reality, at the same time doing much to put the coastal passenger ship out of business.

The introduction of wharf labourers subsequently played a key part in forcing the small coastal steamer off the trade routes of this country. Thanks almost entirely to these "labourers" the number of intra-state shipping movements in the port of Sydney fell from 4,568 vessels with a total gross tonnage of 3,127,372 tons in 1938/9, to 2,220 vessels in 1946/7 (gross tons of 1,956,132) rising to only 2,420 vessels (2,028,883 tons gross) in 1949 when these vessels which the R.A.N. had used during the war of 1939/45 were returned to go about their lawful occasions. This represents a decrease of no less than 2,148 sailings per year in only 10 years. The 1,099,489 gross tons of cargo space lost has forced this amount of cargo (and it would be much more than this now, 41 progressive years later) to be carried by road and rail. Another important point is that the average coaster required a crew of approximately eighteen men. With the number of ships involved, quite a few seamen were employed in this trade, and these men are now forced to find work away from shipping. At one stage the N.C.S.N. fleet comprised twenty-seven vessels, and that is just one firm.

Even this is not the whole story, for when the above figures were published in 1950 these companies were still in business. Now they are not, yet they did not "go broke!"—They went into voluntary liquidation because they did not consider it was worthwhile continuing against the opposition and obstructionism arrayed against them by this powerful minority of workers. One example will suffice—the "Allenwood" used to arrive at Allen Taylor's wharf at Rozelle Bay at 8 a.m. in the morning, unload her entire cargo of timber, reload with a general cargo for the North Coast and sail again at 4.30 p.m. the same day. This work was performed by her own crew. The very first time the "wharfies" took over this work, the job took a week!

To be perfectly fair to all concerned, the crew members on these little vessels worked hard. The late John Allcot, the famous marine artist, was once a sailor and at one time he was on the South Coaster "Merimbula"; of life aboard her he had this to say— "with her it was one month aboard and three months in hospital to recover afterwards". It seems that we have gone from one extreme to the other, and the former is perhaps the more acceptable, as jobs are always needed in a young, growing country. Certainly, good honest work is preferable to unemployment, and progress only comes by hard work.

Back in the Charleston era, those wild years the "roaring 20s", a completely new outlook on life was born—a new era—although many

97

were to regret the passing of older, more gracious ways, even if modern improvements did make life easier. In 1921 the old "Kallatina" was sold and she left Sydney for the last time, bound for Brisbane. Her new owners were John Burkes and she served them well, going as far afield as the Gulf of Carpentaria and on the Darwin run as part of her new job. What wonderful little ships they were, to sail 13,000 miles out from the builders, serve their owners for thirty years and more, and still be fit for years of hard service in a trade for which they were never intended or designed, running many times as far as the mere 300 or so miles per trip for which they were built.

At Byron Bay jetty, on Saturday 14th May, 1921, the "Wollongbar" was loading a typical cargo of butter, meat and sundries, and it was intended that she should sail as usual for Sydney that night. As it fell out, this was not to be, and her remains may still be seen in the surf at the spot where she stranded that day so long ago. Many stories have been told of how she met her end that Saturday, but they are nearly all wrong. I believe that the following version, told to me by two independent witnesses (one each on the ship and the jetty at the time) tells the correct story.

Some time before the loss of the "Wollongbar" her master, Captain Hunter, had reported on arrival in Sydney, that at low tide alongside the Byron Bay jetty, the ship had touched bottom occasionally, even though she had a draft of only about 14 feet. The Company had at once requested the appropriate authority to have the area around the jetty dredged to bring it back to a safe depth but, at the time of the "Wollongbar"'s loss, this work had not been undertaken. The officers and men knew this, but there was nothing that they could do about it except to cancel the service, so they continued to operate as usual pending the commencement of the dredging operations. The ship had to berth, therefore, at an open sea jetty in a depth of water which was, even in the calmest of weather, perilously shallow.

On the day in question a fresh southerly developed but this was not in itself any cause for worry as the jetty was completely sheltered from the south by the impressive bulk of Cape Byron. Nevertheless, the captain decided to hasten the loading of his cargo and get out of the area as soon as possible. Normally this would have been safe, but at 11 a.m. the wind hauled around the east and big seas drove straight into the Bay.

James Hunter well knew the danger of remaining any longer. He at once gave orders to cast off, ringing down for main engines even as he did so. No sooner had the ship cast off and commenced to move away from the jetty than she was struck by a succession of big seas, which caused her to bump heavily several times, severely damaging her stern gear and wrecking both her propellers. Thus crippled and without power, too far from the jetty to get her lines back onto the bollards, she at once paid off and, beam on to the sea was blown ashore a couple of hundred yards away. Although an anchor had been dropped as soon as the trouble developed, in the space available to her it had no hope of checking her way before she hit the beach, facing north. Firmly aground, with a pronounced list to starboard (seawards) the seas broke right over her, filling her with water, ruining the cargo which was valued at £80,000 ($160,000).

Some have alleged that she had insufficient steam up, and that this caused her to go ashore. This may have contributed but was not

T.S.S. "Wollongbar" steaming along the beach—a total loss after stranding at Byron Bay 14.5.21. Note after lifeboat falls. *Acknowledgement: Arthur Jones, the ship's purser.*

the prime cause. Arthur Jones, the Purser, says that she had been bumping badly earlier and while he was on an errand he had noticed that the cemented main deck in the vicinity of the engine room was bulging upwards about 12 to 18 in, and this was before she went ashore!

In the light of this it was perhaps a good thing that she did go ashore as, with bottom damage sufficient to cause the decks to bulge, she may have foundered out near the Juan and Julia Rocks if she had got away and in the sea then running some would have drowned.

Captain Cuthbert, the surveyor, wanted a photograph showing the seaward side of the wreck. He said that the underwriters would want to see evidence of a wreck, not a photo of a ship steaming along a beach, before they would pay a claim. The photo he wanted, since unfortunately lost in a Grafton flood, showed the railings smashed down, and bulkheads and deckhouse sides sprung and forced inwards, together with other extensive damage not visible from the shore.

Mr Jones also tells of destruction on the main deck where cabins were wrecked and partitions demolished by waves that had got inside the ship and there was 3 ft of water sloshing around on the seaward side of that deck. No photos show anything like the damage that really was sustained.

The crew successfully abandoned the vessel via the port after lifeboat, although when swinging the boat out against the list to seawards she took charge and smashed forward into the poop railings narrowly missing Mr Jones and another man. Fortunately no one was hurt.

As there was no question of commencing salvage operations until the weather moderated, the wreck was abandoned. It was later confirmed that her back was forced up and severely strained—possibly broken—and the underwriters declared her to be a total loss. Shortly afterwards, she was sold for £1,600 ($3,200). The buyer dismantled the wreck, leaving only that part which was under water at low tide, and there it remains.

Immediately after the loss, the N.C.S.N. Company ordered a new vessel and they decided to retain the name, general arrangement, and appearance of the old. Nevertheless some improvements were made to the design, and the new vessel, fitted with a single screw, was some 250 tons heavier, and two feet wider, but not as fast. There were numerous smaller changes incorporated in the new ship which was built by Lithgows Ltd. of Port Glasgow. A fine ship in her own right, she never equalled her illustrious namesake in prestige or reputation. The new "Wollongbar" arrived late in 1922 and at once slipped into the gap left by her predecessor, running to Byron Bay in partnership with the "Orara".

On Monday 27th June, 1921, Sydneysiders were shocked to read in their morning papers that two shipping disasters, involving heavy loss of life had occurred off the coast.

The vessels were the steamers "Fitzroy" which foundered off Cape Hawke, and the "Our Jack" which also sank in the same area.

Pathetic scenes were witnessed throughout the day as anxious relatives of passengers and crew sought information from the offices of the two shipping companies concerned.

The cargo boat, "Our Jack", foundered in heavy seas in the vicinity of the Manning River Heads early on Sunday morning. The captain and four others were drowned, the remaining nine being rescued by the steamer "Brundah" after a perilous struggle. When the ship encountered bad weather, the skipper had decided to run for safety but found it impossible and it soon was realized that she would have to be abandoned.

The "Our Jack" was about a mile and a half eastward of the "Brundah" when first sighted. The "Brundah" was proceeding to Sydney, with a mixed cargo from the Richmond River. The story of the rescue is one of heroic struggle against frightful conditions; high seas running through the half-darkness, and driving rain surrounded the "Brundah". When the "Our Jack" was sighted at 7 a.m. she was in a bad way, and appeared to be settling down. She had distress signals flying and was wallowing heavily in the mountainous seas that were running. As the "Brundah" approached, the crew of the "Our Jack" were on the point of abandoning her. Captain Purdie of the "Brundah" ranged as close as possible and saw the boat take the water. In a moment it was dashed with considerable force under the counter of the "Our Jack" and turned over by a big sea. Some of the occupants were thrown well clear from the upturned boat, some were hurled against the stern of the sinking ship, and a few were momentarily held by the suction below the surface. Most regained the boat and clung to it for dear life. The boat was capsized twice more by the sea and finally the survivors were left clinging to the upturned boat.

The weaker ones fought until they could fight no longer, and then went under. The Captain, Alexander Forbes, was seen putting up a splendid fight against the waves, but finally he gave up the unequal struggle and disappeared.

By this time the "Brundah" was right alongside; Captain Purdie displayed superlative seamanship throughout. It was impossible to launch a boat from the "Brundah" owing to the tremendous seas

that were running and the captain quickly decided to manoeuvre his ship and rescue the men from the water by lifelines. All hands on the "Brundah" fell to with a will in the rescue work and by skilfully working the vessel Captain Purdie got nine men safely on board. Meanwhile five of them, including Captain Forbes, had disappeared. They were drawn under principally by the wash under the counter of the "Our Jack", and by exhaustion in their desperate struggle with the sea. It would appear that the lifeboat was also smashed against the "Brundah", causing some casualties.

Albert Bale was a fireman on the "Our Jack". "I had just come off watch", he said, "when engineer Rudder rushed along the firemen's quarters and shouted 'all hands on deck!'—up on deck I went and joined the rest of the crew dumping cargo over the side. Terrific seas were striking the ship and it was apparent to us all that it would not be long before she would founder. We were dumping for about three-quarters of an hour, and in this time the seas were continually sweeping over us. Orders now came to launch the lifeboat and this was swung over the side with its crew of fourteen. We had just cleared the ship when the lifeboat capsized, but we managed to get a grip on it and waited for the 'Brundah' to pick us up. The captain soon weakened and disappeared.

"The 'Brundah' was nearing us by this time but the seas were so heavy that it was a difficult job for the skipper to reach us. William Gray was lying across the keel of the lifeboat when the 'Brundah' came down on us, and as the steamer struck the lifeboat, Gray was badly injured. I saw what was coming and, letting go, came up on the other side and was then hauled aboard.

"The 'Brundah' fell away, and the second time she came the rest of those alive were taken aboard. Except for the skipper I think the rest of us must have been crushed between the lifeboat and the 'Brundah'."

One man was rescued in a remarkable way. Caught by a big sea, he was swept high on the crest of the wave almost level with the rail of the "Brundah", and one of her hands smartly gripped him by the clothing and he was hauled on deck. The "Our Jack" by this time had disappeared from sight. Captain Purdie remained in the vicinity for an hour searching unsuccessfully for the remaining five members of the crew, then he headed for Sydney.

The officers of the "Brundah" described the weather as the worst experienced for years. The gale was cyclonic in character and was accompanied by squalls of almost hurricane force.

Paul Cassar, the chief officer of the "Our Jack", said "had the 'Brundah' not come up at the time, we would all have been at the bottom now. The Captain of the 'Brundah' behaved magnificently and rushed his ship to our rescue. When the 'Brundah' came up, Gray, a fireman, Erickson, a sailor, Nelson the boatswain and the cook who was a Russian, were hanging on to the overturned boat with me. Nelson and Erickson disappeared, and I lost sight of the cook."

Later, a well-known Newcastle shipping man, expressing regret at the death of Captain Forbes paid tribute to his skill as a navigator who was, he said, one of the best bar skippers on the coast. Some years earlier when he was in command of the "Electra" that vessel, crossing out of the Manning, almost went ashore. Captain Forbes, by skilful handling, got her over the bar stern first, against a heavy sea.

Two days after the wreck, part of the hull of the "Our Jack" was found where she had drifted ashore near Harrington and had gone to pieces in the surf.

In the same gale, Langley's steamer "Fitzroy", a fine modern steel ship of 623 tons, was in similar straits only about 20 miles away. For her, there was no would-be rescuer at hand to give the help that she so desperately needed. The "Fitzroy" was on her way south from Coff's and as she came down the coast she ran into rapidly worsening weather. She had left Coff's Harbour at 3.40 p.m. on Saturday, 25th June, with thirteen passengers, twenty-one crew and a mixed cargo consisting of logs and sawn timber in the forehold, butter and sundries in the afterhold, and a deck cargo consisting of seventy head of cattle, thirty pigs, eight or nine logs about 30 feet long and 4 feet around the girth, three cases of bacon, three cases of fish, a sling of sawn timber and a horse. The cattle were carried on the starboard side of the forward well-deck while the logs were on the port side. Shipping water heavily, she was all right until near Cape Hawke, when a huge sea swept the vessel and washed the cattle and everything else on the starboard side over to port thus giving the ship a heavy list. Captain Colvin then ordered that the logs be jettisoned, but the crew could not get steam on the winches as evidently the steam-pipe had been broken. The chief engineer, R. T. Saunders, then ordered the men to shift the coal in the bunkers but when they got there, they found too much water in the stokehold to allow this to be done. Captain Colvin then tried to work the ship in shore, and maybe beach her, but she became unmanageable; so all hands were ordered to their boat stations. The survivors told of their subsequent battle with the sea. By this time there was about 9 ft of water in the stokehold and engine-room, and the rising water had put the fires out some time earlier.

Karl Jansen, a Dane, an A.B. on the "Fitzroy", was on watch when she sailed from Coff's. A strong south-west wind was blowing with very little sea, and these conditions continued until he went off watch at midnight. He came on deck again about 6.30 a.m. when all hands were called to try to get the logs overboard, but they could not get the winch to work. "The captain then ordered all of us to put on our lifebelts and clear away the boats for launching but we could not launch them, as the ship had too much of a list to port", he said.

By this time the passengers were mustered near the boats and the ladies were being put into the boats when the ship suddenly rolled over and sank. Jansen continues his story:-

"One of the lifeboats floated clear but what became of the other I do not know, I tried to jump clear but was taken down with the ship. When I came to the surface I got hold of a piece of plank. I then saw a lifeboat with three men in it floating close by, to which I swam. When I got into the boat, which was waterlogged, I saw a boy about 12 years of age floating nearby and got him into the boat and tried to bring him around but could not. We kept him about an hour then he was washed away. We picked up Peter Hansen, an A.B., who was swimming. I called to him and held out an oar and we got him into the boat. We passed another boat bottom up with the chief engineer and the second mate clinging to it and called to them to come over to us, but they made no reply. There were several other people floating about but we could not render any assistance. We could not work our boat as she was waterlogged.

"We drifted along the coast and towards the land. When we got near the beach I got everything out of the boat and told the others that as soon as we got to the first breaker, they must jump out and swim clear of her, making for the beach. The first breaker turned the boat over, but we were all clear of her, and when I got ashore I found Hansen there. He called to me to help him haul a man ashore, and we found that he was all right. This was Herbert Ramsay, the only passenger to survive. I saw the other two floating in the surf and we pulled them up well clear of the sea. As they both appeared to be dead we left them there and walked along the beach until we came to a track, which we followed until we found ourselves at the Tuncurry Prison Camp.

"When we told the officer-in-charge who we were and about the two bodies on the beach he immediately sent some officers and prisoners to bring them in. They tried for three and a half hours to resuscitate them, but without success."

The survivors were full of praise for the staff and inmates of the prison who showed every kindness and attention to them.

Herbert Ramsay, the passenger, said: "The passengers included two ladies and my brother Albert. It was blowing hard on Saturday afternoon but the sea was not rough. I went to bed directly after tea and did not get up until about 6.30 the next morning when we were aroused by the cry of 'All hands on deck' and 'lifeboats'. I snatched two lifebelts, and gave one to my brother, helping him to secure it, then stayed to put on my pants and fix my belt. I then climbed to the boat-deck and gave what assistance I could to launch the boats. The attempt was unsuccessful owing to the list of the ship. I looked over the poop deck and saw Olaf Johansen assisting the lady passengers to the boats. He handed me a lady whom I carried to the port side lifeboat, placing her near it. I then did the same with the second lady and went to get the stewardess who was supported by Johansen, but as I reached the starboard side the steamer turned turtle and we were all taken down with the ship.

"On rising for the second time I came up alongside a lifeboat and got into it, though it was waterlogged. The only occupants were the two who later drowned. After drifting a few minutes, we picked up Karl Jansen. We then picked up the body of a boy about 12 years old, whom we tried to resuscitate but though we worked on him for over an hour, we could not fetch him round. During this time we picked up Peter Hansen. We drifted along and were eventually washed ashore about three miles north of the Tuncurry forest station prison camp."

Olaf Johansen, a Norwegian, was also an A.B. on the "Fitzroy" and he came on duty at 4 a.m. on the 26th, and took the wheel. The course at the time was south half west, and the weather was very bad and a heavy south-east gale was blowing. While he was at the wheel, Captain Colvin and the second officer were on the bridge. About 5 a.m. the course was altered to south.

"We were still on that course when I was relieved at 6 o'clock but I remained on the bridge as lookout. About 6.30 a.m. we shipped a heavy sea which washed the cattle from the starboard side to the after part of the logs on the port side. The captain then gave me orders to call all hands to get the logs overboard. We could not get any steam on the winch, so we could not shift the logs. The captain then gave orders to call all passengers and the crew to don lifebelts and get the boats ready. I do not know how many passengers were aboard but I do know there were two ladies. I assisted them up the ladder to the boat deck. At that time we were about four miles off Cape Hawke. The lifeboat could not be launched owing to the heavy list of the ship and the heavy sea. I passed the two lady passengers up to Mr Ramsay on the boat deck and I had hold of the stewardess when the ship went down, taking us with her. I lost hold of the stewardess and did not see her again. When I came to the surface I saw the chief cook and chief steward; a lady, the second mate and the chief engineer. They were floating about when I last saw them, hanging onto an upturned boat. I spoke to them, and we tried to turn the boat over, but were unable to do so. I left them and swam towards shore, eventually landing near Black Head at about 8 p.m. I must have swum about 10 or 12 miles.

"When I got ashore I crawled up near the scrub and lay down for a couple of hours weak and exhausted and famished. Those two hours were the longest I have ever experienced; but they brought me strength, and when I was able to stand I started along the beach for Tuncurry. Arriving there at 2 a.m. I met Mr C. Wright, manager of the local dairy company, who gave me every attention including a dry change."

Captain Colvin had started in the North Coast Trade as a seaman about 30 years previously and sheer merit carried him to the command of the ill-fated "Fitzroy". Previously he had served in the "Augusta", "Dorrigo", "Duranbah" and the "Cooloon" which was wrecked on the Manning Bar in 1917 or 1918. Captain Colvin was a particularly strong swimmer and many people owed their lives to his prowess. He had survived several wrecks, on one occasion swimming a long distance to the shore with two lady passengers—at that time one of the most sustained and plucky rescues on record. It is no exaggeration to say that he was the most popular skipper along the North Coast and passengers went out of their way to travel on his vessel.

The Langley family was connected with two business enterprises on the North Coast, and this fact causes some confusion. The two firms were Langley Bros., owners of the "Fitzroy", and other ships, and W. Langley & Sons whose interests lay in timber at Langley

Vale, on the Lansdowne River, a tributary of the Manning. Langley Vale was a Company town in the most literal sense, and Langley's owned the sawmill, wharf and extensive logging railway system incorporating massive trestle bridges. There was also a store, post office and shipbuilding yard. This firm was the first on the east coast of Australia to have a steam tramway, which included 17 miles of line. The rails were of wood, specially sawn to reduce wear and were used as the locomotive could climb a stiffer grade than would have been possible using steel. The locomotive, an imported "Climax" wood burner with eight wheels, was fitted with an automotive type gearshift, had 8 in. treads on the wheels for traction and could climb a 1 in 6 grade and negotiate extremely tight curves. The Australian feature movie "Tall Timbers" was made on location at Langley Vale. Langley's also installed the first "log hauler" in Australia, having got the idea from New Zealand. This operated on the principle of a payout wire, a hauling wire, two winches and a donkey boiler and the wires were led around curves using steel blocks weighing 30 cwt each. A man rode with each log and sent signals by bell wire to stop, slow or speed up the log. In fact the whole idea was very similar to a system of cable trams. Superb axemanship was needed to shape the nose of each log so it would travel along the correct path; also a channel had to be cut in each to take the hauling wire.

W. Langley & Sons supplied many of the wooden street blocks and also the blackbutt cross-arms for PMG telephone poles. Even the insulators were of tallow wood and all cut in one operation on a special machine.

Captain James Colvin, lost with the "Fitzroy".
Shown here on the bridge of that ship.
Acknowledgement: Colvin Family.

W. Langley's family home was in Foy Street, Balmain. They later moved to Smith Street where they owned a terrace of houses named Sussex, Kent, etc., for their ships. During the depression the mill at Langley Vale was sold to Ellis's; later to Allen Taylor & Co. In later years it was burnt down, rebuilt and electrified and was finally moved by the last owner into Taree. Langley's had owned the ketch "Phil Forbes" – sunk off Newcastle and the steamer "Cora Lynn" very like the "Cooloon".

Langley Bros., the shipping firm, started when Robert Langley was operating from the Shoalhaven district and had offices in Sussex Street. On his deathbed he won the contract for the Tweed River service from the Colonial Sugar Refining Co. and it was this contract that put the Company on a sound financial footing.

Langleys "Cobaki" almost as big as a Sydney Harbour ferry
Acknowledgement: R. Dufty

On the death of Robert Langley Snr the Company passed to his two sons Robert Jnr and Alfred and became known from then on as Langley Bros. I am told by Mr R. J. Langley of Balwyn, Victoria, who provided this information, that Alfred ran the business side from the Sydney end while Robert Jnr travelled to and from the rivers and around the Tweed. Langley Bros. specialized in shipping, trading mainly to the Tweed, Woolgoolga, Coff's Harbour and also Port Stephens. In the early days their fleet consisted of the topsail schooners, "Vale", "Sussex", and "Kent" together with the "Dolphin", a fore and aft schooner. On the 29th January, 1890, the "Kent" of 104 tons and the "Sussex" of 97 tons sailed from Trial Bay in company bound for Sydney. There was a gale blowing at the time and neither has been seen since. Later vessels included the steamers "Duroby", "Cooloon", "Boambee", "Cobaki", "Fitzroy", and "Dorrigo", among others. Prior to this they had, in the eighties, first gone into steam with the "Harrington" of 1884, "Murwillumbah" built in 1887, "Terranora" a tug built in 1896, and the "Rocklily" 1, a wooden paddler of 132 tons built in 1898.

In 1912 the firm went into the passenger trade in a bigger way when they had the "Fitzroy" built in Scotland for the Woolgoolga and Coff's Harbour service.

One of their skippers was Sam Coulter. A whole book could be written about this wonderful seaman's life and adventures. His name will be mentioned again in the following pages, but his early life at sea reads like almost something out of a novel.

He first went to sea at the age of 13 as a cabin boy on the ketch "Mary Davis", bringing logs from Erina Creek (just out of Gosford) down to Balmain. This was in 1893 and the ketches engaged in the trade used to sail through the old drawbridge—since replaced by a modern concrete structure — on the Gosford to The Entrance road, and on up the creek to the area being cut. Later he was on another ketch in the Lake Macquarie/Sydney coal trade (long since defunct) when coal was loaded near Morisset. Next, he joined a schooner, the "Young Rock" running to Port Stephens and Cape Hawke. Early in 1901 he got his master's ticket at the age of twenty-one, and not long afterwards was given his first command — another small ketch.

In 1904 young Sam Coulter went to Langley Bros., relieving for three months on the steamer "Duroby" while her mate was in hospital. When the mate returned to duty, Coulter was paid off and returned to his ketch. However, the "Duroby"'s regular mate seems to have been a confirmed alcoholic and less than a week after he rejoined his ship he was sacked for neglect on duty. Not altogether surprisingly, upon this character's dismissal, Sam Coulter was approached and offered the job full time. He accepted, and remained with Langley's for almost twenty years, during which time he earned the nickname of "Cyclone Sam" — a tribute to his uncanny ability to bring a ship in, the state of the weather notwithstanding. He eventually rose to command the "Duroby" then the "Cooloon" and — for a short time — the "Fitzroy" whose loss has already been described. He also had the "Dorrigo", ex "St Francois". On many occasions he performed extraordinary feats of seamanship, for one of

which he was awarded that rarest of awards: a Lloyd's Medal.

He could be a sanctimonious old bloke when he wanted to be, and in ticklish situations was sometimes known to exhibit mock terror — "I can't look! I can't look!" was one of his lines, but as his record shows, this was an act. He was a bold seaman who many times saved his ship from what appeared to be sure destruction.

"Wallamba" sporting her distinctive stovepipe funnel extension.
Acknowledgement: R. Dufty.

107

Another of the Masters to learn his trade in the Brisbane water firewood ketches was Captain Rube Lucey, whose father also skippered one of these fine little vessels. Young Lucey started the

"Uki" coming south on a good day.
Acknowledgement: R.A.N. Historical Section

hard way, like Coulter, in one of the roughest schools of all; the sea.

Everyone knows of the famous regattas held on the Derwent near Hobart by the Tasmanian ketches of old; not so well known were the very similar regattas held by the owners of the Brisbane Water ketches, which were not unlike the modern ocean racing yacht in size.

During one of these races from Brisbane Water to Sydney, young Rube was sailing with his father when the old man fell overboard in Broken Bay. Before young Lucey could put the ketch about his father shouted to him to carry on with the race, and proceeded to swim home. Rube did carry on and won the race, and returning to Brisbane Water received quite a welcome from his pleased father.

During 1922, the "Nambucca" was built by E. Wright & Son of Tuncurry for Allen Taylor's. She filled the gap left by the loss of the "Our Jack", but was built to co-operate with the North Coast Company, who were her managers. In 1923 the "Tintenbar" was available to take a charter with the Commonwealth Government, who sent her to New Ireland where she hit a reef the following year and was lost. Also in 1923, the wooden steamer "Wallamba" built six years earlier at Tuncurry, was lost on the 11th July when she tried to "go overland" at Morna Point. She was completely demolished, with timber and cargo scattered for hundreds of yards among the rocks and only the boiler and main steam-pipe visible in the surf. The cause of this wreck was that age-old enemy of all who go down to the sea in ships — fog. Happily, no lives were lost on this occasion, but the swell rolling in from the wide Pacific made short work of the little coaster, and she was quickly reduced to so much wet kindling. The "Narani" was sold to the South Coast Company during the year.

Two new vessels were built in 1923, and both were workhorses giving splendid service to the Company for the rest of its life, when they were both sold for further trading under other flags. Indeed, when the N.C.S.N. Company went into voluntary liquidation in 1954 these were the two oldest vessels in the fleet of nine that were still trading under the familiar red and blue house flag. They were the "Uki" and the "Ulmarra" of 545 and 924 tons respectively, and they both had more than their share of adventures. In the "Uki" the influence of Sir Allen Taylor first became manifest. Sir Allen, so it is said, always judged a ship solely by the length of the turpentine piles that she could carry, and this influence can be seen in all of the remaining vessels built for the Company (even the new "Wollongbar" showed this tendency!) right up to the "Bangalow" and the "Uralba" which were the last two vessels ever built for the fleet.

The "Uki" and "Ulmarra" were totally dissimilar in appearance, the former having only one large hatch virtually amidships and the bridge and machinery well aft, while the latter was more conventional in appearance, being little more than

"Uki" loading scrap iron, a typical "problem" cargo.
Acknowledgement: Captain D. Gibson.

a "three Island" ship with a raised quarter deck from the bridge aft. These ships became the prototypes for two distinct classes of vessel, and the company persisted with these silhouettes from this time on, with only minor modifications as they became necessary. The "Uki" class was developed from Sir Allen's wooden boats like the "Wallamba" but the "Ulmarra"'s owed their shape very largely to the old

"Poonbar", and even the little "Gunbar" before her.

The wooden steamer "Boambee" of 236 tons, went ashore about a hundred yards south of the southern breakwater at the Tweed, on 18th December, 1923, and by night-fall the vessel was high and dry. The "Boambee" left Sydney on the Friday previously, arriving at Tweed Heads on the afternoon on the 18th. Attempting to cross in,

109

"Ulmarra" passing down through the Grafton Bridge in later years
Acknowledgement: Owen Sanders, Grafton.

she hit the bar and washed ashore. By 6.30 that evening heavy seas, whipped up by a strong nor'-easter were pounding the vessel which was owned by Langleys. The vessel was very lucky as the weather moderated sufficiently to allow her to be refloated not long afterwards.

1924 saw the building of the drogher "Oxley" for service on the Manning River, and also the second vessel in the "Uki" class, the "Urana". In this ship, some 26 tons smaller than the "Uki", a few

"Ulmarra" landing a small van – Clarence River.
Acknowledgement: Captain Sam Coulter.

improvements were made and the totally enclosed wheelhouse as fitted to that steamer was not copied, the "Urana" having the more usual canopy with glass windows in front while the back and sides were left open. This arrangement was continued in all further ships built for the Company, as it gave the better all-round vision so critical when crossing river bars.

During the year another of the steamers was sold. This time it was the old "Kyogle" which was purchased by the Commonwealth Navigation and Lighthouse Department for use as a lighthouse tender on the Queensland Coast. For the next six years she performed this task until, in 1930 she was again sold – this time to the Queensland Cement & Lime Co., of Brisbane. She ended her days carrying rotten coral from Moreton Bay to the Cement works at Darra, where it is used in the manufacture of the company's produce.

The year 1924 also saw the old flagship of the R.A.N., the twelve inch battle cruiser H.M.A.S. "Australia" towed out of Sydney Harbour to be scuttled in the graveyard of old ships that lies off the Heads. Her scrapping was required under the terms of the Washington Naval Treaty and accordingly this magnificent ship was systematically stripped of all her fittings, the gun barrels were cut with oxy-torches, and the hulk that remained was given the honour of a "funeral"

Even though she had been stripped she still made an impressive sight, and many thousands of Sydneysiders vied for positions around the Harbour foreshores and on the various small ships that were to follow the gallant old warrior on her last voyage.

One of these followers was the "Pulganbar" and such a large crowd of sightseers turned up at the Company's wharves in Sussex Street that she was forced to move out into the stream and anchor some time before the advertised hour for departure to prevent over-

Clarence River, "Kyogle" near Maclean, circa 1912.
Acknowledgement: O. Notley.

crowding. The master had not arrived at this time — he would normally go aboard one hour before sailing time — so the ship was moved by the marine superintendent. On special occasions such as this it was normal practice to allow as many people on board as was consistent with safety, and the "Pulganbar" must have been carrying in the order of a thousand passengers that day; also she was in light trim, with very little cargo in her holds, and she must have been a bit tender and inclined to list somewhat if the crowd moved too much to one side. She was a fine vessel, however, and there was no danger.

Many among the crowd must have had a lump in their throats as they watched the rusting hulk of our once proud flagship moving out to sea that day. The Australian Navy has not since had a ship to equal her. Today the age of the battleship has passed and the "Pulganbar" had witnessed the passing of a little bit of history.

The "Bonalbo" of 960 tons, and the "Tyalgum" of 544 tons were both new in 1925, the former being a slightly larger edition of the "Ulmarra and also better finished. She also survived to the end being sold to Messrs Patson Ltd of Sydney in 1955. The "Tyalgum" was less fortunate, and after many adventures she was lost in 1939 at the entrance to the Tweed River. She was another "Uki" class.

The old shipping firm of Langley Bros. was taken over by the North Coast Company in the same year, and their trade was looked after by Allen Taylor's and the N.C.S.N. Company between them. One of Langley's ships, the "Dorrigo" was sold to John Burke & Co. in Brisbane after being laid up in Sydney for nearly six months, she had once been the French "St Francois" of New Caledonia and had been purchased by Langley's in 1921 to replace the ill-fated "Fitzroy". She had not been built for work out of bar harbours and was rather too deep for this type of employment, but she was a fine little steamer nevertheless. Unfortunately she was lost in heavy weather in 1926 when she flooded and capsized near Wide Bay on the Queensland Coast, taking 22 lives with her. Only the captain and his son—who was the mate—

survived. It was rumoured at the time that she was overloaded by three inches, and that the water that came aboard could not get away owing to clogged scuppers.

The "Boambee" and the "Cobaki" were also included in the Langley fleet and they went to the N.C.S.N. Company while the "Duroby" had gone to the South Coast Co. the "Boambee" was sold in 1926 to F. Viggers, later being resold to the Newcastle & Hunter River S.S. Co., who altered her name to "Illalong".

Two more of the old steamers were sold in 1925, the "Brundah" and the "Yulgilbar", both of which went to Burns, Philp (South Seas) Ltd. The "Brundah" was renamed "Malinoa" and the "Yulgilbar" was called the "Makatea". Both of them were eventually scuttled near Suva when they had outlived their usefulness.

The next year, 1926, saw the disposal of several more of the older boats which were no longer up to the Company's high standards. As well as the "Boambee" which has been mentioned, these included the "Gunbar" and "Myee" which was turned into a harbour lighter.

"Arakoon" at the Company's Sussex Street (Sydney) discharge wharf, unloading mixed cargo.
Acknowledgement: Bruce Grant.

This year, as well as seeing the last of these older vessels, also saw the building of two new ones: the "Arakoon" and the "Uralla" to be lost so soon afterwards. The "Arakoon" was a particularly fine vessel of 875 tons, twin screw, and 190 ft long. She was built especially for the Macleay River, and ran there for nearly all of her long life. She was finally sold in 1954, after a career that was remarkable for its lack of drama. The little "Uralla" was the last of the initial four ships of the "Uki" class, and she was the first to be lost.

1926 was the year that the Company decided to place their first order for a motor ship. This historic order, placed in Copenhagen,

"Nimbin", N.C.S.N. Co.'s first motor ship, loading at Lismore.
Acknowledgement: G. Hughes

called for a large vessel of 1,000 tons which was to be an improved "Ulmarra". The new ship, the famed "Nimbin" sailed for Sydney via Suez on the 29th June, 1927, and she arrived not long afterwards. This vessel, later widely known as the "Tin Hare" on account of her speed, was a big advance on any ship that had up to that time been engaged in the Lismore run. She had better refrigerated space, more speed, electric winches and diesel engines. This change over from coal burning was a success in every way, and all but three of the later ships built for the Company were of this type. The three exceptions were the "Bangalow"; "Nambucca" 2; and the "Uralba".

The "Melinga" was ordered in 1927 for delivery in 1928, and it was at this time that the "Poonbar" was sold for the reasons described earlier, the "Nimbin" of course, replacing her.

The traffic during 1928 was somewhat below expectations owing to the unusually heavy rainfall that was experienced all over the coast, and the most destructive flooding that followed, particularly on the Clarence and Richmond Rivers. The whole coast was lashed by gales and, to those at sea, life became rather precarious. The "Melinga" arrived at the end of May, and she entered service shortly afterwards.

It was in June of 1928 that the "Uralla", still almost brand new, and under the able command of Captain Francis Patrick O'Beirne, one of the patriarchs of the coast, sailed from Coff's Harbour for Sydney on the voyage that was to be her last. Loaded with stringy-bark logs and sawn timber, she called at Newcastle for more cargo, where Paddy O'Beirne had a yarn with his old friend Captain Sam Coulter, who was in Newcastle loading the "Nambucca" of which he was master. The conversation got around to the state of the weather which looked decidedly threatening, but both had seen worse and neither thought that it gave any reason to delay sailing on the short run down to Sydney.

The "Uralla" cleared Nobby's at 5.24 p.m. on Wednesday, 13th June followed shortly afterwards by the "Nambucca". Heading down the coast the weather deteriorated steadily until, nearing Cape Three Points, the little coaster was struck by the full force of the gale. The account can best be continued from descriptions given to me by the vessel's chief officer, Simon Simonsen.

"Nearing Sydney Heads it became impossible to make any headway, so the skipper decided to put about and run before it. As the "Uralla" made her way up the coast the gale steadily increased in violence, while blinding rain-squalls reduced visibility to almost zero. Big seas broke over her, keeping the decks continually awash. Rising one moment to the crest of a big one, she was the next minute buried foc's'le-deep in the following comber."

About daybreak on Thursday they reckoned their position to be off Newcastle again, but with the torrential rain, poor visibility and huge seas that were running, Captain O'Beirne realised that any attempt to cross the bar would be to invite disaster, and he accordingly decided to remain at sea. Few people can comprehend the power unleashed by such a storm — those who can are usually seamen. This gale delayed the "Suevic", a large liner, and for some days the "Canonbar" and the Collier "Corrimal" were missing and their fates in doubt. On the upper deck it was not possible to move about without using the lifelines that had been rigged. Things were uncomfortable for all on board — no one from the skipper down had a stitch of dry clothing between them but the ship was still sound and no one was in any real danger. However, when they were a few miles north of Newcastle, one of those rare freak cross seas, a monstrous

115

grey mountain of water struck the "Uralla" amidships.

The wonder of it was that it did not swamp her and cause her there and then to disappear forever, but nevertheless it sealed the steamer's fate. The starboard lifeboat was torn from its chocks, bending the heavy davits like licorice, and was dumped heavily onto the main valves of the steam steering gear, which was mounted abaft the funnel and between the two lifeboats. The delicate mechanism was wrecked and the steering gear hopelessly jammed. The ship was now virtually a derelict and at one stroke her chances of survival had been shattered.

The same wave smashed the cabin doors on the starboard side and, flooding the chief and second engineer's cabins, smashed fixtures lamps and furniture, washing away personal gear (even the mate's alarm clock) then broke through the wooden partitions to the cabins on the port side where further damage was done. The second engineer J. Laycock, was in his cabin at the time and had a very narrow escape from serious injury. Indeed, he was nearly drowned in his cabin! The galley, saloon and engine-room skylights broke under the weight of water and the after awning frame collapsed. Tarpaulins were hurriedly rigged over the wrecked skylights but the entire food supply was ruined, the galley being completely washed out. All attempts to re-light the galley fire proved ineffective.

Efforts were made to rig a jury rudder, but the rough seas breaking over the vessel prevented this, and the anchors were let go. The stream-anchor, having been lowered with 200 fathoms of cable attached to it, parted company with the ship and shortly afterwards the second one followed it. With only her two bower anchors to hold her, the "Uralla" started to drag towards Morna Point at nearly four knots! If she went ashore there it would be all over. Captain O'Beirne knew that the only hope now lay in beaching the ship, and accordingly Mr Simonsen went forward and successfully slipped both cables – no mean feat on a bucking, wave swept foc'sle.

By careful manoeuvring of the engines, one ahead and the other astern the ship was kept on a rough course for the twenty-mile stretch of rock free sand known as Stockton beach. All hands wore lifebelts for at any moment the vessel might have broached to and foundered. After some hours of this nightmare navigation the "Uralla" 529 tons gross and only 59 horsepower, grounded on the sandy bottom roughly ten miles south of Port Stephens, about 4 p.m. in the afternoon. She was soon carried up high and dry, so that at low tide a dog was later seen to walk right around the ship. However their troubles were not yet over for the ship carried no radio, and the whole grim trip was as yet unknown to the outside world.

The ship's whistle was blown to warn the engine-room crew to abandon their machinery as it was feared that another wave might come aboard and drown them at their posts. This attracted a couple of local men to the scene of the shipwreck, Messrs Upton and E.W. Holloway, both dairy farmers. Mr Upton got a shouted message from the ship that they were all O.K. Later, Captain O'Beirne wrote a note which he threw overboard in a bottle, saying "Get a message through to Mr Hough that we are short of provisions but I think the crew will be right for the night." This message, retrieved by Mr Holloway became the first intimation of the disaster to reach the outside world when it was phoned to Newcastle about an hour after the vessel grounded.

The Rocket Brigade arrived, hurriedly summoned from the scene of the "White Bay" disaster at Morna Point, but they were not needed. (The "White Bay" had been driven into the surf and capsized and all but one of her crew were drowned, while the vessel herself was smashed to matchwood in no time at all.)

Back at the "Uralla" large stringybark logs from the cargo were slung over the side to form a gangplank from the beach to the top of her bulwarks, in readiness for the visitors — both official and unofficial — that the morning was sure to bring. Sure enough, the local residents turned out in force, and fed and cared for the crew when they decided to come ashore. After the grounding the captain had decided that they were now out of danger, and the hands he preferred to stay aboard for the following night and day where they were considerably more comfortable than they would have been on the beach.

Only one man had been injured throughout the ordeal, a seaman named Carlsen who, at the height of the storm had lashed himself to the emergency steering wheel, and when the fatal sea came aboard, was spun around by it and knocked unconscious. His only injuries were bruises and a badly gashed thumb, possibly caused when the starboard boat hit the steering engine nearby. It was soon discovered that the "Uralla" was a hopeless wreck, firmly embedded in the sand, while even a cursory inspection revealed that her back had been broken, or at least severely strained, and her deck was bulging at least three feet upwards according to the mate.

For at least two crew members, J. Halliday, a fireman, and William Erickson A.B., the wreck was no new experience, as they had both been on the Company's steamer "Wallamba" when she "tried to go overland" at Morna Point, only five years previously.

Meanwhile the little "Nambucca", under "Cyclone Sam" Coulter was also having a rough time of it. She too, was battling her way south until near Cape Three Points she was forced to heave to, as

"Uralla" high and dry on Stockton Beach, 14th June, 1928.
Acknowledgement: N. Brien.

she was in danger of opening up under the severe pounding that she was taking, or being driven ashore like the "White Bay". Captain Coulter now decided to try to reach shelter in Broken Bay. In shocking visibility, at night, when Barrenjoey light could only occasionally be seen glowing wetly through the rain, Sam Coulter edged the "Nambucca" towards where he believed the entrance to Broken Bay to be. He told me that at one point the worried helmsman asked

117

"Are you certain you know where you are?" However, the "old man" was complete master of the situation. By expert seamanship, and in his own words, "By the smell of the damp earth ashore" he worked his vessel slowly into the shelter of Barrenjoey head, then carefully picked his way down Pittwater to Coaster's Retreat where he decided to anchor until the storm had blown itself out.

Some local residents came out to him in a boat and told him the "Uralla" was ashore, but no other details were known at the time. The "Nambucca" remained there for 24 hours until the storm had abated sufficiently to venture outside at 10 a.m. on Friday and even then she had a rough passage to Sydney, where she discharged her cargo intact.

Captain Francis Patrick O'Beirne was given another command, but in 1930 he retired from the sea. He was one of the best known skippers on the coast. After serving his apprenticeship on deep sea vessels, he entered the Cape Hawke tug service in 1885 where he remained for twenty years. He then went to Allen Taylor & Co. commanding their steamer "Tuncurry" on which, for the next 15 years, he set and held the record for the run averaging 100 trips per year from Sydney to Cape Hawke. He joined the North Coast Company in 1921 and remained there, the bearded old Irishman, until his retirement. In 1932 he and his wife celebrated their golden wedding anniversary, and not long afterwards he passed away. He will long be remembered for his famous understatement: "I think steel ships have come to stay."

About three months later, on the 23rd September, the "Coombar" had an accident very similar to the one that later sank the trans-pacific liner "Tahiti", but in this case the accident was not serious. and no further damage was caused. The "Coombar" was 2½ miles east of Barrenjoey light when her port tail shaft broke allowing the propeller to drop off. Fortunately there was no leakage and the vessel managed to reach Sydney on the remaining engine, and she was then towed (owing to the resulting lack of manoeuvrability) to Mort's Dock for repairs. Once there the spare tail shaft and propeller were fitted and the vessel was soon back at sea.

On the 15th October, 1928, the "Nimbin" had a close shave, when the steering gear broke down as she was entering the Richmond River. She sheered over and hit the breakwater but, although leaking freely, she managed to get into the river and reach Ballina. No cargo was damaged, but several frames and plates were bent and she needed docking for proper repairs to be made. A temporary job was done by fitting a cement and timber patch well shored up, and the leak was stopped.

One night the "Nimbin" under Captain Purdie (late of the "Brundah") was passing down the Richmond near Woodburn when a patch of fog ahead obscured the "leading marks" to the next reach, and Purdie was peering ahead trying to find them when a farmer on the bank trying to be helpful, hung a light on a post to guide the ship. Unfortunately his good intention went for naught as the skipper, mistaking the light for one of the leading marks said "Well, there's one of them anyway, steer for that light." Shortly after, the ship came to a very sudden stop as she rammed the bank, burying her bows deep into the soft mud.

Moments later the mate Simon Simonsen came up to the bridge and said,

"Will I hang a light over the bows skipper?"

"What on earth for", demanded Purdie.

"Well, sir, we'll be run down by a car soon if I don't — we're into the roadway!" The Pacific Highway at this point is right on the river bank.

About this time (1929/30) seven members of "Nimbin" 's crew including the captain were in the habit of buying a regular lottery ticket. After some time with nothing to show for their efforts, Captain Purdie withdrew from the syndicate and the next ticket won second prize of £1,000. One can imagine the captain's feelings and it is said that he threw his cap on the deck and jumped on it.

During 1928/29 the Northern Rivers were frequently in flood, and this of course affected production which, coupled with the coal and timber strikes of the time, resulted in somewhat decreased trading. Increases in taxation together with the beginnings of the depression were starting to be felt but the fleet was mostly made up of new vessels and it was this fact that enabled the Company to retain its strong position. The "Coolebar" was sold to New Zealand early in 1929.

Visitors throng Byron Bay jetty for the first visit of the new "Wollongbar" 11.1.1923.
Note motor car being unloaded.
Acknowledgement: H. B. Young.

CHAPTER EIGHT

The Lean Years

It would be true to say that the Company did not meet with any serious ill effects from the depression which swept the world at this time, as the vessels were all sound and no replacements were needed for several years, thus eliminating the need for heavy expenditure while, as mentioned earlier, the Company's loadings were mostly essentials — necessities of life such as food-stuffs and primary produce, etc. No doubt some of the finer lines of general cargo fell off, and possibly the back loading of timber also (the building industry was very hard hit) but this would not have seriously affected the net profits as there was not much margin in timber anyway. The shareholders' dividend remained steady at the usual 10 per cent per annum until 1932 when it was reduced to 8 per cent and the staff's wages were reduced about 10 per cent per annum but in the latter case these deductions were made up later when times became better. I have not heard of any staff being put off due to the depression and in any case the M.V. "Wyrallah", which arrived from Copenhagen new in 1934 must have been ordered in 1933.

One other well-known coastal shipping firm, however, fell victim to hard times and in December, 1929, went into voluntary liquidation. The Company was "Nicolas Cain's Coastal Co-operative Steam Ship Co. Ltd" and their assets and business connections were purchased by the North Coast Company who carried the trade to Port Macquarie from the 1st February, 1930, onwards.

Cain's had been associated with the North Coast Company for a long time and back in 1908 the drogher "Gladstone" was sold to them by Cain's, while in November the following year the "Hastings" was also purchased, but later she was resold to John Burke & Co. The North Coast Company had a shareholding in, and a seat on Cain's Board, and Nicholas Cain was himself a director of the North Coast Company at one time.

The Blue funnelled steamers of "Cain's Coasters" traded to Port Macquarie and the small timber port of Camden Haven. Their vessels in later years were the "Macquarie", a nice compact passenger and cargo vessel, and the cargo-only "Pappinbarra" which was very like the "Uralla" of the N.C. Company. She was, in fact, a sister of the South Coast Company's "Bergalia". The "Pappinbarra" was lost near Port Stephens when she went ashore almost under the lighthouse in 1929, and it was this wreck which precipitated the Company's demise.

The "Macquarie" was sold to New Zealand, but shortly afterwards was acquired by the well-known firm of W.R. Carpenter.

The N.C.S.N. Company carried on trade to Port Macquarie mostly for the back loadings of timber and oxide for several years but finally vacated this port in 1939 or 1940 owing to the reduction in the number of smaller ships, which were then being commandeered by the R.A.N. and also on account of the state of the bar as vessels were continually stranding there, and were in trouble practically every trip. From 1944, the beacons were no longer being moved to meet the changes in the channel and, as a sea port, the Hastings River at Port Macquarie ceased to be. Today, only small fishing boats use the port.

In June, 1930, the drogher "Jap" fell victim to a flood on the Manning River, when her hull was pierced by a wharf pile and she sank. Her salvage was necessary as she was foul of the wharf and, in any case, she was still a sound vessel, with a good winch, etc. and these were removed and put aboard the other drogher, "Manning" temporarily. "Jap" had impaled herself and the floodwater was now beginning to recede, and there was a possibility that she would be left high and dry. Ernest Wright was called in from Tuncurry and the job continued under his leadership. After 17 days the drogher was pulled free and was put on a slip for repairs. This was only a very minor incident, yet it could have had a very great effect had the attempt failed, as the wharf could have been most effectively put out of commission for a long time.

About this time some more trouble was experienced with tail-shafts. The "Coombar" which seems to have been most unlucky with her stern gear, broke two tail-shafts within a period of three months in 1930. In June she broke one off the Clarence River, and in September when twelve miles off Sydney Heads, outward bound, she did it again, and returned to port. Luckily the propellers in both cases remained with the ship but the "Kinchela" near Tacking Point bound north lost both the shaft and the propeller in October in the same year when the starboard shaft snapped. She was escorted back to Sydney by the "Maianbar".

Some of the old vessels which had been sold had interesting stories and while not strictly connected with our story, some mention should, I feel, be made about them and especially the "Coolebar" and "Gunbar", as these two ships were later bought back by the N.S.C.N. Company as previously mentioned. The "Gunbar" was sold in 1926 to Deplechet McLeod Co. in New Zealand. She became well known in New Zealand waters. The "Coolebar" after some years as the "Himitangi" was resold in 1936 to Cam & Sons, fishermen, in Sydney. She then resumed her old name.

At the end of 1931, the "Ulmarra" was crossing out of the Clarence River at 4.30 a.m. on the 2nd December when she became stuck on the bar. Although she was refloated at 8.30 a.m., they must have been a rather exciting four hours. All the deck cargo was swept overboard, all, that is, except eighteen tons which was jettisoned. As she was found to be leaking she returned to the river, where the after hold was found to be full of water, although the butter room and fore-hold were dry and undamaged. By this time the ship was resting on the bottom at Iluka.

At 2.30 a.m. on the 4th, she was refloated and moved up to Maclean where she berthed at 4 a.m. and a diver sent down to inspect the damage. Captain D. W. Gibson, the well known marine surveyor and salvage expert came up from Sydney, while the diving gear was rushed up from Nambucca Heads. All available pumps were put on the job of pumping out the after-hold, and extra equipment was sent from Sydney in the "Melinga". Most of the rivets in the bottom plating were found to have popped and no less than 500 bolts were used to make a temporary repair, pending drydocking in Sydney.

A most unusual incident occurred the following year when, on the 5th February, the "Tyalgum" was passing through the Pyrmont bridge to berth at the Druitt Street Wharf. The ship was returning from the Tweed, laden with dairy produce, and was on the point of passing through the bridge when it began to close on her.

The master, Captain John Magee, sounded the siren and went full astern, but the little steamer could not stop in time. She went hard to starboard, hitting the stonework of the bridge, but the closing span caught her and swept the fore-rigging, funnel, ventilators and main mast away; the funnel fell over to starboard, wrecking the lifeboat, and the mast went over the stern, while the large ventilators were neatly bent over to 45 degrees, clouds of smoke and steam belching from the yawning hole in the deck where the funnel had been. When the bridge was re-opened, the "Tyalgum" passed through under her own steam, and proceeded to her berth. Quite a number of people were on the bridge at the time, and saw the whole episode, which all in all, must have provided them with a rather amusing spectacle. All too often, an accident was accompanied by injury or loss of life, but on this occasion fortunately, not a soul received even a scratch, although two men were nearly hit by the falling funnel. It is not often that an accident such as this occurs and this one, although expensive, had all the elements of a first-rate slap-stick comedy. The owners sent the repair bill to the Department of Public Works, and they accepted responsibility and paid £655 1s. 6d. for repairs and demurrage — loss of use of the ship. What was said to the bridge operator is not recorded.

John Magee lived as a boy on his parents' farm on the Brisbane River near the 17-mile rocks. One day when he was fifteen a ship's double-ended lifeboat (with lugsail) manned by three men from the barque "Orari" sailed up that way, was caught by a squall and cap-sized throwing the crew into the water. Young John piled into a dinghy and rowed out to the rescue, saving two men, but was un-fortunately too late to save the third. His survivors proved to be the captain of the barque and an apprentice, another apprentice having been drowned. At the inquest John Magee had to give evidence and later the captain of the "Orari" invited him to dinner on board.

During the meal the captain asked John to name his reward for saving his life, and the youngster replied that he wanted to go to sea. The captain thereupon agreed to ask Mrs Magee's permission for her son to sail with him in the "Orari". This she granted, and Jack went to sea. He was very seasick at first (the only time in his life that he was) and on arrival in London the crew paid off. Young Jack got a job shipkeeping, then to Valparaiso, thence to St Michael's for orders, to New York, finally paying off in Rotterdam. Shipped back to England DBS (Distressed British Seaman) he joined the dredge service. Subsequently he returned to Australia as second mate/bo'sun on a dredge being run to Geelong. He then went into coasters. He had been five years in square rigged ships.

During 1932, the old "Coramba" was sold to the Belfast & Koroit S.N. Co. of Melbourne and she sailed for southern ports. She was lost on 30th November, 1934, when she foundered in a heavy gale near Philip Island in Bass Strait, with all hands.

Damage amounting to several thousand pounds was caused on the 5th May, when the collier "Abersea" out of Newcastle, bound for Sydney deeply laden with coal, and the "Tyalgum" on her way to the Tweed with general cargo, collided off Norah Head at 5.15 a.m. causing considerable damage to both vessels. The night was dark, but clear, and both vessels had the other in sight for at least fifteen minutes prior to the collision.

The master of the "Tyalgum" said at the subsequent inquiry that when he first saw "Abersea"'s lights she was one point on his starboard bow and heading towards his port side. He came onto the bridge 20 minutes before the collision and saw the "Abersea"'s masthead lights. Three or four minutes before the collision, he lost sight of the red (port) light on the other ship.

The master of the "Abersea" was in his bunk when the crash came; He went on deck and saw the "Tyalgum" lying alongside his port side. The mate, who was on watch at the time, said that he had steered S.W. x S. until the Norah Head light was raised. The "Tyalgum"'s lights were sighted near Norah Head and the "Abersea"'s course was altered half a point. He saw the "Tyalgum" alter course, and he then ordered hard a'port. He said the "Tyalgum" continued on her course and the "Abersea" struck her with the stem abaft of the fo'c'sle on the starboard side. The vessels then accompanied each other to Sydney. Although the "Tyalgum"'s side was badly stove in she remained tight, but the "Abersea" had her stem sprung and the plating folded across it and was leaking badly. The captain tried an old trick and had bags forced into the leak, finally "fothering" his vessel with a tarpaulin, after which the pumps managed to keep ahead of it. Fortunately water does not harm coal and no further damage was done, and repairs were soon well in hand at Mort's.

Some of the smaller rivers and ports were always giving trouble and in early 1933, the Tweed River bar was almost impassable. The "Melinga" crossed in early in March and found herself bar-bound for a while. She managed to get out again, but with only a part cargo. It was to be three months before the next vessel could get in, but on the 24th June the "Tyalgum", dragging heavily in only 7 ft 9 in. of water, crossed in although the sea was fairly rough. She needed 8 ft 6 in. to go out with a full cargo of molasses, so it was decided to only half fill the tanks for the return to Sydney. However, such is the fickle nature of sandbars, that two days later on the 26th, conditions were most favourable and a depth of 10 ft was available at high water.

In March of 1933 the "Kinchela" had a narrow squeak when she got stuck on the bar at Port Macquarie, for the second time in five months. Captain Gibson again went to the rescue. This man had the credit for refloating literally scores of stranded coasters, and he was readily acknowledged to be one of the great salvage men on the coast. He was at one time employed by the N.C.S.N. Company before he went into practice as a surveyor and was always ready for the unexpected. Once, while serving as second mate on the "Burringbar", a stoker failed to turn up at sailing time so Gibson arranged a substitute second mate at short notice, and he went as a fireman. The other firemen were furious at having their delay nullified but any further action would have been mutiny, as the ship had sailed at once.

When he arrived at Port Macquarie to free the "Kinchela", he found that the rudder was lost and the vessel leaking freely, but she was floated off the bar after the deck cargo was jettisoned and repairs were soon effected.

On the 9th January, 1934, one of the finest examples of seamanship seen on the coast was performed by the "Urana", when the launch "Venture" en route from Sydney to Brisbane lost her rudder near Port Stephens in a 40-knot southerly gale and anchored to prevent being blown ashore. That night, making her way down the coast into the teeth of the gale, the "Orara" was making fair progress under the circumstances when a flare was sighted inshore by the lookout. Captain Cole at once altered course to assist and proceeded to work in as close as safety would allow to the flickering flare. When he saw that the distressed vessel was a fairly large launch, and not a raft as he had at first supposed, and that the four men on it were in no immediate danger, Captain Cole abandoned his first idea of towing it against the gale to Newcastle, deciding instead to await the arrival of Captain Coulter who, now in command of the "Urana" was due to pass the position running before the gale on his way north.

The "Urana" was several miles out to sea and would probably have passed without seeing the "Venture", but Captain Cole steamed out to meet the other steamer and signalled her inshore. While the two coasters stood by the launch, the masters worked out a plan of action. It was decided that Sam Coulter, in the "Urana" would tow the cripple to Port Stephens and safety, but as she closed in to pass the tow-line, one of the men leapt aboard the steamer, landing on the heavy wooden belting strip, and refused the offer of a tow, asking simply to be put ashore. The other three then abandoned the launch, leaving her still at anchor. The "Urana" took them to Nelson's Bay where they were landed.

Captain Coulter, in describing the incident to me years afterwards emphasised the fact that the launch could have been towed to safety, adding that the men came aboard the "Urana" quite uninvited and, on being offered the tow, refused it. Maybe they were worried about the possibility of a salvage claim. Anyway, when they returned for their launch the next day she had disappeared, having been swamped and sunk overnight.

It was a tough job getting the men aboard the little North Coaster once they had decided to abandon the launch, but the "Urana" manoeuvred close and lowered a boarding ladder. The heavy sea often carried the two vessels yards apart, and it was only Sam Coulter's skilful seamanship that enabled the three remaining men to be hauled one by one on to the heaving coaster's deck.

At 4 p.m. on the 7th May, 1934, the "Nambucca" was being towed into the Nambucca River (tugs always assisted the ships to enter the rivers) when the tow-line parted and the vessel was swept onto the south beach. Attempts were made to refloat her during the next few days but they proved futile. The "Nambucca" was a wooden ship and the strain caused her to open up and fill with water. Although pumps and salvage anchors were sent up by the "Uki" they failed to move the stranded steamer and shortly afterwards the water had risen until it had almost covered the engines. By this time her back was broken and she had commenced breaking up. On the 22nd May the underwriters decided it was hopeless and declared her a total loss. Shortly afterwards the hull was sold for £100 and dismantled.

During the year the freight rates were substantially reduced to assist producers who were still feeling the effects of depressed prices and, at the end of December, the brand new "Wyrallah", sister of the "Nimbin" arrived from the builders. She was commissioned immediately, and proved to be a distinct success.

Just prior to this, the "Glenreagh" was sold to Penguin Ltd. for breaking up, She had been rather seriously damaged when she sat on a rock while being loaded in Sydney Harbour and she broke her back as a result. About this time the hulk of the old "Burringbar" was towed outside and scuttled off the Heads, having also been stripped by Penguin Ltd.

In mid December, 1934, the "Ulmarra" hit a submerged object, probably a snag, in the Clarence River near Brushgrove, stripping the propeller and damaging the rudder. Since repairs could only be carried out in dry dock it was decided that she should be towed to Sydney, and the "Arakoon" was earmarked for this job.

However, the "Arakoon" was delayed and was unable to take the tow so it was decided that the "Nimbin" would do the job instead. The Government tug was detailed to tow the lame duck out of the river, and when the "Ulmarra" was safely outside, the "Nimbin" took over, arriving in Sydney Harbour two days later. The tow was uneventful except for a short time when the tow broke. Luckily the weather was fine and no trouble was experienced in picking it up again.

1935 was a quiet year, but an unusual amount of worry and delay was experienced through inclement weather conditions and the further silting up of several bar harbours, notably those at Port Macquarie, Nambucca Heads and the Tweed.

The "Melinga" had a close brush with disaster on the 1st November when she grounded at Port Macquarie while attempting to cross in. Being empty, nothing much could be done to lighten her, and she was still fast eight days later. Captain Gibson, left for the scene on the 4th and the "Uki" sailed with the necessary salvage gear on the 6th. Two days later, on the 8th the gear was laid, and at 5.30 p.m. the same day the "Melinga" was afloat once more. She had lost her starboard anchor in attempting to refloat herself, but this was subsequently recovered.

At 7.45 p.m. on the 9th she crossed out, bound for Sydney where she was slipped at Mort's for an inspection. Only one month later she was again ashore, this time on the Tweed bar but, on this occasion, she was hauled off within twenty-four hours. During the year the old "Kinchela" was hulked, and her machinery was saved for the new "Nambucca", then being built at Tuncurry.

Early in 1936 the new "Nambucca" was launched at Tuncurry and the hull towed to Balmain where the machinery was installed by Mort's Dock. She was

commissioned about September. About the same time that she took the water an order for a new motor vessel was placed with Harland & Wolff in Glasgow, for delivery about the middle of the following year. This vessel was the "Comara" and she arrived in Sydney on 30th June, 1937. She was a particularly fine little ship, rather smaller than the "Wyrallah" which she closely resembled, but eminently suited to the smaller rivers. Her "light" draft was only three feet forward and about six feet aft, while fully loaded she drew hardly more than nine feet.

Her machinery was not of the finest finish when she arrived, but

M.V. "Comara" taken off Port of Newcastle during 1940s.
Acknowledgement: Newcastle Maritime Museum.

her chief engineer, Mr D.R. MacFarlane, dismantled the complete installation progressively and had it reassembled "just so". The result was a vast improvement in performance and reliability, but the main engine was very small — the "Comara" was always a trifle underpowered, and showed it if there was anything of a wind or tide opposing her. However, this is not the fault of the builders. Unfortunately diesel engines are made in certain standard sizes, and the "Comara" was just "in between" two of these sizes, with a leaning towards the smaller. I knew her engine-room well, and it was a model of ingenuity in its layout, and all readily accessible, but it was always rather cramped. This is one advantage which will always remain with the old steam "up and downer" as this type of machinery is nearly always tailored to the ship and is therefore the ideal size for the hull. The machinery installation in the old "Uki" — often referred to as the U.K. One — was beautifully done; one of the finest engine-rooms it has been my pleasure to see.

During 1937 the "Maianbar" was sold to Newcastle interests, and the "Coombar" was sold to W.R. Carpenter for use in the Islands.

In August, the "Urana" was on her way to the Tweed. She passed and spoke to the "Melinga" off Cape Hawke, and was in company with the "Tyalgum" at the time. She was keeping fairly close inshore and at 9 p.m. there was a crash followed by severe bumping and she came to rest on a reef not far from Old Bar near Taree, about a quarter mile off shore. The crew of seventeen officers and men abandoned the ship and rowed ashore while the "Tyalgum" stood by. She was, however, unable to assist, and left to proceed with her own voyage soon afterwards. The wreck was visited by Captain Gibson who advised that the "Urana" was a total loss. The hull and machinery were accordingly offered for sale. To this day her steering wheel may be seen in the Old Bar Surf Club . . . . and thereby hangs a tale.

At 9 p.m. the postmaster at Old Bar, Mr C. Parish, was gazing out the window of the post office, which overlooked the fog-shrouded bay, when suddenly he saw the lights of a vessel looming out of the fog and heading for the beach. About 600 yards from the shore she struck a sunken reef and ground to a stop.

Mr Parish raised the alarm by phoning the rocket brigade at Harrington, and the tug at Forster, and then raced down to the beach. By this time the stranded ship was sending up rockets in quick succession and using her Morse lamp to call for help as well.

At Harrington, the pilot, M.C. Black, mustered the rocket brigade. having notified the police at Coopernook that a vessel was ashore at Old Bar. Constable first-class Bond commandeered a truck, collected the rocket brigade, and set out to drive the thirty or so miles — over rough roads — to the wreck, and they did well to arrive when they did at 12.30 p.m. Meanwhile, at Old Bar, the gathering crowd watched helplessly and could not understand why no attempt was being made to abandon the steamer. The fog had lifted and the crew could be plainly seen hurrying about the ship. About 10 p.m. the crowd saw another vessel standing in towards the reef, in answer to the first ship's S.O.S. Up to this time the identity of both ships was unknown. It was not until later that it became known that they were the "Urana" and "Tyalgum" and that they had left Newcastle in company that morning.

Postmaster Parish, in a statement to the "Manning River Times", said:

"We waited anxiously for the rocket apparatus. Our surf-boat had been taken to Taree for renovation for the coming season.

"Suddenly, we saw a man's figure on the bridge of the wreck.

When the ship's boat reached the beach our first question was about the man still on board. The men told us simply, 'he wouldn't come'."

The 16 crew members who had reached the shore were soaked and exhaused after their ordeal on the wrecked ship. They were taken to the pavilion, wrapped in warm blankets, and given steaming tea and sandwiches. However, for the sailor still trapped aboard the wreck things appeared grim. Everything was against a rescue attempt.

The fog had lifted, but the sea was still heavy, the local surf-boat was ten miles away and there was no chance of making a rescue in the "Urana"'s lifeboat, but in Taree help was being organised.

The licensee of the Royal Hotel, Mr W.A. Scahill, was first to hear news of the shipwreck. He immediately took a taxi to the home of Vic. Rushby, captain of the Taree Old Bar Surf Club. Within two minutes Rushby was ready, gathered a crew for the surf-boat and arranged for the boat to be taken to Old Bar, just as it was, on a lorry.

When they arrived, they discovered that the Harrington rocket crew had been there for some time. However, they had not attempted to lodge a rocket over the wreck for fear that the rope may create difficulties for the oarsmen of the surf-boat. Rushby conferred with pilot Black on the best means of rescuing the sailor, now identified as A.B. Tornoe, from the wreck, which was showing only one white light, making it impossible to tell whether she lay end on or broadside on to the beach.

The only light in the surf-boat would be Rushby's small torch which seemed hardly adequate but it was the only one available. By 1 a.m. the surf-boat was ready and the five lifesavers pushed off into the surf. They made rapid headway and as they approached the wreck quickly sized up the situation. They were extremely cautious as there was tremendous danger of the boat being smashed to pieces on the side of the ship if they ventured too close. Rushby eventually decided to bring the boat up on the lee side of the ship's stern, thus minimising the danger. This manoeuvre was quickly and cautiously executed.

The crew called to Tornoe to jump, but for some time he wouldn't do so. However, he was finally persuaded that this was his only means of escape and he leapt from the deck into the sea. The boat was thirty feet away from him when he hit the water but a wave brought her dancing down to within a yard of him. One of the surf-boat men attempted to haul the sailor over the gunwale of the surf-boat, only to discover that there was a rope secured around his waist. The other end of the rope was tied on to the ship, as a safety measure in case he couldn't reach the boat. However they dragged the man aboard, untied the safety rope and discovered that he was rigged out in complete heavy weather gear — seaboots and all. This explained his unusual weight.

The crew swung the boat around and bent to the oars, pulling for the shore through the breakers. They had almost made it when the last breaker burst over them. One said later that it looked as high as the Comboyne Mountain. This last furious wave struck with such force that it smashed several sweeps, broke off one of the rowlocks and spilled the men into the water. Eventually the ship's crew were taken into Taree, the crowd of onlookers dispersed and all was quiet again on the beach. However, the gallantry of the rescuers did not go unmarked. On 5th October, 1937 the Surf Live-saving Association awarded each of the men the Bronze Meritorious Award. The committee described the circumstances under which they had laboured to effect the rescue as unprecedented in surf-boat work on the New South Wales coast.

An order was placed immediately for a new ship at Harland & Wolff Ltd Glasgow, for delivery in March 1939, and this was the "Bangalow".

In August 1938, the "Wyangarie" arrived from Burmeister & Wain's in Copenhagen, thus following her two sisters "Nimbin" and "Wyrallah", while in the same month the old "Coolebar" was bought back from Cam & Sons of Sydney. (Cam's had acquired her about two years earlier from the Holm Shipping Co. of N.Z.) These two vessels soon took their places in the fleet. The "Wyangarie" entered the Richmond run and her smaller consort resumed her old run to the smaller streams. The "Wyangarie" earned the nick name the "Randwick Express" both on account of her speed and the fact that her master regularly arrived in Sydney in ample time to attend meetings at that famous Racecourse.

When the "Bangalow" arrived from Scotland in May, 1939, she too was immediately pressed into service, but unlike the earlier "Uki" class — of which she was a copy — she was never a conspicuous success as her increased

draft made her just a wee bit deep for the smaller rivers and she spent much of her time ashore as a result. Later, she was used on the

"Bangalow" running speed trials on the Clyde, prior to delivery.
Acknowledgement: R.A.N. Historical Section.

128

Coff's Harbour run and to the larger rivers, but she was too small to be an economic proposition there. She represented one of the Company's few bad mistakes, and was the only vessel to be built for them which did not "fit in" somewhere or other. She was a steamer too: the first since the second "Nambucca" and it appears that steam was chosen in preference to diesel in this case, owing to the growing possibility of a European war cutting off the supply of spares for these engines, most of the builders being either in Germany or Scandinavia. Also, in war time, oil might have been in short supply, while coal was freely available.

A very new M.V. "Wyrallah" at Lismore circa 1936.
Acknowledgement: Malcolm Burgess.

CHAPTER NINE

The Second World War (1939/42)

In September, 1939 the world was plunged into war and this time our little coasters were to be intimately involved in it — not at all like the Kaiser's war — in which they largely escaped the effects, if not the inconveniences.

Immediately, the Navy Department swung into action, requisitioning ships to expand our small Navy. The first ship to be called up (on the 9th October), was that wonderful old steamer, the "Orara", which became, after a hasty refit, the leader of a flotilla of minesweepers. Her motto epitomised the spirit of her company, many of whom were, like her, civilians in Naval uniform — "As they sow, so shall we sweep".

The "Uki" commissioned on the 11th December, and the "Coolebar" on the 18th of the same month, also became minesweepers. It must be remembered that a not inconsiderable delay occurred between a ship being requisitioned and her commissioning, while she was converted to her new role and guns, "sweeping gear" and extra accommodation were added; so we may assume that the date of requisitioning would have been about one month earlier in all cases.

Within a month it happened again. This time it was the "Nambucca" (10th January, 1940) and she too, became a mine-sweeper. Although these requisitions were paid for (at rates fixed by the Imperial Government) their withdrawal from service naturally imposed a severe strain on the Company's ability to cope with the trade that was offering. The position was not improved by the fact that the "Tyalgum", while entering the Tweed River on the 28th August, 1939, with a

H.M.A.S. "Uki" – a gun on the fo'c'sle, a hole in the stern for minesweeping gear = instant warship.
Acknowledgement: Newcastle Maritime Museum.

cargo of coal, cement in bags and petrol in cases, had got into trouble and grounded on the north side of the north breakwater and close to Lover's Rock. Although the underwriter's salvage gear was sent from both Sydney and Brisbane she remained fast and on the 6th September, was declared to be a total loss. Nine days later the wreck was sold at auction for the sum of £240, and it was dismantled where it lay.

Thus, with the effective "loss" of no less than five vessels within as many months, the Company found it necessary to secure additional tonnage so an order was accordingly placed with Mort's Dock & Engineering Co., in Sydney for a steel vessel of about 600 tons

H.M.A.S. "Nambucca" of the 50th Minesweeping Group.
Lost by fire in 1945 whilst in U.S. Army hands.
Acknowledgement: the late John Allcot.

deadweight, with delivery date about July, 1941, and another with Ernest Wright at Tuncurry for a wooden hull of similar size, to be delivered about a month later, in August. The author has in his possession a copy of the general arrangement plans for the Mort's vessel, and she appears to have been an improved sister of the "Bangalow", but as will be explained later she was never completed. It was also considered advisable to repurchase the old "Maianbar" from the Port Stephens S.S. Co. and to reconstruct her for further service, and it was decided to tow her to Sydney where the work could be done more conveniently. However, when she left Newcastle on the 5th May, 1940, in tow by the "Arakoon", disaster struck. It was late in the afternoon, and they had just rounded Nobby's when the tow parted and the "Maianbar" started to drift inshore. Although she had a skeleton crew of two men aboard, she had no steam and, before anything could be done, she was among the numerous reefs which plague this spot. The "Arakoon" had to watch helplessly as the old steamer drifted right through this maze of reefs — amazingly without hitting any one of them — to finally strand herself right alongside the marine drive with her bow almost touching it. Although she was quite high and dry at low water, her stern was occupying the best part of the surfing area at what is Newcastle's most popular beach and, obviously, she could not be allowed to remain there. All attempts to refloat her proved ineffective so she was broken up where she lay while the city fathers urged the work on.

Russell Vasey, later Commander, R.A.N.R., recalls the wreck:

"My most distinct recollections are of going down to the ship relatively shortly after she beached at Nobby's.

"As I recall there were three wires run about ten feet from the fo'c'sle head to pegs driven into the Marine Drive. We would clamber

across these and in heavy weather it was a bit of an exercise to traverse the forward well-deck without being soused with spray.

"We would sit in the port shelter deck just outside the stokehold entrance with our backs against the shell-plate. Seas would crash against the hull, shaking the ship from one end to the other. Torrents of water would escape down skylights and vents and drip through the fast opening deck overhead.

"It was a great thrill and we thought ourselves very brave indeed. One of her lifeboats lay for months in the grass under Fort Scratchley. I was unsuccessful in my persistent endeavours to convince my father that he should buy it for £5 so that I could convert it into a yacht.

"After the ship was broken up the three-furnace Scotch boiler was rolled across the beach and up to the road leading to the Signal Station.

"A year or two later as an ordinary seaman second class drafted to H.M.A.S. "Maitland", the Newcastle shore establishment, I can remember, on the night the Jap. sub. shelled Newcastle, peering seaward over the fence of the Naval Barracks and thinking that the "Maianbar"'s boiler might provide some shelter if the sub. 'got the range'."

It is a proud fact that the service was maintained in spite of the local strike that occurred about this time and lasted for ten weeks and which, coming as it did on top of the drastic reduction in tonnage then in service on the coast, raised almost insuperable

Captain Tolmie and his crew abandon the "Tyalgum" after going ashore close to Lover's Rock, 28th August, 1939.
Acknowledgement: W.R. Duggan.

difficulties for shipowners. Adding insult to very real injury, the war also caused sharp increases in the cost of wages, fuel, stores, repairs and insurance rates, but this was only the beginning as the Company's difficulties all seemed to have started about this time, and they continued to grow steadily worse.

On the 30th September, 1940, the grand old man of the coast, the Hon. Sir Allen Taylor M.L.C., worn out by overwork and the worries of the last twelve months, passed away. He had seen the shipping of this State through its greatest era, and like the grandfather clock in the old song shipping almost seemed to pass away in sympathy. It is certain that it will never be the same again.

In November the "Gunbar" was taken by the Navy, commissioning on the 18th December as H.M.A.S. "Gunbar". She was sent to Darwin, minesweeping there to keep her date with destiny. About the same time the "Pulganbar" was also requisitioned for use as an Admiralty store ship.

The emphasis placed on minesweeping by the Navy was not misplaced as it had long been feared that the Germans might try to repeat their successful W.W. I effort and again mine our sea lanes and, predictably, try they did. Mines were laid in October, 1940, when during the night of the 28th the commerce raider "Pinguin" laid four minefields between Sydney and Newcastle. Having completed this job, she went south and laid two more fields off Hobart.

The first realisation that raiders had been active came on the 7th November when steamer "Cambridge" out of Melbourne for Sydney, was sunk near Wilson's Promontory which had also been mined. The "Orara" reached the area at 9.20 the next day and rescued the survivors who were landed that night. The following day the "Orara", with the ex-trawler "Durraween", swept two

133

mines within fifteen minutes, and sank both with rifle fire. Success did not come with the first attempt, of course – the "Orara" and her consorts had been training and sweeping endlessly for thirteen months before they reaped this harvest — bitter backbreaking months of toil and sweat and sheer drudgery. That is the lot of the mine-sweeper — he is a fisherman who hopes and prays that he will never catch anything, but is nevertheless very proud when he does.

Christmas too was spent at sea; a typical minesweepers' Christmas with very little "Peace or Goodwill", but they could still joke. The story is told that the "Orara" and "Swan" were searching near Kangaroo Island and "Swan" had her coloured minesweeping lights burning as it was after dark and she looked very pretty to the blacked out "Orara" which, being merchant built, was not so fitted. The "Orara"'s skipper light signalled —

"May I hang my stocking on your Christmas Tree?"

Back came "Swan"'s reply —

"Yes. And I will shortly be hanging a sprig of mistletoe over my stern."

I have been told that the "Orara" was laid up for some time after her early minesweeping efforts, and later in the war, about 1943, was refitted as a training ship. She was certainly seen up in the Islands and it is known that she took supplies to Port Moresby. My informant, a commander in the R.A.N. who died recently, stated that her back was broken and had been when the Navy got her. This is certainly not true of the vessel before the war, though it may have been after.

Three weeks earlier, the "Nimbin" became one of our first war losses. At 3.20 on the afternoon of the 5th December, 1940, while quietly proceeding down the coast from Coff's Harbour, she was racked by a violent explosion. She had hit a mine about eight miles off Norah Head, and quickly settled by the stern. Within two minutes she had disappeared, taking with her seven of her ship's company including the master, William James Bysantson, Mr Chapman the mate, Mr McAllister third engineer, A.B.s Carlson and Gorry and firemen Hutton and Hallett. The Cook was saved by Fred Gough, one-time steward of the "Orara". The survivors were in the water only about 2½ hours altogether, during which time a seaplane sighted them and landed on the sea nearby, then left for assistance. The "Bonalbo" arrived on the scene about 6 p.m. having been directed by the air-craft, and she picked up the thirteen swimmers and brought them to Sydney where she arrived at 10 p.m. The "Bonalbo" was very lucky that she did not suffer the same fate as the "Nimbin" as it was not realised that a mine was responsible for the sinking for some time.

As a matter of course, the Navy sent a sweeper to check and she caused considerable consternation all round by finding a minefield! The "Nimbin", Sir Allen's favourite ship, was long referred to as the "Tin Hare" on account of her speed. Her model may be seen in the Museum of Applied Arts & Sciences in Sydney. Immediate plans were made to build a replacement and the drawings were prepared by Mort's for a steam powered vessel of similar size with only minor alterations to suit the different machinery and with the recently adopted idea of housing the hands aft. It was to be a steamer because most motor engine builders were then in occupied Europe, or were engaged in urgent Naval work.

The sister vessel "Wyrallah" went to the Navy during the year, and was commissioned as a fleet auxiliary, complete with a 4-inch gun. Later in the war (February, 1942) she was renamed H.M.A.S. "Wilcannia" because there was now a corvette named "Whyalla".

Shortage of materials and labour, and more pressing Admiralty

H.M.A.S. "Wilcannia" (ex-Wyrallah) commissioned 2nd September, 1940 as a patrol vessel.
Acknowledgement: R.A.N. Historical Section.

requirements delayed work on the two 600-tonners ordered the previous year. The steel job at Mort's never did get completed and the wooden vessel from Tuncurry could not now be launched before the middle of 1942.

On the 5th February, 1941, the "Melinga" had what must rate as one of the closest shaves ever as, when entering the Manning River in tow at 4 p.m. she struck the sand heavily, right in the middle of the bar. There was a strong northerly set, whipped up by a real southerly buster and these carried her onto the rocks which had been progressively washed away from the end of the breakwater over the years, but clear of the wall itself. The tug was forced to slip the tow to avoid being dragged ashore herself, and the "Melinga", opened up about the middle of the hold by the rocks and leaking freely, ran onto the north beach where she lay broadside on and facing north.

The little tug tried valiantly to put another line aboard but was forced to abandon the attempt before she herself became a casualty. Eventually, showing some more of his superb seamanship, the master (Coulter) managed to get his "Melinga" off the beach under her own power and back into deep water. Sam Coulter then made a very reasonable decision. The owners had already lost, or had requisitioned far more ships than they could afford to lose, and were maintaining a difficult and

"Melinga" – petrol drums and oil tanks adrift – at point of sinking.
Acknowledgement: A. Beckenham, Engineer.

136

"Melinga" – on the bottom at Crowdy Bay.
Acknowledgement: Captain D.W. Gibson.

complicated service with a ridiculously small number of vessels. Clearly, they could ill afford any further losses and, accordingly, the "Melinga" must not be allowed to sink anywhere where subsequent salvage operations might prove to be difficult or impossible. The fact that the ship was at the moment sinking under him worried the captain not one whit. He set off up the coast heading for Crowdy Bay, which offered a safe beach, protected from the existing weather conditions and here, he realised, was the best place for his purpose.

The "Wyangarie" (R. Lucey), which was passing, stood by to render any needed assistance, but the "Melinga" managed the five mile trip under her own power. With her fo'c'sle awash and the propeller almost completely out of the water, the crew were forced to flood the after peak tank (a ballast tank fitted in most ships) to bring the propeller and rudder back into the water to regain some control, and incidentally to help to stabilise the vessel by "counter-flooding".

The "Melinga" was loaded at the time with butter boxes, completely knocked down in bundles or "shooks" and these provided some buoyancy forward. She was also fitted with a pair of "deep tanks" for fuel oil and these were located near the collision bulkhead. The forepeak remained dry, too, but over 50 per cent of the ship was flooded.

Her deck cargo included a large number of 44-gallon drums of petrol, together with a big tank of oil fuel destined for the Taree Butter Factory, and this tank broke adrift and ran amok on the starboard side of the foredeck. The vessel was acting in a pretty lively manner in the sea that was running and several of the petrol drums were burst open by the runaway oil tank, increasing the hazard and nauseating all hands with the smell of petrol.

A little later the electric steering gear short-circuited and failed, and the "Melinga" began sheering wildly, to the consternation of Captain Lucey in the "Wyangarie" who was escorting her only 50 yards away. Undaunted, and now steering by hand, she eventually arrived and, like a tired old fisherwoman, settled to the bottom at 4 p.m. about 200 yards off shore. The weather continued to deteriorate and the tug and the other steamer, seeing that the "Melinga" was safe, proceeded on their way. The crew remained aboard overnight and came ashore next morning. The whole episode attracted much attention and as the little motor vessel went up the coast towards Crowdy Bay, many of the locals followed to watch the drama. The ship lay on the bottom facing seaward, her bows nearly submerged and her stern still afloat, while big seas were dashing over her.

The first thing to be done was to salvage the cargo, which included some 240 forty-four gallon drums of petrol. This was taken, 18 drums at a time, to Taree by three lorries. Other cargo was salvaged as it floated ashore. Captain Gibson came up from Sydney by car on the day of the accident and set about the job of refloating the ship. The Navy was not interested at all, saying that a vessel of only 500 tons was not worth the time or effort involved, and they refused to allow more than four men to work on the job. Nevertheless, by the 18th she was afloat, and Captain Gibson brought her to Sydney with his three assistants, aided by the tug "Heroic" which, with the "Doepel" the Navy had at last allowed to assist.

When the "Melinga" arrived at last off Sydney Heads, the Naval examination vessel "Falie" made herself very unpopular with Captain Gibson when she told the "Melinga" to stop and wait to go through the normal routine examination. As the "Melinga" was still leaking, and had several large salvage pumps going full bore to keep her afloat, this order was ignored by Captain Gibson, who swept past the "Falie" and told her that if she insisted on "examining" his ship, she could do it in Watson's Bay, and that if he waited around too long the "Melinga" was liable to sink! Mr Albert Beckenham was the engineer at the time, and was one of the three who helped David Gibson bring her home.

In November, 1941, H.M.A.S. "Wyrallah" (not yet renamed) based at the time on Fremantle was called upon to join the extensive search which was then being conducted with the aim of finding the missing cruiser H.M.A.S. "Sydney" but the only thing that was ever found was a badly damaged Carley float. It was known that she had been in action with a German raider, and, while most of the raider's company were picked up, no other trace of the cruiser was ever found. The story is too well-known for me to go into further details in a book such as this.

The ex-north coaster "Tambar" which you will remember had been sold some years previously, was also requisitioned by the Navy and commissioned as a minesweeper of group 74 on the 7th November, 1939.

Sometime later (date unknown) she was based on Brisbane and made it her habit on her way up the river to stop off at the Army camp at Cowan Cowan. She often used to give lifts to Brisbane to soldiers going on leave. Coming up the Brisbane River about 10 a.m. one beautiful clear day she was approaching Cowan Cowan when the Army fired a six-inch shell across her bows. At least that was the intention. As the "Tambar" was about to anchor her cable party was close up on the fo'c'sle, and the shell, instead of crossing the bows passed lengthwise down the ship. One of the cable party was cut down and the shell then went through the captain's cabin, and chart-room, finally coming out through the wireless-room on the starboard side.

During its passage through the captain's cabin the steward was killed and Warrant Officer Seaman lost both legs. He died on the way to hospital. Seven or eight of the deck personnel had flesh wounds from splinters. The engine-room crew heard a tremendous bang and the rust of ages showered down on them from every nook and cranny. The engine-room skylight collapsed and fell into the engine-room and they thought that the ship had been bombed.

This tragic accident was immediately veiled in wartime secrecy and after attending a military funeral for the dead the entire crew was broken up and posted to different ships, the captain getting a new command.

By this time the wages of the seagoing staff had risen 50 per cent above pre-war rates, and an appeal to the prices commissioner was necessary to gain the 22½ per cent increase on pre-war freight rates which enabled the firm to carry on.

Early in 1942 yet further requisitions were made, this time on behalf of the U.S. Army Small Ships Command. The first two were probably the "Bangalow" and the "Melinga", but the dates of their commissioning are not known. Mr H.T. Parrott, who now resides at Manly, served in the "Melinga" in the South West Pacific Theatre, and he confirms that these requisitions were made by the R.A.N., although they went to the U.S. Small Ships Command. Mr Parrott also pointed out to me the fact that the "Noorebar" was not scrapped in 1932 as originally believed, although it is true that she was struck from the register at that time.

Mr Parrott who, incidentally, also did his time at Mort's Dock as an apprentice and knew the future Sir William McKell, says he saw the "Noorebar" in Rabaul in 1935/37 at the time of the great eruption when Matupi volcano exploded and, on the west side of the harbour a new volcano named Vulcan was born. This would be in 1936. Not far from where Vulcan rose out of the harbour was the site of the old slipways and the "Noorebar" was on the slip at the time. She was launched in a great hurry, covered in pumice and volcanic ash and, right where she had been, the harbour bottom rose many feet and became dry land. If they had not launched her when they did she would be there yet, and indeed one ship is still there, buried in ash, about a mile from the water. The "Noorebar" was owned at the time by W. R. Carpenter but her ultimate fate is unknown. If this story is true, the Japanese probably got her.

CHAPTER TEN

The Second World War (1942/45)

The Raid on Darwin:

Thursday, 19th February, 1942, dawned bright and clear over Darwin and normal work at the jetty and Naval base continued as usual. At 10 minutes to 10, however, with no warning, the Japanese arrived for the first raid of the day.

The story of that fateful morning, with its similarity to the earlier raid on Pearl Harbour, has been told too often in the popular press to merit a repetition of the major events here, but one of the ships that was present was a North Coaster, and her story, usually passed over in favour of others, makes stirring reading. The steamer concerned was the little "Gunbar" which was at the time doing duty as a water carrier after her stint as a 'sweeper. She was still in the Navy, under the command of Lieutenant N.M. Muzzell R.A.N.R. (S), and was passing through the boom gate when she met the Japs coming in.

She shared, with five U.S.A.A.F. "Kitty Hawk" fighters, the dubious honour of being the Japs' first target, as she later reported:—

"At 9.57 a.m. nine fighters attacked giving, in all, eighteen separate attacks from ahead, astern, and starboard. The Japs used armour-piercing, tracer, and common ammunition and the first run hit our single Lewis gun, rendering the ship defenceless. At 10.10 the attack finished."

In this attack, no less than nine of the "Gunbar"'s crew, including the skipper, were wounded and one subsequently died. Lieutenant Muzzell, although in great pain from wounds in both knees, refused to leave the bridge until his ship was safely anchored after the raid had ended, but not before the Japs had succeeded in wrecking the jetty and gaining hits on the "Neptuna", "Barossa", "Zealandia" and the U.S.S. "Peary", all of which were sunk as well as others which were damaged. Scarcely a ship in the harbour got off unscathed and the town took a severe beating as well.

The "Gunbar" was subsequently steamed south for repairs, and Joe Martin, who was one of the N.C.S.N. Company's engineers, (and later chief engineer of the N.S.W. Public Works Department dredge service), was in the ship for the run. He recalls that the ship was still riddled with bullet holes, especially the funnel. Nor could sufficient coal be spared for the run, and she was ordered to call at Townsville to bunker, so as to have enough coal to make Sydney. She scraped in almost on the last shovelful. When they said that they wanted full bunkers the Naval officer-in-charge said that there was no coal to spare, pointing out that the entire stocks held were required for a large convoy that was expected. Apparently the ship was eventually bunkered as she completed the trip and went into dock for repairs.

In April, the drogher "Wauchope" sank off Port Stephens in heavy weather, while being towed to Sydney by the "Arakoon". The order for a steel vessel placed with Mort's three years earlier, which had been delayed several times by now, was finally shelved for good early in 1942 owing to the press of Admiralty work, but by early July the wooden vessel building in Wright's yard at Tuncurry was complete except for machinery, and had been launched. Named the

H.M.A.S. "Gunbar" – first vessel attacked in the original Japanese raid on Darwin.
Acknowledgement: R.A.N. Historical Section.

"Uralba" she was towed to Sydney and there fitted with second-hand machinery from the old Sydney ferry "Kuramia" together with a boiler from the old coaster "Malachite". Before her owners could take delivery, she was commandeered, but was handed over to the Company in 1947.

In October, the "Comara", on passage to Coff's Harbour, got lost for 24 hours. This is the way it happened. Although due to arrive at Coff's on the morning of the 12th, nothing was heard from her until the following day when a phone call was received at Sussex Street from the Navy at Garden Island, to say they had received a message from the "Comara" through Australian National Airways —

"Rudder stock broken. Drifting 14 miles south-east of Smoky Cape."

A message was sent to the "Ulmarra", south bound from the Clarence, to endeavour to locate and assist. Meanwhile phone calls were made to Kempsey, Coff's Harbour, Port Macquarie and Newcastle in an attempt to gain more information. The next day this continued and the "Wyangarie" was also asked to search, but it was not until the 15th that Garden Island could advise that the dredge "Trinity Bay" was standing by with gear to assist. The "Wyangarie" radioed at 10.20 a.m. —

" 'Comara' now in sight — proceeding to her, send instructions." to which, half an hour later, came the reply: —

"If weather conditions suitable, tow to Sydney, otherwise take to Coff's Harbour."

The "Wyangarie" replied that she would bring the "Comara" to Sydney and the two vessels arrived at 6 p.m. the following afternoon, where the "Comara" went straight up to Mort's for repairs.

A few weeks later, when the "Comara" was again fit for sea, the U.S. Army had her requisitioned, and subsequently she spent much of her time in the islands — Rabaul, New Ireland, the Solomons, New Hebrides, Guadalcanal — she was there, at all of them.

The American ways of direct action applied to shipping requisitions just as they did in any other field. Their method was simple and effective but was not appreciated by shipowners. A marine sergeant simply walked up the gangway, accompanied by a private armed with the American Flag. The ship's national flag was hauled down (often against the captain's protest) and the Stars and Stripes raised in its place. The sergeant then informed the Captain that his ship was now the property of the U.S. Army and he was not to do anything without their approval. He would proceed on his way leaving an armed sentry on the gangway to see that his orders were observed. In due course a formal letter would arrive from the R.A.N. ratifying the sergeant's actions.

Captain John Magee was skipper of the "Comara" in the South West Pacific theatre, and has a fund of anecdotes about this period.

Her carrying capacity was tested far beyond normal limits, and it was nothing to fill her holds to capacity, fill the decks with 100-Octane gasoline in drums, cover them with a tarpaulin, put a hundred troops on top of that, and an awning over all for shade. She also carried 8-ton trucks, fully loaded as deck cargo.

One time in the Trobriand Islands, she arrived with a large consignment of empty drums. Magee was much amused when the boarding officer insisted on knowing what was in them — "What", he asked, "would normally be in *empty* drums?"

The Official History "Royal Australian Navy 1942/45" (G.H. Gill, Australian War Memorial) mentions "Comara" on page 267, stating that she: —

Was loaded to her marks and there was not a square foot of deck space. Hatches were covered with trucks and vehicles of all descriptions, and with Ship's Company & Troops there was twice the number of men on board for whom there was lifeboat accommodation.

I have heard that she sometimes had her marks well below the water but she did an excellent job, and was highly regarded.

The "Nambucca" also went over to the Yanks, and she too, spent much time near the "front" but she was merely seconded from the R.A.N. who no longer needed her for minesweeping. She gave sterling service.

The Company was now down to six ships to maintain their service — the "Arakoon", the "Bonalbo", "Doepel", "Ulmarra", "Wollongbar" (2) and "Wyangarie" and this was shortly to be reduced by one, for, in April, 1943 the "Wollongbar" was torpedoed by a Japanese submarine off Crescent Head. The following story was related to me by Captain "Will" Mason who was acting chief officer at the time, while his own vessel "Arakoon" was undergoing overhaul.

All went well until two days before Anzac Day when the "Wollongbar" was on her way up to Byron Bay. Owing to the war, she had no passengers and the entire crew was using the passenger accommodation. The trip was uneventful until off the Clarence River entrance, she received an S.O.S. from a steamer which was on fire. The "Wollongbar" proceeded to the position and picked up survivors. A corvette arrived and joined in, taking those survivors from the "Wollongbar" as well. The "Wollongbar" then proceeded to Byron Bay, where she discharged her cargo and loaded frozen meat and butter for Sydney.

At 5 p.m. on the Sunday the Australian minelayer H.M.A.S. "Bungaree" was seen passing Cape Byron, and three hours later, at 8 p.m. the "Wollongbar" sailed, with "Will" Mason on watch. The night was uneventful, and at 8 a.m. he took over from the second mate, one Captain Sargent who had been serving in oil tankers after having left the North Coast S.N. Company some years earlier. Captain Sargent then went below to breakfast.

Mason was still on watch, and the master, Captain Benson, was walking on the boat deck just below the bridge, talking to the Chief Engineer when it happened. The time was about ten in the morning and the chief was making his usual morning report on his machinery to Captain Benson. Apparently no one saw the torpedo — most likely there was only one, although it is possible that two were used — but Will Mason dimly remembers an explosion and instinctively grabbed the dodger in front of him. Captain Benson immediately dashed into his cabin, most likely to get the log and other confidential books in their weighted bag, preparatory to dumping them, but neither he nor his Chief Engineer was seen again.

The next thing that Mason remembers was when he woke up in the water. There was no sign of the ship or, for that matter, her attacker. The whole area was littered with wreckage — pieces of wood, fittings from the ship, floating boxes of butter as well as sundry other bits and pieces. Wreckage was still coming to the surface, too, and there was no lack of means of keeping afloat. He grabbed a butter box and it supported him until he noticed a lifeboat floating nearby. It was full of water and he swam to it. He remembers he had a battle to climb into it . He then saw Frank Emson, a greaser, in the water and helped him aboard. Emson, in his cabin above No. 1 boiler when the torpedo hit, was badly burnt by 'flash' before jumping overboard. The gun crew had just been given a "stand easy" and had gone below for tea and a smoke just minutes before the submarine was sighted. It was unfortunate, but they would not have had time to lay their three-inch gun, load and fire it at the sub. before the ship sank, and the gun was on the stern whilst the sub. was on the bow anyway, but if they had been on deck they may have survived too.

Only one person on shore saw the sinking — a little boy, walking on the beach at Crescent Head with his father. The child looking seaward said:—

"Look at the big ship, daddy".

But by the time the father had looked up, the ship was gone! It was as quick as that.

In the lifeboat, they could not see any more survivors for a while. Then Mason saw a man — he forgets his name now — paddling a raft. This man had made a pierhead jump to join the vessel. He paddled his raft over to the lifeboat and shortly afterwards they sighted two more men on another raft. They too, came over to the boat and the five of them, after looking in vain for any more survivors, sat and waited. Mason, who was the only officer to survive, knew that they were about ten miles off Crescent Head, and that, being in a shipping lane, help would come if they waited long enough. To increase their field of view they stepped the mast, discovering in the process that the boat had almost no bottom left. One man shinned up the mast, but all he could see was thousands of boxes of butter floating among other pieces of wreckage — no ships, no bodies, no more survivors, no submarine. It was hard to believe that a disaster could strike so swiftly and leave so little trace.

They decided, since the mate and greaser were injured, to row and sail for the beach, but eventually gave up rowing and more or less drifted, waiting for help. At noon they were sighted by an RAAF Catalina, which called for help, and a fishing boat with a volunteer crew set out from Port Macquarie to bring them in. The fishing boat saw their sail intermittently and survivors were picked up. The lifeboat was abandoned and was later washed ashore near Point Plomer. For weeks the area was littered with wreckage.

The trawler, which turned out to be Claude Radley's oddly named "Xlcr", returned at full speed to Port Macquarie, where Dr Eric Murphy was waiting on the breakwater. The survivors remember that it was rough crossing the bar, but they crossed in safely and tied up at 3.30 p.m. A group of V.A.Ds were waiting with an ambulance and all except Emson were taken to the Royal Hotel — Emson went straight to hospital to begin a four month sojourn while his burns healed. His skin was all dried out like parchment by the scalds, and sitting in the open boat for most of the day had not improved it. Will Mason was taken to hospital later by car, after he had phoned the owners and also the Navy in Sydney. He spent ten days "in" while doctors worked on his legs, which had been damaged when he had fallen through the bottom of the lifeboat while stepping the mast.

The other three survivors who were uninjured were taken to Wauchope and put on the night train to Sydney. One of them, a fireman named Blinkhorn, had an amazing escape when the torpedoes hit. He was blown at least thirty feet upwards and clean out of his stokehold, landing on a raft bone dry, and completely uninjured except that he was somewhat dazed, as well he might be.

When he got back to Sydney, Captain Mason had to tell the Naval authorities the whole story as he knew it, and was then told to keep quiet about it (wartime secrecy) and to this day the facts are often misquoted when the story is retold. Sometimes to the extent of claiming that it all occurred at night! The survivors owed the presence of the lifeboat to the fact that the boats were not griped down and had no falls rove in the davits, on the principle that in the event of such an occurrence as this there would be no time to formally abandon ship, and this way the boats would float clear on their own, as also, did the life-rafts.

Thirty-two men died in this sinking, including the master, second officer and all engineers, and of these, those who were not killed outright must have been trapped below. As recently as November, 1962, barnacle-encrusted blocks of putrid butter were still being washed ashore near Crescent Head and Point Plomer. One was covered with marine growths and so evil smelling that it had to be buried, another was reported to be in "fair" condition.

An unusual accident for a shipping company occurred at Coff's Harbour on 22nd December, 1943, when an Airforce plane crashed into the back of the local manager's residence. The damage to the house was not great, but both airmen were injured, and the plane (naturally enough) was wrecked.

During the war years an incident occurred which highlights the different attitude to seamanship taken by the Merchant Service and the Navy. The former have an inbuilt hatred of regimentation, while, to the fighting Navy, discipline and obedience to orders is fundamental. The following goes to illustrate this point:

Captain Buckingham, of the "Bonalbo", regularly called at New-castle and had for weeks been answering the challenge made by the port examination vessel before he was allowed to enter. Finally the day arrived when Buckingham, never a patient skipper, said "to hell with this rot – they ought to know by now that the "Bonalbo" is not a Japanese submarine," ignored the challenge and held course for the harbour entrance. Next instant, a three-inch shell was put across his bows and he realised that he had better go along with the ritual, and stop. The identification was made but "Buck" was not amused when he subsequently got a bill for £40, the cost of the shell! He had the last laugh, however, when next trip he stood miles off the harbour entrance, and the examination vessel had to go out and identify him. Both sides were irate about the whole thing, but no real damage resulted.

Towards the end of April, 1944, the Government placed the remaining vessels under the control of the Shipping Control Board (later to become the Australian Shipping Board) for which the Company now acted as agents. This had little effect on the service but it did mean that the Company no longer had control of its own vessels.

On the 30th May, the "Bonalbo" got herself stuck in the mud near Woodburn on the Richmond River during a fog and bent her rudder post, making it impossible for her to steer. A diver and crew were brought from Byron Bay to examine her, and the "Doepel", waiting to load at Coff's Harbour, was instructed to proceed instead to Woodburn and to render assistance. She arrived the next day, by which time the divers and the ship's engineers had the offending rudder post nearly ready for removal. On the 30th it was sent to Ballina by road to be straightened while the "Bonalbo"'s cargo was taken aboard the "Doepel" for Lismore. She had to make two trips to do this. Then, on the 6th June, while in Europe men were locked in mortal conflict on the beaches of Normandy, and the gigantic struggle was just beginning to unfold, the little wooden "Doepel" towed her larger consort to the slipway at Ballina.

The rudder post was reinstalled on the 10th with the aid of the diver, inspected by the surveyor, and another episode was over. Not long afterwards, the "Doepel" was chartered by the "Pig and Whistle" Company and she ran to the South Coast ports for the next few years, during which time little was heard of her by her owners.

In 1945 the Department of the Navy released the "Uki" to resume trading, but the other vessels remained under requisition. This vessel also had seen service with the American forces for a while, having been seconded from the R.A.N., and was known to them as the U.K. (1), as they could never get used to the correct pronunciation, which is "you-kye"; not "ucky" or "youky".

On the 30th December, in the same year, while still under requisition to the armed forces, the "Nambucca" became a total loss, but the Company was not informed for nearly a year, and even then no details were given. However it was later learned unofficially that the little wooden steamer, while being operated by the American Army in the Islands, had caught fire and burned to the waterline.

While awaiting discharge from the Army in the winter of 1946, Mr J. Ralph of Forestville was temporarily attached to a small craft park located at Primrose Park at the head of Willoughby Bay in Middle Harbour just near Cammeray. One of the craft in the bay was an old wooden steamer named "Cobaki", she was resting on mud and needed pumping out twice a day by means of a petrol driven fire pump parked on deck.

It is not known what use the Army had made of her but she was then derelict and in fact was towed with some difficulty in her waterlogged condition on a cold and windy day into Salt Pan Creek,

The wooden T.S.S. "Doepel" built on Brisbane water.
Acknowledgement: R. Dufty.

Northbridge, about half a mile away and allowed to settle on the bottom alongside the remains of a sailing ship. Her bones are still there.

In 1946 the "Comara" and the "Bangalow" were returned and resumed trading, still under the control of the Australian Shipping Board. On the 17th June that year, Mr Arthur McElhone, who had been a member of the board of directors of the Company since the 1920s, and chairman since the death of Sir Allen Taylor, passed away, and was replaced by Mr Orwell Phillips, a man well known for his ability in this capacity.

During the early part of 1947 further ships were returned by the Navy, namely the "Melinga" and the "Uralba", followed later in the year by the "Wyrallah", after a most extensive refit, which included the fitting of a completely new bottom. This completed the de-commissioning of vessels taken over for war purposes, as the older ships were declared unfit for reconversion to a trading role and were accordingly sold. This was not as unfair as it sounds as the vessels concerned were all very old, and the alterations carried out by the Naval authorities on requisitioning these ships would have reduced their carrying capacity alarmingly. It must be remembered that these ships were originally built to strict draft requirements, and any tampering with the design—as in converting the ships to warships—could only have had a detrimental effect on the commercial qualities of the vessel.

It would appear that the Navy Department protected the owners against any likelihood of these vessels ever coming back as competitors even if they were reconverted, as all disposals were to be outside Australian waters, mostly to Hong Kong or Mainland China. There were no less than four vessels of the N.C.S.N. Company fleet sold in this manner, all of which came under the Chinese (Nationalist) flag, although not all of them did actually leave Australia.

The old "Orara", after being de-commissioned by the Navy, lay in Sydney Harbour until she found a buyer in 1947, in Shanghai, and she then proceeded "up top". On reaching her new owners in 1948 she was renamed "Pearl River". Following a frequent Chinese practice she was renamed the following year, becoming "Hong Shan", then in 1950 she was renamed "Santos". On the 19th June in that year, and under this name, she hit a mine about twelve miles off the Woo Sung Forts at the mouth of the Yang-tse River, and sank with a regrettably heavy loss of life.

The "Pulganbar" was also sold to Chinese interests about the same time, but she lay in the Harbour for a considerable time before leaving our shores sometime in 1948. On her delivery voyage she ran into Coff's with her crew "mutinous" and they were repatriated to China and a new crew engaged. It is known that she was renamed "Yang-tse River", and later "Tamara" and was finally broken up for scrap in 1951 or 1952.

The "Gunbar" was another ship that was sold to China, but she never left Sydney. She was unfit for the long voyage and was broken up in her old home port, while the "Coolebar", also sold east, was renamed "East River" but apparently never left these waters either, for she sank at her mooring in Newcastle on 25th September, 1949, and was raised in pieces nine years later for scrap.

CHAPTER ELEVEN

"Ave Atque Vale"

The "Doepel", under charter to the South Coast Company, grounded on the bar at Bateman's Bay in May, 1947, but the owners were not advised until August. She was leaking and an examination in dock showed damage amounting to £1,419. During the year Mr F.A. Sargeant resigned as a director of the Company owing to ill health. He had been a director for many years and rendered valuable service to the firm.

In October, the "Ulmarra" hit the bottom when she was about two miles north of Woolgoolga, coming down inside the Solitary Islands. She began making water in the engine-room and after hold, and was beached alongside the Coff's Harbour Jetty. The damage was not great and the pumps were able to cope, but the master, Sam Coulter, acted prudently and once again picked a good place to beach his ship. Shortly afterwards she was refloated and sailed for Sydney for repairs.

About this time the government charter ended and control of the vessels was handed back to the Company. Freight rates were increased to cover rising costs as the familiar post-war spiral got under way. It now took much longer to overhaul a vessel, and another problem was the slow turn-around in port. Trade was variable and all these factors made it increasingly difficult to provide the regular, frequent service so essential with small vessels in the coastal trade.

The results of the 40-hour week, and other variations in awards which reduced ordinary productive hours, were now being felt and these, together with continual increases in costs, had a serious effect on all forms of transport and in business generally. The post-war repair programme initiated as a result of the unavoidable postponement of certain work during the war years, was completed in early 1949. Very heavy expenses were necessary on one vessel and dockyard strikes caused major delays. The disastrous coal strike that developed towards the end of June, with serious results to industry, generally curtailed cargoes and this continued until factories could resume normal production.

The last of the Company's wooden vessels, the "Doepel" and "Uralba" had been sold in late 1947, and the fleet now comprised five steamers and four motor ships. The "Uralba" was sold to the Melbourne Electricity Commission and the "Doepel" went to Dickson Primer & Co. for work in Borneo. In September, 1948, Mr W. C. Sturrock retired as general manager, and Mr J. Gordon was appointed to replace him. John Gordon had been with the Company since 1908, having joined about the same time as his illustrious brother. He served in the "Brundah" for a short time then went into the office as an accountant. As he was the Company's last manager he had the sad task of winding up the Company and it is to his eternal credit that he did so in such a painless manner.

John Gordon was a disciplinarian himself and was not always popular with the staff, but he saw to it that no member was hurt financially by the winding up, as could easily have happened. He has

Coff's Harbour 1950 – "Bangalow" well and truly ashore after the cyclone.
Acknowledgement: J. Kennedy–Engineer.

148

been accused of winding up a going concern unnecessarily, but as the remainder of the story will show, the writing was on the wall, and no one could have avoided it. Delayed it yes, maybe for up to five years, or even more, but it would then have been an involuntary liquidation, with big debts and many little people left "holding the bag".

An attempt was made by the Department of Shipping to provide new tonnage to replace war-time losses, the idea being, apparently, that State-owned ships could be chartered to private owners. The idea was basically sound, and the five vessels of the "E" class — "Eugowra", "Enfield", "Edenhope", "Elmore" and "Euroa" were built by Walkers Ltd Maryborough in 1948 and 1949. They were good little vessels of 584 tons, about 175 ft long by 29 ft 6 in. beam, the design being based on the A.U.S.N. "Babinda", but no allowance was made for the specialised nature of the N.C.S.N. Company's requirements, and they were not really suitable for working shallow bar-harbours, being 11 ft 3 in. deep. They were intended for any trade offering and were insufficiently adapted to the North Coast Trade. They were used for a time, at least, on the Clarence River and possibly the Richmond, but only because of the shortage of more suitable vessels and the incredible cost of building new tonnage in the post-war period. They were all eventually transferred to the Australian Coastal Shipping Commission (later the A.N.L.) and tramped from one end of the coast to the other. None remains now on the Australian Register, as they were "sold foreign" over the last few years.

In the latter half of 1949 and all 1950 the coast was lashed by gales and unprecedented wet weather that had a marked effect on trading and, in June, the disastrous floods on the North Coast seriously disrupted the running of the Company's vessels. The whole area suffered severely and trading conditions remained difficult for some time. On the 24th June the "Bangalow" was blown ashore at Coff's Harbour during a cyclonic gale and it was nearly a month before she could be refloated by Captain Gibson. She had been carried high and dry.

Great difficulty was experienced in giving any sort of service to Kempsey, as dredging did not overcome the shoaling of the river caused by the August, 1949, floods. Since then no vessel has been able to proceed beyond Smithtown and cargoes had to be landed at small wharves and carried the last twenty-odd miles by truck.

Industrial troubles also had a serious effect on this river. To cap it all, rising costs forced further freight increases to avoid making a loss. Trading in the latter half of 1950 was still severely handicapped by the aftermath of the floods. Unfortunately the unprecedented wet weather continued, causing a heavy loss in man-hours and this necessitated excessive overtime working to cope with the cargo which was offering.

The coastal steamer "Allenwood", with a crew of 16 under Captain Boutrup, ran ashore in fog, before dawn on 14th September, 1951, on sand at the foot of Wybung Head, five miles north of Norah Head, and remained stuck fast. She lost her starboard propeller, and later in the day was reported to be bumping heavily.

She had cleared Sydney at 8.15 p.m. the previous night, bound north for timber. At 5 a.m. a distress call was picked up, stating that she was ashore on a sandy beach not far from Bird Island. The freighter "Bungaree" offered assistance but was refused because of the risk, she being a large vessel. By nightfall the "Allenwood" was moving about in a fair sea and moderate nor'-easter, and her bow was embedded in about 4 ft of sand. The tug "Wonga" was sent from Sydney but, by the time she arrived, the "Allenwood" was firmly embedded, with seas breaking over the port side. She lay only about twenty yards from the jagged rocks of Wybung Head. The tug was unable to get her off and some days later she was declared a total loss. She eventually broke up and very little of her now remains. There were no injuries in this wreck, but had she piled up, say, fifty yards further north, it must have been a different story.

The rivers to which the Company was still trading, required considerable dredging as a result of the floods and this was repeatedly brought before the Government department concerned. However very little improvement was made in the Macleay and vessels still could not reach the terminal port of Kempsey. During the year steep wage increases had a marked effect on operating costs. Industrial troubles on the waterfront showed no improvement, and the turn-round of vessels again deteriorated, while trading operations were further restricted owing to prolonged periods occupied by over-hauls and repairs. Consequently, less cargo could be carried compared with the previous year. It may be appropriate at this point to say a word on the cost of new vessels.

It will be remembered that in 1834, the 200-ton steamer "Ceres", built at Clarencetown, cost £8,150. In 1937 the "Wyangarie" cost the vicinity of £70,000, while in 1953, a similar ship would have cost no less than £250,000, and fully half the fleet was old and in need of replacement, as five of them, "Arakoon", "Bonalbo", "Melinga", "Uki", and "Ulmarra" dated from the 1920s. Replacement vessels were considered, even at these prices, and plans and specifications drawn up, on the understanding that the Government would fulfil its obligations and dredge the rivers properly. When it failed to do so, and the wharf labourers and seamen were causing so much unrest, it is hardly surprising that the orders were cancelled. I have drawings of two of these vessels; both were originally intended to be built in 1941, and then deferred as already seen, so there is no doubt of the Company's intentions, but events rendered these plans impossible.

E. S. Crawford, Esq., so long general manager in the Company, was forced to retire owing to ill health. He had been elected a director in December, 1942, after having been general manager since the early 1920s. It is perhaps significant that so many of these leading men were lost to the Company in its last ten years or so, but even they could not have done much in the face of the forces arrayed against them. A.E. Chown was elected to replace him.

Trading from July to December, 1951, was satisfactory and fine weather was enjoyed all along the coast. Good inward cargoes of sugar, timber, and other produce were available, while outward general cargoes from Sydney, in addition to coal for the industries served by the Company, provided adequate outward loadings, but these conditions were only an Indian summer in the winter of the times. Early 1952 showed a marked decline in timber shipments, mainly owing to a total ban on overtime by the waterside workers from April. At the outports there were only a limited number of these gentlemen, and night shift facilities were not available, so the refusal to work overtime had very serious effects on turn-round, as was only to be expected under the circumstances.

So critical did all these troubles become, that the Company was forced to lay up vessels for varying periods, for sheer lack of work. Naturally costs continued their upward climb, and additional expenses

151

of all kinds forced yet another increase in freights. The screw was being tightened.

During this year no attempt was made to dredge the Macleay River, which had shoaled even further, and vessels could now trade to the lower river only, even then on restricted draft. The latter part of 1952 showed a considerable decrease in sugar production owing to several factors and this affected loadings from the Clarence and Richmond Rivers, which were always the Company's mainstay. Indeed, sugar production was the lowest for over thirty years, while timber shipments were also down owing to the lifeless state of the building industry at the time, and all the while the various industrial troubles continued. The foregoing is supported by the following information from the pamphlet – "Centenary 1854–1954" by Howard Smith Ltd. I quote directly –

The latest ship acquired, the "Cycle", had cost £200,000 in 1939; the price of a replacement would now, in the United Kingdom be £600,000, and if built in Australia £850,000.

Working hours and output decreased to such an extent that the proportion of time spent by ships in port increased from 33% to 66% so that approximately 50% more tonnage was required to do the same work as in 1939. Under such conditions, with the demands of crews and watersiders increased and ships reduced to a state of minimum efficiency, the Government de-requisitioned shipping on 18th August, 1947, leaving it to re-establish itself in normal operation as best it could.

In the industrial field the Company's interests had expanded through war-time demand, but with little current profit to shareholders. Coal and steel industries and building, in peace, as they had been in war, were all subject to disruption, to restrictive price regulations and a discouraging burden of taxation. Strikes almost continuously affected some part, if not all, of the Company's business. In an attempt to reduce production costs of coal, the Invincible Colliery was wholly mechanised in 1949, the year of a prolonged strike by mineworkers and severe flood damage on the northern coalfields. Other firms fared no better.

Early 1953 showed no improvement in timber, and both inward and outward loadings showed a further marked decline. The sugar season, however, was a little better, and an average crop ensued. Then came the axe.

In February, the New South Wales Government Department of Railways granted bulk loading contracts at rates quoted in the press at the time to be no less than 50 per cent below ordinary rail rates. This naturally reduced the amount of cargo sent by sea to Lismore – and Lismore was the most important centre of them all. The press reports stated that these rail concessions were given with the express purpose of obtaining the loading that was then being sent by sea. It appeared that the Railways Department was making a determined effort to eliminate sea competition at all costs from the New South Wales coast, irrespective of the effects this would have on the economy of the State.

How can private enterprise trade profitably (and, whether we like it or not, a reasonable profit is the only inducement to progress) when it has to compete against a Government department which is prepared to operate with a deficit like this? Representations were made without avail to State Cabinet, but no relief was granted. The shackle had at last snapped shut. This was the straw which was to break the proverbial camel's back.

The loss of the regular shipping service to the North Coast of this state which had been in existence for so long — and incidentally had carried the railway when it was being built — had a markedly adverse effect on large industries in the area and on many communities in general.

Operating costs, over which the firm had no control, increased again during the year due to the rising basic wage and increases in awards. Stevedoring costs in particular advanced sharply because of increases in wages and man hour levies for attendance money and holiday payment.

Industrial disputes, especially at the outports about this time, added to the already slow turn-round times, and vessels were often delayed for lengthy periods on most trivial pretexts. Captain George Wilson succeeded in beating these tactics on one occasion when in command of the "Arakoon", in the Macleay River, and earned the wrath of the stevedores ever after for doing so. The men had the vessel's forward hold loaded properly but the after hold was still nearly empty, and the vessel was badly trimmed down by the head as a result, when the lads decided to knock-off for the weekend. This would have delayed the vessel three days at least, and Captain Wilson spoke to them about it, asking them to at least trim the ship properly so he could sail on time even if it meant leaving some cargo behind but the men refused, believing that they had the ship at their mercy.

They did not know the ship however, for the

"Arakoon" had a very large ballast tank in No. 2 hold between her propeller shaft tunnels. Captain Wilson planned to use this if he could not get the men to co-operate and when they refused to let them think that they had won, but got the engineers to flood this tank. The result was near-perfect trim and the ship sailed as planned, to the accompaniment of cries of "scab" from the wharfies who had been most unpleasantly surprised at this development.

The scores of employees who derived their living from the shipping

"Wyangarie" clearing Coff's Harbour on the last "North Coast Run" — March, 1954.
Acknowledgement: A. Short.

153

industry should have realised that continued premeditated disruptive tactics and direct action would ultimately deprive them of earnings and conditions which many of them must have found difficult to replace. Shareholders could not be expected to continue to carry on a business that showed them little or no return on the capital they had invested, while their employees persisted in disregarding the fact that their co-operation was a fundamental obligation necessary in this, as in any other, industry.

The firm continued to trade in this manner, against insurmountable odds for the remainder of the year, but conditions became so bad that at a special meeting of the shareholders, held on the 18th February, 1954, it was decided to go into voluntary liquidation, and the staff began reluctantly to wind up its activities. As the ships arrived in Sydney, they were unloaded, laid up, and their crews paid off. The ships then lay at the Sussex Street wharves pending their sale. The last vessel to sail under the familiar red and blue house flag was the "Wyangarie", bringing the Company's equipment and records down from Coff's Harbour. She arrived in Sydney on the 9th March and as she tied up an era came to an end.

Other vessels had brought items of gear down from the Clarence, Richmond and Macleay River ports, and the branches and offices on these rivers were closed down. Almost in reprisal, it seemed, the Richmond staged a mighty flood which hit Lismore a day or so after the office in that town had closed up, and the angry waters entered the office and wrought havoc on it. Later when the water receded, the model of the old "Brundah" which had been on display there for years, was found buried in the mud nearby. It was badly damaged and was sold at auction. This flood ruined the river for shipping and would have stopped vessels from using it for a very long time.

The "Wyangarie" was the first ship to be sold, and she went straight to Messrs Howard Smith Ltd becoming their "Mourilyan". She was finally sold to Panamanian owners in 1963, and until broken up in 1976, ran as "Fagaras" of Panama. The other vessels continued to lie at the Sussex Street wharves for varying periods, but by August, 1956, they had all found new homes.

The "Bonalbo" went to Patson Ltd in Sydney, then to Messrs Hetherington Kingsbury Ltd and continued to run to the Clarence River until 1957, when she went to Hong Kong as the "Leewana".

The "Uki" and "Melinga" were bought by Maurice Bern of Sydney, the former running to the Macleay under Captain "Black Jack" Magee, bringing powdered milk from the Nestlé's factory at Smithtown, whilst the latter ran to New Guinea for sometime before returning to Sydney where she was eventually renamed "Etmor".

The "Etmor" lay at Circular Quay for some time, as she had had mechanical troubles, and did not prove as reliable as her older sister — mainly due to her blast-injection engine and its habit of burning out exhaust valves. This problem required very careful attention, as only perfect adherence to detail would ensure reliable running. None but the best engineers managed to cope with this vessel's engines without burning out these valves.

History repeated itself and the N.S.W. Railways again undercut the freight-rate forcing M. Bern Shipping to suspend the service. The "Uki" (and the "Etmor" at times) had run regularly and profitably in this trade until November, 1959, when the "Uki" made her last trip from Smithtown, left the River for the last time, and sea-trade to the Macleay ceased completely. The "Uki" and "Etmor" were both sold, cut down to hulks and ran on the Brisbane River — the "Uki" as a self propelled lighter (diesel) and the "Etmor" as a dumb barge.

The Comara was sold for further service in Western Australia, being resold in 1956 to Captain Emile Savoie of Noumea, and re-named "Damadora del Mar". In 1960/61 she was resold, after lying in Sydney for almost a year, assuming her old name, and was towed to Singapore by the "Nyora" for scrap. However, she is still trading in 1979 as "Comara", often visiting Surabaya.

The "Wyrallah" went to John Burke & Co. of Brisbane in 1954, and was resold in 1961 to Captain Emile Savoie in Noumea, becoming the "Colorado del Mar". In 1964 she was again sold, becoming the "Tamata" of Suva. Later she was the "Ocean Life", out of Singapore, and is still running under yet another name, "Sinar Surya".

The next three, the "Arakoon", "Bangalow", and "Ulmarra" all went in 1955 to John Manners & Co. in Hong Kong, being renamed in order, "Glebe Breeze", "Cambay Breeze" and "Rozelle Breeze". Later they became the "San Ricardo", "Lucky Chen" and "Papagayo"; the "Bangalow" was the last afloat as the "Lian Min" until 1976.

The Company's records were given to the Mitchell Library in Sydney, and the models of the ships to the Museum of Applied Arts and Sciences at Ultimo, in Sydney.

The staff, scattered to the four winds, held a reunion annually until 1986, until falling attendance brought it to an end.

There are of course, gaps in this story, but in the early days records were not always kept, or have since been lost; while few people still living pretend to remember details of happenings longer ago than 1910 with much accuracy. A few, but not many.

There were of course, other vessels which ran from time to time on the North Coast, mostly colliers delivering large consignments of coal or little privately owned vessels like the "Kincumber" which was lost with several lives at Harrington, but I have omitted many of them as I have been unable to glean sufficient reliable information, and I would have been forced to rely too much on hearsay to give their story, not really significant in any case. They did not make a great contribution to the development of the Coast, and are now largely forgotten even by people who once knew them.

The North Coast Steam Navigation Company Ltd, and its pre-decessors played a major part in the development of this State. If the reader is in any doubt of this, he should look at the map of New South Wales and notice the distribution of settlement. Apart from the region extending from Wollongong to Newcastle, the North Coast is by far the most heavily populated, and also the richest area of the State. We should also realise that all the initial development was made long before roads or railways existed in the area, and while these later additions have consolidated and speeded recent develop-ment, they would not have produced the Coast as we know it. If readers doubt the truth of this statement, let them look at the South Coast, which, since the cessation of sea transport in 1952, has largely stagnated in spite of the trucks. Granted, it lacks a railway, but if one was built to Bega, I very much doubt if it would cause any great change. The only method of moving goods cheaply is by sea, and if you take away this cheap bulk transport, business simply moves to an area where it is available. The railway is capable of ade-quately supplying an existing community, viz., the North Coast, but not vastly fattening it, and the poor road transport cannot even do that. We have had a transport revolution, and now we all must pay for it.

S.S. "Noorebar" at thy Company's main wharf at Grafton circa 1908. The small steamers are "Iolanthe" (inside) and "Woolwich".

Acknowledgement: Clarence River Historical Society.

APPENDIX ONE

List of vessels owned and operated* by the N.C.S.N. Co. and their predecessors. Page number given where illustrated in text. Overall measurements of vessels given in feet. Vessels shown thus * not owned as above, shown for interest only.

ADA: 89351
   Wood S.S. 17 tons (12 nett) 52.6 x 10.0 x 4.0 12 h.p. Built in 1879, Macleay River. Regd. Sydney 1885, owners C & R R S N Co. fate unknown, presumed broken up in 1890, still entered in 1953 register.

AGNES IRVING: 43237 (Page viii)
   Iron PS, 439 tons 203.5 x 24.5 x 11.7: 2 masts sch. Built 1862. Deptford Green (London) 2 Cyl each 140 h.p. Named after Clark Irving's eldest daughter. C & R R S N Co. Wrecked 1 p.m. 26/12/1879 Macleay River Bar (Old Entrance).

ALLENWOOD: 150156
   Wood T.S.S. Built 1920 at Tuncurry for Allen Taylor & Co. 398 tons gr. 147.0 x 35.0 x 8.2. Name derived from her owner's. She was lost early on 14/9/1951 when she went ashore in fog just south of Wybung Head, near Budgewoi. Her master was Captain Boutrup. 48 h.p. Wreck sold for £601.

ANNANDALE: 106220
   Aux M.V. Wood 108 tons 92.3 x 24.0 x 6.7: 2 masts ketch built by J. Sullivan, Tomakin N.S.W. 1899 for Allen Taylor. Lost off Smoky Cape 12/3/1907. Was a very early Motor Vessel: 50 h.p.

ARAKOON: 152036 (Page 113)
   Steel T.S.S. Built in 1926 at Port Glasgow for the N.C.S.N. Co. 875 tons gr, 190.0 x 34.2 x 9.9. Fo'c'sle 30', Bridge 13', R.Q. Deck 92', named for a village near Smoky Cape. Sold in 1955 to John Manners & Co. renamed "Glebe Breeze" then "San Ricardo". 86 h.p.

AUGUSTA: 93620
   Composite S.S. Built 1889, in Sydney for Quigley & Kelly, 173 tons gr. 109.5 x 22.7 x 9.5. Vessel sold 1905 to N.C.S.N. Co. and cut down to a lighter in Sydney in 1921. Her engines were transferred to the "Nambucca" built the following year.

AUSTRALIAN: 78693
   Iron S.S. built 1879 at Dundee for G.W. Nicoll. 352 tons gr. 160.3 x 22.5 x 10.5. Fo'c'sle 21', Poop 61'. She was sold to Tasmania and wrecked on Wardang Island, S.A. 8/5/1912. December 1879 sold to Nicoll Bros, in 1880 to J. See: in December 1891 N.C.S.N. Co. and in February 1902 to Launceston.

AVON: 53981
   Iron P.S. 115 tons, 100.3 x 18.2 x 6.8: 2 masts sch. Built Nov. 1867, in Melbourne. 2 diag. Osc. eng. 30 h.p. to J. See in 1888: Wrecked Bellinger River 3/6/1891.

BALLENGARRA:
   Wood T.S.S. 221 tons gr. (98 nett) 126.8 x 27.0 x 7.2; 2 masts built Manning River for N. Cains 1911 Compound engines, 16 h.p.

BALLINA: 52707
   Iron P.S. 299 tons, 179.4 x 24.0 x 9.6: 2 masts brig. Built June, 1865. Machy 2 cyl. 80 h.p. Owners J. Alexander, Feb. 1866 to C & R R S N Co. Wrecked 14/2/1879 at Port Macquarie.

BANGALOW: 171252 (Pages 128 and 149)
   Steel S.S. built 1939 in Glasgow for N.C.S.N.Co. 648 tons gr. 162.0 x 36.2 x 9.0. Fo'c'sle 31', Poop 31'. Named for a town 6 miles from Byron Bay. Sold 1955 to Manners, renamed "Cambay Breeze" later ('57) " Lucky Chen". was 48 h.p. Was still trading from Singapore, late 1976.

BELLINGER 1: 89319
   Iron S.S. 225 tons, 125.0 x 22.1 x 8.7: 2 masts sch. Built 1884 Paisley. Compound 45 h.p. for G.W. Nicoll, sold to Victoria 1887 returns same year to B.B. Nicoll, then to Hobart 1890.

BELLINGER 2:
Wood S.S. 141 tons. Built 1901, was under charter to Allen Taylor & Co. when lost. Wrecked Nambucca Bar 26/4/1912. All hands saved from rigging, next day.

BELLINGER 3:
Wood T.S.S. 33 h.p. for H. Doepel. 240 tons. Built 1915 by D. Sullivan Coopernook. 128.0 x 28.7 x 7.2. Reg. Sydney. Machinery aft. Lost Macleay Bar, 1918.

BELMORE 1: 64349
Wood P.S. 66 tons 101.7 x 15.6 x 6.1: 2 masts sch. Built 1870 by Stuart & Ferguson, Macleay River. 30 h.p. engine by Chapman Sydney, for C.& R.R. S.N. Co. Sold January 1889 to C.R.& M.R.S.N. Co. Ltd September 1891 to N.C.S.N. Co. Wrecked at Coff's Harbour March, 1893.

BELMORE 2:
Wood T.S.S. 189 tons gr. (81 nett) 106.7 x 29.5 x 8.3. Built 1914 at Swansea (N.S.W.) owned by B. & N. Einerson and others. Compound 27 h.p. Reported lost Macleay River entrance March 1916 with load of coal, on charter to N.C.S.N. Co.

BOAMBEE: 125187
Wood S.S. built 1908 at Bellinger River for Langley Bros. 236 tons gr. 127.4 x 27.2 x 7.7. Native name for the Coff's Harbour area. Sold F. Viggers of Newcastle in 1926. Later resold to the Newcastle & Hunter River S.S. Co. and renamed "Illalong". Wrecked Belmont Beach, 12 miles south of Newcastle, 1948.

BONALBO: 152003
Steel S.S. built 1925 at Port Glasgow for N.C.S.N. Co. 960 tons gr. 205.0 x 34.6 x 12.0. Fo'c'sle 33', R.Q. Deck 127'. Named for a town 35 miles nor'-west of Casino. Sold to Patson Ltd (Sydney) in 1954/5 then to Hetherington & Kingsbury Ltd being resold in Hong Kong in 1957 and renamed "Leewana". 121 h.p.

BONNIE DUNDEE: 75200
Iron S.S. built in Dundee for Nicoll Bros. 121 tons gr. 130.3 x 19.0 x 9.9. 40 h.p. Compound built 1877. 2 masts. Named after Nicoll's birthplace. Run down and sunk by the S.S. "Barrabool", 8 miles south of Newcastle on 10/3/1879, with loss of 5 lives.

BORTONIUS: See "Lawrence"

BOWRA:
Wood stern wheel drogher, used on the Nambucca River. Named after town on that river. Details unknown.

BRUNDAH: 121147 (Page 65)
Steel S.S. built 1906 in Glasgow for the N.C.S.N. Co. 883 tons gr. 200.2 x 30.1 x 17.9. Name is a native word meaning "Sweet Home". Sold 1925 to Burns Philp (South Seas) Ltd renamed "Malinoa". Was badly damaged in a stranding at Vila on 30/4/1932, refloated but beyond repair so was scuttled off Suva in 1933. She was 110 h.p.

BRUNSWICK: 89241
Iron S.S. 174 tons, 104.7 x 20.6 x 7.8: 2 masts ketch. Built 1883 at Balmain. Sold 1886 to J. See. Lost 18/12/1886 on Manning River Bar. Built for A. Kethel & Partners.

BURRAWONG: 96404 (Page 47)
Steel T.S.S., built 1889 at Dundee for J. See, 391 tons gr. 155.0 x 28.1 x 8.8. Fo'c'sle 26', Bridge 37', Poop 44', 70 h.p. Wrecked 27/3/1909 on the breakwater at Harrington. Was sold to N.C.S.N. Co. December, 1891.

BURRINGBAR: 125224 (Page 67)
Steel S.S. built 1909 at Grangemouth, for N.C.S.N. Co. 876 tons gr. 205.1 x 33.1 x 11.4. Flush decked passenger ship (Name – town near Mullumbimby). Hulked 1932, scuttled off Sydney Heads 16/11/1934. Was 131 h.p.

BYRON: 101024

Wood S.S. 145 tons 96.2 x 20.4 x 8.1: 2 masts F & A schooner built 1891 (November) by T. Davis, Terrigal, Comp. machinery 22 h.p. for G.W. Nicoll. Foundered off Newcastle 24/5/1896.

CANONBAR: 125242

Steel S.S. built 1910 Ardrossan, for N.C.S.N. Co. 708 tons gr. 185.8 x 32.1 x 11.0. Fo'c'sle 20', Bridge 12', R.Q. Deck 93', 108 h.p. Sold 1926 to J. Burke, resold 1946 to Hong Kong in 1949 renamed "Rosita" then "Valiente", 1958 registered Panama still appears in Lloyds of 1967/8. Reported missing in Mekong River, Vietnam (Sydney "Sun").

CASINO 1: 86361

Iron S.S. built 1881 at Dundee for B.B. Nicoll. 425 tons gr. 160.4 x 24.1 x 10.2: 3 masts schooner, compound machinery 65 h.p. July 1882 sold to Belfast & Koroit S.N. Co. Sunk 19/7/1932 in Apollo Bay, Victoria, with loss of 10 lives.

CASINO 2 (Page 27)

Wood S.S. Drogher on Richmond River. Details unknown.

CAVANBA

Steel S.S. built 1901, Paisley for G.W. Nicoll. 573 tons gr. 172.1 x 26.1 x 12.1. Fo'c'sle 32', Poop 100', 103 h.p. Native name for Byron Bay area. Went to N.C.S.N. Co. in 1904, sold China 1916, renamed "Tungyuan" then "Lai H'sing".

CHINDERA:

Wood S.S. 186 tons, 118.0 x 20.8 x 9.7: 2 masts schooner built 1895, H. Hardman, Jervis Bay, compound 35 h.p. G.W. Nicoll. Total wreck at Tweed Heads 9/9/1896.

CITY OF GRAFTON: 73845 (Page 33)

Iron P.S. built 1876 at Port Glasgow for the C.& R.R.S.N.Co. 825 tons gr. 207.4 x 26.9 x 19.3. Flush decked passenger ship of 250 h.p. Laid up in 1913 hulked in 1920, scrapped in 1930. 2 masts, Compound Oscillating machinery.

CLARENCE: 59549

Iron P.S. built 1865 for the Parramatta R. Steam Co. 64.0 x 9.1 x 5.1 double ended 12 h.p. Wrecked Clarence River "some years ago" entry dated 1891. 19 tons, Jan. 1873 to C.& R.R.S.N.Co.

COBAKI: 136441 (Page 106)

Wood S.S. built 1918 in Sydney for Langley Bros. 257 tons gr. 127.0 x 28.3 x 8.5 Fo'c'sle 15', 37 h.p. Sold out of the service shortly after the takeover of Langley's. Her ultimate fate scuttled 1946 in Salt Pan Creek Middle Harbour. 1926 to N.C.S.N. Co., 1926 to I.& S.C.S.N.Co., 1939/45 with Army. Stricken from Register 1937.

COMARA: 171215 (Page 125)

Steel M.V. built 1937 at Port Glasgow for N.C.S.N. Co. 751 tons gr. 173.0 x 35.6 x 9.1 Fo'c'sle 28', Bridge 10', R.Q. Deck 80', 126 h.p. Named for a village on the upper Macleay. Sold 1954 to the W.A. State Shipping Service, resold 1956 to Noumea and renamed "Damadora del Mar". Again sold 1960/1 and renamed "Comara". Towed to Singapore for new owner by the "Nyora" in 1962. Still trading 1979, under Panamanian Flag.

COOLEBAR: 131531 (Page 76)

Steel T.S.S. built 1911 at Ardrossan for the N.C.S.N. Co. 479 tons gr. 150.3 x 30.0 x 8.7. Fo'c'sle 27', Poop 41', 89 h.p. Native name for a type of tree. Sold to New Zealand in 1929 and renamed "Himatangi". Returned to N.S.W. to Cam & Sons in 1936, repurchased by the N.C.S.N. Co. in 1938 and renamed "Coolebar". Requisitioned as H.M.A.S. "Coolebar" for 1939/45 war; sold East 1947; renamed "East River", but sank in Newcastle 29/9/49. Raised in pieces and scrapped in 1958.

COOLOON: 047673

Wood S.S. 141 nett tons, 127.4 x 25.3 x 8.8: 2 masts. Built 1904 at Manning River. Lost on Manning Bar 1917/18, engines to "Cobaki".

COOMBAR: 131537

Steel T.S.S. built 1912 at Port Glasgow for N.C.S.N. Co. 581 tons gr. 166.0 x 30.1 x 10.1. Sold to W.R. Carpenter 1937, W. Crosby & Co. 1941, R.A.N. for remainder of war, Barret & Co. of Singapore 1946, then Manners & Co. in 1948. Renamed "San David", French Indo-China 1949, renamed "Orion", finally registed in Saigon as a powered lighter "Trung Thin". Possibly still afloat, she was (or is) 99 h.p.

COOPERNOOK:

Wood S.S. built for Allen Taylor & Co. measurements not known. Named after town on Manning River. Acquired by N.C.S.N. Co. 1904, used as a drogher on the Macleay River. Later history not known.

COORONG: 45037

Iron S.S. built 1862 for J. Derwent (Adelaide) at Port Glasgow. 391 tons gr. 171.1 x 22.4 x 12.2. Named for a locality in South Australia. Sold to McMeckan Blackwood, then others, then J. See, May 1884, to N.C.S.N. Co. Dec. 1891. Hulked at Sydney 1911.

COPMANHURST:

Wood S.W.P.S. Drogher on Clarence River. Details unknown.

CORAKI: 75052 (Page 37)

Iron T.S.S. 275 tons. 139.6 x 26.1 x 8.5: 2 masts schooner built 1879 by W.B. Thompson, Dundee. 65 h.p. Lengthened 1883 – 326 tons. 159.6 x 26.1 x 8.5 for C.& R.R.S.N.Co. Jan. 1889 C.R.& M.R.S.N.Co. Sept. 1891 N.C.S.N. Co. Wrecked Macleay River 29/11/1900. Hit end of wall, floated off and foundered in fairway, wreck blown up.

CORAMBA: 131495 (Page 56)

Steel T.S.S. built 1911 at Troon for N.C.S.N. Co. 531 tons gr. 160.3 x 30.0 x 10.0. Fo'c'sle 28', R.Q. Deck 76', 73 h.p. Named for town ten miles west of Coff's Harbour. Sold in 1932 to the Belfast & Koroit S.N. Co. Foundered in a heavy gale 30/11/34 in the vicinity of Philip Island. No trace of the ship although some time later some wreckage was found on Philip Island which could have come from the missing steamer. No survivors.

CORNSTALK: 74928

Iron Stern Wheel P.S. built 1877 in Sydney. 145 tons gr. 95.0 x 21.4 x 5.2. Drogher on Macleay River, cut down 1921.

CROKI:

Built 1903, 303 tons, 135.3 x 24.7 x 9.0. 4 masts Steel S.S. lost 13/9/1903 Little Seal Rock.

CUDGEN:

Wood S.S. Drogher on Tweed River, 77.0 x 18.0 x 6.0. Destroyed by fire at Tweed Heads 16/1/1928 and abandoned.

CYGNET: 38818

Wood P.S. 30 tons 88.8 x 11.8 x 9.0. no masts. Built 1866 by G. Thompson Balmain Comp. 30 h.p. Lengthened 1871 to 118.3 x 14.5 x 5.0. 57 tons. Deckhouses added in 1877, re-engined 1879, 28 h.p. Various owners, then April 1870 sold to C.& R.R.S.N.Co. Resold 1874, eventually hulked Aug. 1891.

DEFENDER: 112520

Wood S.S. built 1901 at Kincumber for Allen Taylor & Co. 190 tons gr. 118.5 x 25.4 x 7.4 36 h.p. Sold to New Zealand in 1904. On the 2/8/1918, while loaded with a cargo of case oil, she caught fire in Wellington Harbour and burned to the waterline.

DIAMANTINA: 43213

Iron P.S. of 239 tons (1870 increased to 285) 158.1 x 23.6 x 8.7: 2 masts schooner 60 h.p. Built Low Walker in England 1861 for A.S.N. Co. March 1870 C.& R.R.S.N.Co. stranded and wrecked on Manning River 31/3/1881, but salvaged and sold. Various owners thereafter, scrapped at Townsville 1907. Sold Jan. 1875 to Manning R.S.N. Co.

DOEPEL: 150141 (Page 146)

Wood T.S.S. built 1919 at Blackwall (Woy Woy) N.S.W. for F. Doepel of Urunga. 389 tons gr. 145.0 x 33.0 x 9.2. Machinery from the wrecked "Bellinger" 3, was installed in her 33 h.p. Sold to New Guinea in 1947, renamed "Batang" (Reg'd Singapore 1954). Fate uncertain, as several tales are told about her end. Believed foundered, off Kutching, under tow.

DOLPHIN: 89249

Wood S.S. 38 tons 61.7 x 14.6 x 4.5: 1 mast cutter built 1884 by D. Sullivan, Berry's Bay. 8 h.p. for D. Lynch, then March 1886 to G.W. Nicoll, April 1905 to N.C.S.N. Co. Broken up 1914.

DORRIGO 1:

Wood S.S. built 1902 at Balmain for G.W. Nicoll. 302 tons gr. 136.1 x 24.9 x 12.6 48 h.p. Named for the town of that name, she was sold in 1910 to Burns, Philp and renamed "Misima". Wrecked in New Guinea in 1917.

DORIGO 2:

Steel S.S. 683 tons gr. 180.5 x 29.6 x 15.3. Fo'c'sle 41', Poop 51'. Built 1913 in Yorkshire as "St. Francois", 138 h.p. fitted with wireless. Sold to Langley Bros. 1921 to replace "Fitzroy". Sold to N.C.S.N. Co. 1925/6; resold to John Burke, Brisbane 1926. Lost in Wide Bay 1926 in gale, only 2 survivors.

DOVE:

Wood stern wheel paddle steamer drogher on Nambucca River, tonnage dimensions and fate not known.

DURANBAH: 139409

Steel S.S. built 1905 by Scott's of Kinghorn Ltd. for G.W. Nicoll. 284 tons gr. 130.0 x 23.1 x 9.2'. Sold on arrival in Australia to the N.C.S.N. Co. Sold in 1922 to W.R. Carpenter, and fitted with oil engines. Fate unknown, believed captured by Japanese. 37 h.p. 7 knts. Crew 10.

DUROBY:

Wood S.S. 195 tons gr. 119 net, 121.8 x 24.7 x 8.4; 2 masts built 1902, at Langley Vale, Manning River. Compound 40 h.p. Langley Bros. 1921 to I.& S.C.S.N.Co. burned 1923 possibly rebuilt as motor vessel for Burns Philp & Co. (Plans dated 9/10/25 in posesion of Author, definitely this ship.)

ELECTRA: 93190

Steel T.S.S. built 1887 at Port Glasgow for the C.& R.R.S.N.Co. 395 tons gr. 160.5 x 27.0 x 10.9. Was the first ship in the country to be fitted with electric light, hence name. 70 h.p. and 2 masts. Jan. 1889 C.R.& M.R.S.N.Co.; Sept. 1891, N.C.S.N. Co. Hulked 1920 used by the B.H.P. as a tar store, scrapped in 1930.

EMMA PYERS: 93527

Wood S.S. built 1886 on Richmond River for B. Nicoll. 73 tons gr. 78.8 x 16.6 x 5.6. Drogher on Tweed River abandoned 1930 beyond repair.

ERIC: 89326

Wood S.W.P.S. 177 tons built Macleay River 1885, 91.0 x 28.6 x 4.6. Drogher on the Bellinger River was round bottom and wrecked at Urunga on the wall. 10 h.p.

EUROKA: 106144

Steel, P.S. built 1897 at Balmain for the N.C.S.N. Co. 170 tons 120.4 x 22.1 x 6.9. Fo'c'sle 12', 30 h.p. Native name for the sun. Sold 1910 to Valentine Geary & Co. and wrecked on Long Reef on 19/10/1913.

FENELLA: 31973

Iron P.S. 261 tons, 159.4 x 19.3 x 11.1; 2 masts schooner built 1846 Liverpool, U.K. 110 h.p. 2 cyl. engines. 1856 registered Sydney for Hunter River S.N. Co., 1859 T. Sullivan; Sept. 1859 Jones & Sharpe; June 1860 C.& R.R.S.N. Co. Sold Shanghai, Feb. 1862. It was reported that she was exchanged for the Iron P.S. "Duncan Hoyle", 188 tons, built 1852 but this is not borne out by old registers.

FERNMOUNT: 89263

Wood S.S. built 1884 at Scott's Creek N.S.W. 269 tons, 134.0 x 25.6 x 8.4. 40 h.p. Named after village on the Bellinger River. Built for Perrett & McCulloch March 1885; Perrett & See. March 1885, J. See. March 1892; N.C.S.N. Co. April 1898, On Chong & Co. Sydney. Wrecked in Gilbert Islands 24/12/1907.

FIRE KING: 52385

Wood P.S. 221 tons 148.0 x 20.1 x 7.9; 3 masts schooner built Jan. 1866 Macleay River. 2 eng. 80 h.p. W. Marshall. Dec. 1869 C.& R.R.S.N.Co; Wrecked North Head, Manning River Bay, 30/4/1873, all saved.

FIRE QUEEN: 69753

Wood P.S. 61 tons, 81.0 x 11.3 x 4.0, built 1872 Macleay River (A. Cochrane). 1 dia. engine, 12 h.p. for C.& R.R.S.N. Co. Transferred to Newcastle September, 1884.

FITZROY:

Steel S.S. 623 tons gr. 342 nett, 170.2 x 30.7 x 10.6, built 1912, Old Kilpatrick, Scotland. Triple Exp. 72 h.p. Langley Bros. Lost in S.E. gale near Cape Hawke 25/26 June 1921, with 30 lives—4 survivors only. (Encyclopedia wrong in saying 31 lost 1 saved.)

GLADSTONE:

Steam Drogher on the Macleay River, named after town on its banks, nothing else is known.

GLENREAGH: 136454 (Page 93)

Wood T.S.S. built 1919 at Tuncurry, for Allen Taylor. 498 tons gr. 154.5 x 37.2 x 10.0. Fo'c'sle 21'. Named after town on the upper Orara River. She was broken up in 1934. 72 h.p.

GRAFTON: 32364 (Page v)

Iron P.S. 212 tons, 140.9 x 22.3 x 10.6: 2 masts brig (cut down to 2 masts schooner in 1877). Built Sept. 1854 Birkenhead; rebuilt Sydney 1876/7 as T.S.S. 145.5 x 27.6 x 13.6 of 397 tons. New engines 65 h.p. Owners, R.S. Ross & Partners. Sold Dec. 1858 David Jones & Partners; June 1860 Clark Irving & Partners (Grafton S.N. Co.); March 1886 C.& R.R.S.N.Co.; Aug. 1874 and thereafter various owners. 1878 to Wellington New Zealand; returned to Tasmania, lost on bar at Strahan, 1898.

GUNBAR: 131507 (Page 141)

Steel T.S.S. built 1911/12 at Ardrossan for N.C.S.N. Co. 482 tons 150.3 x 30.0 x 8.7. Fo'c'sle 27', Poop 41', 89 h.p. Sold to New Zealand in 1926, returned to Sydney in 1935, saw extensive war service as minesweeper, sold China 1946/7, but scrapped in Sydney.

HASTINGS 1: 89327

Wood P.S. built 1883 at Port Stephens, 63 tons, 58.4 x 20.0 x 5.6 drogher on the Manning River. Scrapped 1914. Built for J. See, Feb. 1892 to N.C.S.N. Co.

HASTINGS 2: (Page 89)

Wood S.S. built 1901 by D. Sullivan (Coopernook) for Allen Taylor & Co. 193 tons gr. 117.9 x 24.5 x 7.4 sold to N. Cain in 1904. Owned briefly by N.C.S.N. Co., sold to John Burke and renamed "Gundiah". Fate not known, but she ended her days in Tasmania.

HELEN McGREGOR: 56159 *

Iron S.S. 168 tons (171 tons in Encyclopedia) 123.7 x 20.0 x 9.3 built 1866 Whiteinch. 2 masts schooner. Engines 40 h.p. Lengthened Sept. 1867 to 152.6 x 20.6 x 9.1, 251 tons, 3 masts schooner built for C.& N.E.S.N.Co. Oct. 1867 T. Fisher; Sept. 1873 C.& N.E.S.N.Co. Wrecked Clarence River Bar 12/3/1875. 8 lives lost.

HELEN NICOLL: 86362

Iron S.S. built 1882 in Dundee for G.W. Nicoll but went to Nipper & See on arrival. 384 tons gr. 157.0 x 22.0 x 10.3. Sold 1893 to Adelaide and later to Jones Bros. of Sydney, July 1900. She was scrapped in 1932 in Berry's Bay.

IRVINGTON: 89291 (Page 84)

Wood S.S. built 1884 by J. Piper, Balmain for F.G. Crouch. 70.4 x 15.8 x 5.4 Drogher on the Richmond River. Machinery comp. 15 h.p. 1 mast. April 1887 to C.& R.R.S.N.Co.; Jan 1889, C.R.& M.R.S.N. Co. Sept. 1891 to N.C.S.N. Co.; Oct. 1922 Bell & Shields; Nov. 24 Hawkesbury R. Transport Co. No trace since 1933. Broken up Brooklyn.

JANET NICOLL: 89322
Iron S.S. 772 tons, 184.0 x 29.2 x 13.8; 2 masts schooner built 1884 Jarrow, U.K. 90 h.p. Compound G.W. Nicoll Aug. 1890. Sold to Auckland New Zealand, Henderson 1890 — U.S.S. Co. of N.Z. Sold 1903 (Penang). Wrecked at Kopah Inlet, Siam, 10/5/1914 on passage to Moulmein.

JAP:
There was a drogher of this name on the Manning River, which was a wood stern-wheel paddler. Nothing else is known of her. Not registered.

KALLATINA: 93230
Steel S.S. built 1890 Port Glasgow, for C.R. & M.R.S.N. Co. 646 tons gr. 179.0 x 28.2 x 11.4. Fo'c'sle 48', Poop 112'. 88 h.p. A passenger vessel, she was sold to John Burke in 1920. Sold to Peters Slip 1931 and hulked. Hulk is now lying as a breakwater on Moreton Island, off Tangalooma. Passenger accommodation removed circ. 1908/10.

KEMPSEY: 121181 (Page 45)
Steel S.S. built 1907 by Scott's of Kinghorn, for Nicholas Cain's Coastal Co-operative S.S. Co. About 500 tons gr. (193 nett) 173.3 x 27.1 x 9.4, 2 masts. This vessel ran to the Macleay River no more than 6 months, during which time she gave the impression that she was tender to the point of instability. Sold 1908 to the I. & S.C.S.N. Co., who found her too tender for open roadsteads, (renamed "Tathra") bought to replace "Bega" — lost in 1908 — and she was on charter to an Island firm when on 4/1/1912 she foundered near Ambrym Island (New Hebrides) in bad weather. She was reported to have taken water, became unmanageable, fell off into the trough of the sea and swamped. Her value at the time was £14,000 ($28,000).

KEYSTONE 1: 64350
Wood S.W.P.S. built 1863 at Balmain for W. Yeager, 11 tons; 42.2 x 8.9 x 4.3, 6 h.p. 2 masts. Broken up in Richmond River Dec. 1890.

KEYSTONE 2: 89251
Wood stern wheel paddle steamer built 1884 on Nambucca River, 56 tons 76.0 x 17.0 x 3.5 drogher 8 h.p. Abandoned beyond repair 1908. Built for A.B. Howland, sold 1892 N.C.S.N. Co.

KINCHELA ex-TAMBAN: 136402
Wood T.S.S. built Sydney 1914 for the Macleay Farmers Co-op. Society. 369 tons gr. 145.0 x 31.0 x 9.5. Fo'c'sle 26', Poop 16', 48 h.p. Named after town on Macleay River. Hulked in Sydney 1936 and her machinery transferred to the second "Nambucca".

KING EDWARD:
Macleay River drogher, details not known. Broke back on slip February, 1925.

KYOGLE: 112551 (Page 112)
Steel T.S.S. built 1902 at Glasgow for the N.C.S.N. Co. 702 tons gr. 180.1 x 30.1 x 12.0. Fo'c'sle 32', Bridge 44', Poop 72', 115 h.p. Named after town on the Richmond River. A passenger ship sold in 1924 to the Department of Navigation for use as a lighthouse tender. Resold early 1930s to Queensland Cement & Lime Co. in Brisbane. She ended her days carting rotten coral from Moreton Bay to the cement works at Darra.

LADY MUSGRAVE: *
Iron S.S. 204 tons 137.1 x 20.5 x 9.1, built 1884 (Brisbane) compound 45 h.p. Wm Collins. Total wreck 1908, Ballina Bar. Was lengthened 1891.

LAWRENCE: ex-BORTONIUS 87369
T.S.S. iron 399 tons, 160.0 x 28.0 x 8.6, 2 masts schooner built 1884 Sunderland, 88 h.p. Renamed 1885. J. See, Aug. 1889 to New Zealand. Wrecked 29/4/1891.

LISMORE: 78699
Iron S.S. 339 tons 152.3 x 22.1 x 10.0, 3 masts schooner built 1880 at Dundee, 45 h.p. G.W. Nicoll, July, 1880 to Nicoll Bros. Wrecked 10/5/1885 Shaw's Bay, Ballina after grounding—all saved. The wreck was visible at East Ballina until 1969, when it was demolished as unsightly.

LORNA: 89348
Wood S.S. built 1885 in Sydney for Nipper & See; 41 tons gr. 62.3 x 15.5 x 5.6 drogher on the Clarence River. Hulked in 1912.

LUBRA: 73592

Iron S.S. 466 tons, 173.6 x 27.5 x 11.4, 2 masts schooner built 1875, 45 h.p. G. Nipper (original owner) Oct. 1880 sold H.R. New S.N. Co.; Dec. 1891 N. & H.R.S.S. Co.; Feb. 1907 Jones Bros. Lost at Catherine Hill Bay 19/2/1920.

MACKSVILLE:

Wood sternwheel paddler droghing on the Nambucca River. Was eventually abandoned in the river.

MACLEAY ex-WOODBURN: 89495

Steel S.S. built 1883 at Milwall, River Thames for J. Wallace: Dec. 1883 to B. B. Nicoll, 1884 to C & R. R. S.N. Co. – Name changed 1890. 398 tons gr. 155.0 x 25.3 x 10.7, Fo'c'sle 20', Poop 34', 60 h.p. Named after the river. Fitted with tanks for the carriage of molasses. Wrecked on Boondelbah Island on 11/10/1911 with 15 lives. There were two survivors.

MACQUARIE: 125209

Steel T.S.S. 493 tons, 160.2 x 29.1 x 9.0, 90 h.p. built 1909, Hull, U.K. for N. Cain. Sold 1929, being later owned by W. R. Carpenter, then Mollers – renamed "Marie Moller". Lost W.W. II.

MAIANBAR: 131476

Steel T.S.S. built 1910 at Ardrossan to replace the Minimbah, 487 tons gr. 155.6 x 28.1 x 9.2, Fo'c'sle 32', Poop 67', 99 h.p. Was wrecked on 5/5/1940 on Nobby's Beach, Newcastle, while being towed to Sydney. In 1920 was lengthened to 175.6'.

MANNING: 74962

Iron P.S.: Built Atlas Works, Sydney. 1878: 89 tons 109.5 x 18.9 x 5.9. No mast. 30 h.p. Drogher, Manning R.S.N. Co., finally N.C.S.N. Co. Scrap 1937.

MATILDA: 71825

Wood S.S. 11 tons, 45.2 x 8.6 x 4.0, built 1874, W. Dunn, Lavender Bay. 8 h.p. Various owners, then Dec. 1891 N.C.S.N. Co. Feb. 1894 sold.

MELINGA: 155329 (Pages 136 and 137)

Steel S.M.V. built Copenhagen 1928, for N.C.S.N. Co. 536 tons gr. 154.1 x 34.6 x 8.5, Fo'c'sle 30', Poop 28', 98 h.p. Sold 1954 to Maurice Bern (M. Bern Shipping) renamed "Etmor" in 1956. Resold 1960. Hulked at Peter's Slip, Brisbane, still in service as a dumb sand barge.

MINIMBAH: (Page 48)

Steel T.S.S. built 1909 Port Glasgow for N.C.S.N. Co. 460 tons gr. 155.0 x 28.1 x 9.2, 99 h.p. Wrecked 13/4/1910 while still brand new, her machinery was salvaged and returned to Scotland to be fitted into the "Maianbar" which replaced her.

MURRAY: 55582

Iron paddle steamer 1866, 271 tons, 155.5 x 22.5 x 8.9, 2 masts built by T. Wingate & Co. Whiteinch, 60 h.p. Oscilating Cylinders. Came from Melbourne to Nipper & See 1883 with the "Rosedale". Feb. 1884, J. See. Wrecked at Manning River, 9/2/1886.

MURWILLUMBAH: 93562

Wood S.S. built E. Beattie, Brisbane Water, 1887. 44 tons, 63.2 x 17.3 x 4.6. One mast 10 h.p. R. Langley owner. Total wreck Tweed Heads, 1909.

MYEE:

Steel T.S.S. built 1903 by Bow, McLachlan of Paisley, assembled by Rowntree's Dock, Balmain. 144 tons, 100.1 x 20.1 x 6.4, 24 h.p. Was frequently used to unload stranded steamers owing to her loaded draft of only 6' 6". Built for the N.C.S.N. Co., sold 1926 to Allen Taylor & Co. and cut down to a lighter. Scuttled off Sydney Heads in 1933.

NAMBUCCA 1: 106191 *

Wood S.S. 129 tons 96.0 x 24.2 x 7.2, 2 masts F & A schooner, built 1898, D. Drake of Balmain; 2 Comp. S.C. 24 h.p., for F. Buckle Snr. Transferred to Wellington, New Zealand in 1902.

NAMBUCCA 2
Wood T.S.S. built 1922 at Tuncurry for Allen Taylor, 415 tons gr. 148.0 x 35.0 x 8.7. Fo'c'sle 34', Bridge 66', wrecked on the Nambucca Bar, 7/5/1934, becoming a total loss.

NAMBUCCA 3: 157636 (Page 131)
Wood T.S.S. built 1936 at Tuncurry for N.C.S.N. Co. 489 tons gr. 153.0 x 35.1 x 9.9, 48 h.p. Machinery from the "Kinchela". Saw service as mine-sweeper, lost by fire while serving with U.S. Army in Islands.

NARANI: 136384 (Page 66)
Wood T.S.S. built 1914 at Tuncurry for Allen Taylor, 381 tons gr. 148.6 x 33.2 x 8.7. Foc'sle 35', Bridge 53'. To N.C.S.N. Co. ownership 1920, sold 1924 to I.& S.C.S.N.Co. Resold in 1951 to New Guinea.

NERONG:
Steel T.S.S. built 1903 in Sydney. 219 tons, 119.8 x 22.0 x 7.9, Fo'c'sle 15', Poop 26'. Foundered off Norah Head in gale, 19/9/1917. 27 h.p.

NEW ENGLAND: 60446
Iron S.S. 359 tons, 176.4 x 22.1 x 10.7, 2 masts schooner built 1869 by T. Wingate & Co. Glasgow, 270 h.p. for Clarence & New England S.N. Co. Aug. 1879, C.& R.R.S.N.Co. Wrecked trying to cross Clarence Bar 27/12/1882. 11 lost.

NEW MOON: 41081
Wood paddle steamer 48 tons, 91.0 x 12.0 x 6.0, built 1858 on the Hawkesbury River, engine 25 h.p. for W. Marshall. Wrecked Oct. 1864 off Port Stephens.

NIMBIN: 155313 (Page 114)
Steel S.M.V. built 1927 in Copenhagen, 1052 tons, 215.0 x 35.1 x 11.9, Fo'c'sle 32', Bridge 23', R.Q. Deck 102'. Was the first motor vessel in the Company's service. Sunk off Norah Head 5/12/1940 when she hit a German mine, seven lives being lost.

NOOREBAR: (Page 156)
Steel S.S. built 1904 at Kinghorn, 670 tons, 185.1 x 28.1 x 12.4, Fo'c'sle 43', Bridge Poop 116'. Owned by G. Nicoll, sold to N.C.S.N. Co. on arrival from U.K. Native name means "Place where the Noore Vine grows". Sold 1920 in Fiji, resold 1924 to Djambi, Sumatra. Unregistered 1932, reported in earthquake 1937 at Rabaul.

NYMBOIDA ex-OTWAY: 64783
Iron S.S. 563 tons, 198.4 x 25.2 x 13.2, 2 masts, built 1872 Glasgow, 93 h.p. Various owners 1897. June 1901, N.C.S.N. Co. Hulked 1913, broken up 1919.

OAKLAND: 93630 (Pages 39, 174)
Steel S.S. built 1890 at Dumbarton, 398 tons, 154.0 x 24.0 x 10.5, 70 h.p. W.G. Yeager sold her to the N.C.S.N. Co. She sank in a whole gale off Cabbage Tree Island on the 26/5/1903. Eleven lives lost.

OMEO: 40338
Iron S.S. built 1858 at Hebburn Quay, for McMeckan, Blackwood & Co. 821 tons gr., 213.2 x 30.5 x 16.7, one deck, 3 masts (12 kts) barque rig, square stern, no galleries. 120 h.p. Built to replace the lost "Admella". Sold in 1880 to Nipper & See and nearly lost in gale of Newcastle. Sold to Howard Smith & Co. 1881. Engines removed and vessel re-rigged as 4 mast Jackass Barque. Finally hulked at Fremantle.

ORARA 1: 101129 *
Wood S.S. 66 tons, 70.7 x 18.2 x 4.0, 1 mast. Built 1894 R. Davis, Blackwall, 9 h.p. Wrecked 30/12/1895 Woolgoolga, when screw shaft snapped and she was cast on a reef.

ORARA 2: 106186
Wood S.S. 298 tons, 113.8 x 24.7 x 11.1, 2 masts schooner, built 1898 H. Hardman, Jervis Bay. 2 Comp S.C. 48 h.p. Total wreck at Tweed Heads 16/3/1899.

ORARA 3: 121193 (Pages 30, 53, 54 and 80)

Steel S.S. built 1907 at Kinghorn for the N.C.S.N. Co., 1,297 tons, 240.3 x 33.9 x 19.9. Named after the Orara River. War service 1939/45 as a minesweeper. Sold 1946 to China. She was 201.5 h.p.

OSPREY: 75028

Wood S.S. 35 tons, 66.2 x 13.7 x 4.8, no masts. Built 1879 for W. Dunn, Berry's Bay, 11 h.p. No trace of owner or ship, deleted 1953.

OTUS:

Wood S.S. built 1891 as a drogher for the Richmond River, 51 tons, 63.5 x 16.4 x 5.2. Drogher was built in Sydney, date unknown.

OURIMBAH:

Steel S.S. built 1890, 750 tons. No other details known as she was wrecked off the coast of South Africa on her delivery voyage, 26/11/1909.

OUR JACK (Page 92)

Wood T.S.S. built 1907 at Tuncurry for Allen Taylor & Co., 281 tons, 133.0 x 28.0 x 6.8. Transferred to N.C.S.N. Co. 1920, sank off Manning River on the 25/6/1921 with 5 lives.

OXLEY: 151089

Wood S.S. built 1924 in Sydney, 124 tons gr. 91.8 x 25.3 x 6.3. Was a drogher on the Manning River. She no longer appeared in the Register after 1944.

PAPPINBARRA:

Steel T.S.S. 518 tons, 153.0 x 34.6 x 9.6, built 1925, Glasgow, 70 h.p. for N. Cain Coastal Co-op. S.S. Co. Ltd. Total wreck Port Stephens September, 1929.

PELICAN: 93645

Wood S.S. 96 tons, 76.6 x 21.9 x 5.4, built 1890 Balmain. Compound 18 h.p. Clarence Richmond & Macleay Rivers S.N. Co. Sept. 1891 N.C.S.N. Co. Scrapped 1915.

PENDLE HILL

Sydney Harbour drogher, details not known.

PERSERVERENCE: 643377

Iron S.P.S. 95 tons, 120.0 x 22.3 x 4.3, one mast, built 1872 Mort's Dock & Eng. Co. Balmain, 2/36 h.p. Clarence & New England S.N. Co. Ltd. Aug. 1879 Nipper & See, Jan. 1884, J. See. 1891 N.C.S.N. Co. Ltd. Closed 1944 not required.

PHOENIX: *

Wood P.S. 108 tons, 118.9 x 17.7 x 8.9, built 1846 (Sydney) engines ex-"Sophia Jane" 50 h.p. E. Manning & Partner. Lost 14/4/1852 on Clarence Bar.

PLATYPUS: 48934

Iron S.S. 217 tons, 140.4 x 23.8 x 8.4, two masts schooner built 1864 A. & J. Inglis, Glasgow, 2/50 h.p. engines, for Clarence & Richmond River S.N. Co. Aug. 1887 G.L. Fuller. Broken up in Sydney, March 1898.

POONBAR: 131557 (Page 63)

Steel T.S.S. built 1913 at Glasgow 909 tons 200.4 x 34.1 x 12.2, Fo'c'sle 31', R.Q. Deck 96'. Sold 1929 to S.H. Hammond, Tasmania, then to Nelson & Robertson, Sydney. In 1947 sold to John Manners & Co. Hong Kong, renamed "San Ernesto". Scrapped 1951. 90 h.p.

PULGANBAR: 131509 (Page 52)

Steel S.S. built 1912 at Grangemouth, 1,160 tons, 225.0 x 35.1 x 12.5, Fo'c'sle 35', a fine large passenger ship. War service 1939/46. Sold to China 1948 renamed "Yang-tse River" then "Tamara". Scrapped 1951/2. 325 h.p.

PYRMONT: (Page 90)

Wood S.S. built 1902 at Coopernook, 215 tons, 122.6 x 25.0 x 8.1, Fo'c'sle 21'. Built for Allen Taylor, sold to the N.C.S.N. Co. in 1904, resold Burns Philp & Co. 1910 renamed "Mindoro". Wrecked in New Guinea 1913. 35 h.p.

QUEEN OF THE SOUTH: 74793
    Iron P.S. built 1877 for the Manning & Macleay Rivers S.N. Co. 198 tons, 126.2 x 22.1 x 7.8, Fo'c'sle 13', Poop 14'. Sold to New Zealand and was lost near Cape Campbell 10/5/1919.

RAINBOW: 36852
    Wood P.S. 89 tons 149.8 x 18.2 x 6.6, two masts schooner built 1860, 60 h.p. Engine. Lost 2/6/1864 when she foundered in a gale in Seal Rocks Bay.

RAMORNIE 1:
    Iron S.P.S. built 1869 for Australasian S.N. Co. Pyrmont. Eng. 30 h.p., 86 tons, 92.9 x 22.0 x 4.7. one mast. Owners C & R R S N Co. Jan. 1889, C.R. & M.R.S.N. Co. Sept. 1891 N.C.S.N. Co. Ltd. Closed 1944.

RAMORNIE 2:
    Steel T.S.S. built 1902 at Glasgow 546 tons, 148.2 x 28.1 x 9.6, Fo'c'sle 34', Poop bridge 75'. Named after town on the Orara River. Passenger accommodation removed 1916, ship sold 1919 to W.A. again in 1920 to New Zealand, being renamed "Opua". She was lost at Tora near Pallister Bay 2/10/1926. 86 h.p.

REPTON (Page 85) *
    Bar tug – lost on sea wall at Bellinger.

RICHMOND 1: 78683
    Iron S.S. 240 tons 136.1 x 20.2 x 9.5, three masts schooner built 1878 Gourlay Bros. & Co. Dundee, 2 Comp SC Eng. 45 h.p. for G. & B. Nicoll, April 1881 J. See. Lost Port Macquarie 21/1/1884.

RICHMOND 2: 89094
    Steel S.S., 628 tons June 1887 to 700 tons: 178.0 x 27.7 x 10.5, 2 masts schooner, built 1885 Gourlay Bros. & Co. Dundee, 2 Comp. Eng. 105 h.p. for B. B. Nicoll, April 1887 A. B. McDonald, to Auckland April 1889.

ROCKLILY 1: 106221
    Wood single P.S. 132 tons 82.5 x 23.2 x 4.1 no mast, built 1898, Dennis Sullivan, Manning River, 12 h.p. for R. & A. Langley. Broken up in 1928.

ROCKLILY 2:
    Wood S.S. built 1906 at Kincumber, 218 tons, 117.7 x 27.9 x 9.0. Used in a service to Brisbane for a while, sold 1915 to Westons Sydney, resold 1923 to Saddington Dixon. Scrapped 1927. 30 h.p.

ROSEDALE: 74762 (Page 60)
    Iron T.S.S. 274 tons 140.1 x 26.1 x 8.5, two masts schooner built 1877 W.B. Thompson Dundee, 2 Comp. SC 65 h.p. for Nipper & See, Jan. 1884 J. See, Dec. 1891 N.C.S.N. Co. Missing, sailed Sept. 1911.

SABRINA: 59543
    Wood S.S. built 1869 at Balmain, 16 tons, 53.2 x 12.2 x 4.1. No other information known. Drogher. Engine 9 h.p. Register closed 1952.

SAMSON:
    Stern wheel paddle steamer built 1885 on Myall River, 101 tons, 90.0 x 20.0 x 4.5. Foundered off Crowdy Head, 24/12/1908, drogher.

SAINT GEORGE:
    Steel, S.S. built 1895 Sunderland, 515 tons, 161.0 x 25.5 x 12.7, Fo'c'sle 25', came from W.G. Yeager, sold 1915 to On Chong & Co. and ran to the Pacific Islands. 95 h.p.

SARAH NICOLL: *
    68-ton schooner wrecked in heavy weather near Bellinger River, 19/2/1875.

SEAGULL 1:
    Wood S.S. 96 tons, 86.4 x 21.4 x 7.7, built at Stockton 1910. Sold July 1919 to Allen Taylor & Co.

SEAGULL 2:
    Wood S.S. Lost off Newcastle in August 1926. No other details known.

SETTLER'S FRIEND: 52389
    Wood S.P.S. 49 tons, 84.6 x 13.4 x 5.6, one mast, built 1866 one 12 h.p. engine. March 1882 J. See, Dec. 1891 N.C.S.N. Co. Register closed 1908.

SOPHIA ANN: 83877*
Wood S.S. 165 tons, 121.3 x 21.6 x 7.2, two masts schooner built 1883 W. Peat, Tomakin N.S.W. 2 Comp Eng. S.C. 35 h.p. T. O'Sullivan & Partners. Wrecked entrance Richmond River, 9/4/1908.

SOPHIA JANE: 401/1830*
Wood P.S. 153 tons, 120.3 x 20.1 x 10.3, two masts, built 1826 Barnes & Miller Eng. 50 h.p.

SUSANNAH CUTHBERT: 46466
Wood S.S. built 1864 in Sydney for J. Cuthbert. 178 tons, 131.6 x 18.8 x 10.0, 3 masts. Sold 1866 to the Clarence & New England S.N. Co. (Tonnage 193). July 1867 T. Bawden, Sept. 1873 C.& N.E.S.N. Co., March 1874 J. Frazer. Wrecked on Long Reef, 7/7/1875. Was 50 h.p.

TAMBAN (see KINCHELA):

TAMBAR: 131522
Steel T.S.S. built 1912 at Grangemouth, 456 tons, 145.2 x 30.1 x 8.7, Fo'c'sle 25', Poop 60'. Sold 1919 to New Guinea, 1928 Tasmanian Government thence to Holyman's. Scrapped in Melbourne in late 1960. 73 h.p.

TATHAM: 93603
Wood S.S. 37 tons, 60.6 x 15.5 x 4.7, one mast built 1889 H. Hardman Iron Cove Sydney, 10 h.p. for B.B. Nicoll. Jan. 1904 B.M. Corrigan. Broken up 1915.

TERARA: 89336
Iron P.S. 152 tons 125.3 x 20.0 x 6.7, built 1885 Atlas Eng. Co. Sydney, 30 h.p., Illawarra S.N. Co. June 1896 N.C.S.N. Co. May 1914 N.S.W. Government.

TERRANORA: 75005*
Steel P.S. 349 tons, 141.5 x 27.1 x 10.4, two masts, built 1878 D. & W. Henderson Ltd. Glasgow, 94 h.p. for Colonial Sugar Refining Co. March 1890 Gallagher & Cassidy, Sept. 1890 transferred to Auckland.

THE CLARENCE: 73779
Iron T.S.S. 603 tons, 222.2 x 30.1 x 15.7, 3 masts built 1875 T. Wingate & Co. Whiteinch, 250 h.p. for C.& N.E.S.N.Co. Sold March 1883 A.S.N. Co. then various owners renamed "Currajong" 1883. Run down and sunk by "Wyreema" Sydney Harbour 8/3/1910.

THE GRAND: 79545
Steel S.S. 66 tons 90.2 x 13.0 x 7.8, one mast built 1883 Forman & Co, Yarrabank Melbourne, 2 Comp S.C. 76 h.p. for J. See. Dec. 1891 N.C.S.N. Co. Ltd. Broken up 1892.

TIMARU: 76070
Iron S.S. built 1883 at Sunderland for New Zealand. 459 tons, 150.0 x 27.0 x 10.6. This vessel had many owners including the Brisbane & Clarence Rivers S.N. Co., before being purchased from the Patrick S.S. Co. Ltd by the N.C.S.N. Co. Ltd in July 1922. Resold in December the same year to Adelaide owners, and hulked shortly thereafter. Was 3 masted, 70 h.p. compound.

TINTENBAR:
Steel S.S. built 1908 at Ardrossan 668 tons, 185.5 x 30.2 x 10.7, Fo'c'sle 20', Bridge 11', R.Q. Deck 93'. Named for village 8 miles from Ballina. Chartered to Commonwealth Government 1923, lost ashore on New Ireland 1924. 115 h.p.

TOMKI: 83729 (Page 27)
Steel T.S.S. 589 tons, 180.0 x 27.2 x 14.4 2 masts schooner built 1882 R. & H. Green, Blackwall, 2 pr. Comp. Inv. SC. 90 h.p. for C. & R.R.S.N. Co. Jan 1889 C.R. & M.R.S.N. Co. Sept. 1891 N.C.S.N. Co. Lost Richmond River Bar 14/9/1907.

TUNCURRY 1:
Wood S.S. built 1903 J. Wright at Tuncurry, 162 tons gr. 113.5 x 22.2 x 7.6 Compound engine 2 masts. Ultimately sold to resident commissioner, Gilbert & Ellice Islands, renamed "Tokelau". Resold to Melbourne owners: given back her old name and traded on the Victorian coast. Stricken from Register 1919.

TUNCURRY 2: 125205
Wood T.S.S. 236 tons built by J. Wright Tuncurry. Early 1920s saw her lengthened by 20 feet. Sold in 1932 to H. R. Pountney to carry coal from the Belmont Mines to Sydney. In 1935 Cam & Sons bought her. She was dismantled in Sydney soon after the 1939/45 War.

TWEED 1: 89308 *
Wood S.S. 47 tons 67.8 x 15.9 x 6.5, 2 masts lugger built 1884 by D. Drake, Pyrmont. Comp SC. 20 h.p. for J. Paul & Partners. Broken up Dec. 1931.

TWEED 2: 89374
Steel S.S. 240 tons, 128.2 x 22.7 x 8.9 2 masts schooner built 1885 Newcastle on Tyne, 50 h.p. for G.W. Nicoll. Wrecked Tweed Heads 19/4/1888.

TWEED 3: 93621
Wood S.S. 285 tons, 132.0 x 25.5 x 11.5, 2 masts schooner built 1889 by T. Davis, Terrigal. 2 Comp SC 50 h.p. for G.W. Nicoll. Wrecked Byron Bay, 22/1/1893.

TYALGUM: 152016 (Page 132)
Steel T.S.S. built 1925 at Glasgow, 544 tons gr. 160.0 x 34.7 x 8.5 Fo'c'sle 30'. Named after town on Tweed River, wrecked at Tweed Heads, 25/8/1939.

UKI 1: 101053 *
Wood S.S. 28 tons, 57.8 x 13.6 x 4.5, no mast. Built 1892 by A.W. Settree, Balmain. 10 h.p. for A. & J. Howie. Register closed 1953.

UKI 2: 150200 (Pages 108, 109, and 130)
Steel T.S.S. built 1923 Port Glasgow, 545 tons, 152.9 x 34.6 x 8.5. Fo'c'sle 30'. Named after town on the Tweed River. Sold 1954 to M. Bern & Co. in 1960, was hulked in Brisbane. Stripped and scuttled off Tangalooma, Moreton Island, June 1976 as breakwater. Alongside old Kallatina. 70 h.p.

ULMARRA 1: 38873
Wood P.S. 50 tons, 85.3 x 14.3 x 4.3, built 1861 Waterview Bay, Balmain. One 12 h.p. engine for C.& R.R.S.N. Co. Wrecked Manning Heads, 10/10/1872.

ULMARRA 2: 150197 (Pages 110 and 111)
Steel S.S. built 1923 at Port Glasgow, 924 tons, 200.0 x 33.1 x 12.4. Fo'c'sle 32', Bridge 24', R.Q. Deck 97'. Named after town on the Clarence River. Sold 1954 to John Manners & Co. Hong Kong, renamed "Rozelle Breeze" then "Papagayo" eventually sinking in typhoon near Hong Kong. 121 h.p.

ULOOM: 46445
Iron S.P.S. 115 tons, 102.0 x 18.4 x 6.6, 1 mast, built 1863 A.S.N. Co. Ltd, Pyrmont, eng. 25 h.p., altered 1869 100.4 x 18.4 x 5.6, 90 tons eng. 14 h.p. for C.& R.R.S.N. Co. 1889 C.R.& M.R.S.N.Co. Sept. 1891 N.C.S.N. Co. Passed out of existence through age and decay. 1909 registration closed.

URALBA: 174694
Wood T.S.S. built 1942 at Tuncurry, 602 tons, 62 h.p., 154.8 x 37.0 x 9.3. Fo'c'sle 33', Bridge 82'. Named after settlement on the Richmond River. Requisitioned by R.A.N. on completion 1942, sold to Melbourne 1947. Broken up 1964/5.

URALLA 1:
Wood T.S.S. built 1908 at Tuncurry, for Allen Taylor & Co. 120 tons 125.8 x 26.5 x 8.5. Sold to I.& S.C.S.N.Co., renamed "Tilba Tilba". Wrecked at Wreck Bay, 17/11/1912. 62 h.p.

URALLA 2 (Page 117)
Steel T.S.S. built 1926 at Grangemouth, 529 tons 153.0 x 34.6 x 8.5. Wrecked on Stockton Beach 14/6/1928. 59 h.p.

URANA: 151995
Steel T.S.S. built 1924. 518 tons gr. 153.0 x 34.6 x 8.5. Fo'c'sle 30'. Named after town in South West New South Wales. Wrecked 31/8/1937 on reef off Old Bar.

URARA: 36848

Iron P.S. 382 tons, 180.5 x 24.2 x 11.4, 2 masts schooner built 1859 Birkenhead, two 120 h.p. engines for C. & R. R. S. N. Co. Wrecked Clarence River Heads 1/5/1866.

WAIMEA: 38862

Iron S.S. 158 tons, 131.0 x 21.5 x 9.5, 3 masts. Built 1868 North Sydney J.E. Manning 60 h.p. in 1871, 229 tons, J.E. Manning, 1870 E. & H. Manning, Oct. 1871 C. & R. R. S. N. Co. Wrecked Richmond River Heads 10/1/1872.

WALLAMBA (Page 107)

Wood T.S.S. built 1917 at Tuncurry for Allen Taylor, 331 tons, 142.5 x 34.8 x 7.1. Named after river that flows into Wallis Lake at Tuncurry. Totally wrecked at Morna Point in fog on the 11/7/1923.

WANDRA:

Wood S.S. built for Allen Taylor in 1907, 164 tons, 120.5 x 26.0 x 5.8 ketch rigged. Wrecked 15/12/1915 on Drum & Sticks.

WATER LILY: 75058

Wood stern wheel P.S. built 1880 at Sydney, 96 tons, 72.4 x 19.5 x 5.6 drogher. Abandoned beyond repair 1908.

WAUCHOPE 1: 121103

Wood T.S.S. 269 tons, 127.5 x 25.5 x 9.2 built 1905 by D. Sullivan (Coopernook) for N. Cain. 1913 to Holymans (Melbourne). Lost by fire off Portsea, 1/8/1919.

WAUCHOPE 2: 136461

Wood S.S. built for Allen Taylor in 1920, 120 tons, 100.0 x 26.0 x 6.2. Named after town on Hastings River. Drogher, foundered off Port Stephens while under tow to Sydney by "Arakoon", 5/4/1942. Built in Sydney.

WELLINGTON: 79269

Iron S.S. 182 tons 125.2 x 21.5 x 7.8, two masts, built 1884 Burrel & Son, Dumbarton. Pr. Comp SC Inv. 55 h.p. Ross & Duncan, Glasgow for J. See. Dec. 1891 N.C.S.N. Co. Lost on Nambucca Bar 3/12/1892, all saved.

WILCANNIA, H.M.A.S. (Page 135)

See "Wyrallah" 2

WILLIAM THE FOURTH: 5/1832 (Page 3)

Wood P.S. 54 tons 74.0 x 15.6 x 7.0, 2 masts, built 1831 Clarencetown. Lengthened 1854, 77 tons, 86.0 x 14.8 x 8.2 for W. Grose. 1843 E. Manning & Partners, 1857 Grafton S.N. Co., 1860 I. & S.C.S.N.Co. 1864 sold to China.

WOLLONGBAR 1: (Pages 57 and 99)

Steel T.S.S. built 1911 at Troon, 2,005 tons, 285.5 x 40.2 x 23.8. Fo'c'sle 40'. Named after small village east of Lismore. Capable of 20 knots. Wrecked at Byron Bay 14/5/1921. 332 h.p.

WOLLONGBAR 2: 150190

Steel S.S. built 1922 at Glasgow to replace the above. 2,239 tons, 285.0 x 42.0 x 23.9. Fo'c'sle 51'. Sunk by Japanese submarine off Crescent Head at 10 a.m. 29/4/1943. 32 lives lost, 5 survived. 218 h.p.

WOLLUMBIN

Wood S.S. built 1893 at Jervis Bay for G. Nicoll. 231 tons, 112.9 x 24.7 x 10.3. Wrecked near the Bellinger River 10/11/1905. 45 h.p.

WOODBURN: 89495

See "Macleay"

WYANGARIE: 171238 (Page 153)

Steel, S.M.V. built 1938 at Copenhagen, 1,068 tons, 215.0 x 36.5 x 13.0. Fo'c'sle 30', Bridge 23', R.Q. Deck 108'. Named after village north of Kyogle, she made the last passage for the N.C.S.N. Co. on 9/3/1954, sold to Howard Smith Ltd., renamed "Mourilyan". Sold East (John Manners) April 1963 and renamed "Tong Leong", then "Rita" 1964, "Baringo" 1965, later "Fagaras". Sold by Cia Nav. Thompson, of Panama to Loy Kee, Hong Kong, August 1976, for scrap. 263 h.p.

WYOMING:

Wood S.S. built 1890 at Brisbane Water for W.G. Yeager. 258 tons gr. 132.0 x 23.0 x 10.3. Sold 1908 and wrecked 10/10/1911 on Kiola Beach. 30 h.p.

WYRALLAH 1: 93558
    Iron T.S.S. built 1887 in Sydney for B. Nicoll, 302 tons, 140.0 x 22.3 x 13.2. Named after town on north arm Richmond River, sold to the Gippsland S.N. Co. in 1900, run down and sunk in fairway at Port Phillip by the S.S. "Dilkera" on the 8/4/1924. 45 h.p.

WYRALLAH 2: 157619 (Pages 129, 135)
    Steel S.M.V. built 1934 at Copenhagen, 1,049 tons, 216.4 x 36.7 x 8.3. Fo'c'sle 30', Bridge 31', R.Q. Deck 108'. Sold 1954 to John Burke & Co. Brisbane. Resold 1960/61 to Noumea and renamed "Colorado del Mar". In 1964 sold to Fiji, renamed "Tamata", reported ashore near Fiji Island. Resold back to Noumea, renamed "Colorado del Mar". 1972 to Singapore as "Union Pacific", 1973 "Ocean Life", by 1976 "Sri Mahkota", and 1979 "Sinar Surya", still trading. 224 h.p.

YAAMBA: 49260
    Iron S.P.S. 98 tons, 102.0 x 20.2 x 6.1, 2 masts, built 1864 Australasian S.N. Co. Pyrmont. Two 24 h.p. engines Australasian S.N. Co. Sept. 1877 F. O'Brien & Partners, Aug. 1880 J. Ritchie, Dec, 1891 N.C.S.N. Co. Ltd. Broken up 1910.

YULGILBAR:
    Steel T.S.S. built 1907, 799 tons gr. 137 h.p., 199.5 x 32.0 x 11.0. Named after property on the Clarence River north-west of Grafton. Ran to Macleay River. Sold 1925 to Burns Philp Ltd and renamed "Makatea". Eventually scuttled off Mbengga Island in 1933.

APPENDIX TWO

INSTRUCTIONS & REGULATIONS FOR CAPTAINS & OFFICERS
OF THE NORTH COAST STEAM NAVIGATION COMPANY LIMITED
– 1899

The North Coast Steam Navigation Company's Regulations for Masters (1899) were mostly straightforward, and even today are relevant, but the following selected articles are of interest: today they would be considered a bit puritanical, but were quite everyday orders in 1899.

Article No. 27
    The officer of the watch is not to leave the bridge until relieved, nor must he sit down during his watch, or enter into conversation with passengers beyond civilly and briefly answering any questions addressed to him. He shall not permit passengers to go on the flying bridge.

Article No. 29
    Captains are strictly prohibited from racing their vessels with other steamers, whether belonging to this or any other Company. This order shall not prevent them from driving their ships when it is necessary in the Company's interest that a rapid passage should be made, and where there is no obstacle to exerting the speed of the ships in a prudent manner.

Article No. 31
    Captains are expected to give personal attention to the comfort of both classes of passengers. They shall see that the table is kept in a creditable manner, that the cabins are neat and clean, the attendants orderly, respectful and diligent, and that no dirt nor disorder prevails in any part of the vessel.

To this end, they shall, when practicable, make frequent visits of inspection throughout the ship, including the forecastle, galley, W.C.'s and lamp room: and should there be evidence of dirt or untidiness, he is to have it attended to promptly. Strict attention is to be paid to the ventilation of the passengers accommodation, skylights and ports being kept open at all times when weather permits.

Articles No. 38 and 39

Captains will be reimbursed for all petty expenses incurred for telegrams, cabs, etc. on Company's business. They are also allowed to exercise their discretion in dispensing hospitality where the interests of the Company can be furthered thereby in such cases as prolonged night work, refreshments to pilots or ship's crew during arduous bar work, or other unusual circumstance and are to sign cards for refreshments supplied.

They are, however, expected to exercise a wise discretion in this direction, and be strictly temperate themselves. All liquors supplied to officers or engineers are to be noted by the steward in a book kept for the purpose, and he shall produce the same for inspection when called on to do so by the marine superintendent. When promotions are being arranged preference will be given, other considerations being equal, to men who are total abstainers.

Article No. 41

Masters and officers shall not take part in any game of cards on board ship while at sea.

Article No. 42

Private trading of any description on the part of masters or officers is strictly forbidden, and any employee of the Company breaking this rule will be summarily dismissed.

Article No. 43

Any instance of insobriety on the part of officers is to be reported to the managing director, who will deal with the offender.

172

REGULATION RE UNIFORM

The board of directors have adopted the following regulations as regards uniform, and it is to be observed in all the Company's passenger steamers:—

Captains, Mates, Engineers and Stewards are to wear a uniform suit of navy blue cloth or serge, and blue cloth cap.

Captain is to wear a double breasted sac coat with five gilt buttons on each side.

The chief steward is to wear a similar coat with five silvered buttons on each side.

Mates are to wear (when on clean duty) a similar coat to the captain, but without gilt buttons.

Engineers are to wear a single-breasted jacket. Under stewards are to wear suits of navy blue: shell jackets, double breasted: when on duty in the saloon they must always wear white shirts and shave each day.

Caps are to be of navy blue: the captain's is to have a mohair band mounted with a Company's badge: two gilt side buttons and gilt chin-strap.

The chief steward's cap to have silver buttons, strap and badge. All other caps to be plain.

Seamen when on duty steering, to wear navy blue trousers, jerseys, and caps of Company's pattern.

Generally:— It is imperative that captains and officers should acquaint themselves with the Company's regulations, as herein embodied and that the provisions contained be strictly carried out.

In any case where the regulations are not complied with, the managing director will deal with the person in question according to circumstances.

By order of the Board of Directors.

APPENDIX 3

SUMMARY OF CARGO SHIPPED FROM THE CLARENCE RIVER DURING 1940

102,018	boxes butter	5,090	cases eggs
1,922	pigs	19,506	pieces bacon
17,295	bags maize	19,341	bags potatoes
9,876	tins honey	729	bags pumpkins
1,161	bags beans and peas	14,192	empty drums
204,725	sacks sugar	29,853	bales Megass
1,777	logs	13,649	piles and poles
7,730,419	s/ft sawn timber	2,051	girders
51,400	sleepers	149,000	bags zircon
82,000	oyster sticks	420,000	molasses
40,000	bags of sand	400	tons of bulk sand

plus sundry boxes of fish, odd motor cars and trucks, horses, cattle and scrap metal etc.

The above figures are a fair sample of cargo carried to Sydney from one river only, and this under war time conditions.

APPENDIX 4

(EXTRACT FROM SHIPPING ADVERTISEMENTS WEDNESDAY, 12TH SEPTEMBER, 1917)

THE NORTH COAST STEAM NAVIGATION COMPANY LIMITED.
(Bars and Weather Permitting) From 3 Sussex Street

BYRON BAY	"Orara", Saturday, 2 p.m.
COFF'S HARBOUR	"Orara", Saturday 2 p.m. Passengers only
RICHMOND RIVER	"Burringbar", This day, 9.30 p.m.
CLARENCE RIVER	"Coombar" (Cargo only) to-morrow 2 p.m.
	"Pulganbar" Saturday, 2 p.m.
MACLEAY RIVER	"Yulgilbar", "Coramba" (Cargo only) to-morrow 2 p.m.
	"Yulgilbar", Tuesday, 5 p.m.
MANNING RIVER	"Maianbar", to-morrow 10 p.m. via Newcastle
BELLINGER RIVER	"Yulgilbar", Tuesday, 5 p.m.
	(Transhipping Mcleay River)
NAMBUCCA RIVER	"Coolebar" (Cargo only) To-morrow 2 p.m.

FROM DRUITT STREET

COFF'S HARBOUR	"Tambar", Monday 5 p.m.
TWEED RIVER	"Gunbar", Monday 5 p.m. (Cargo only)
	Passenger Office and Tourists' Bureau
	261 George St. Telephone 6712

Tourist Guide Book, Price 1/−, Posted 1/1

ROBERT A. BELL
Managing Director

SUGGESTED FURTHER READING

Australian Ships Sketchbook, Alan Slevin (Rigby Ltd) 1972
Australia's Pearl Harbour, Douglas Lockwood (Cassell) 1966
The Brisbane Water Story, C. Swancott, (4 volumes) Vol. 4 — 1961
The Ferries of Sydney, G. Andrews (Reed) 1975
Fitted for the Voyage, M. Page (Rigby) 1975
Lion of the China Sea, Olson (P. & O. Aust.)
A Maritime History of Australia, John Bach (Nelson) 1976
Men and a River, Louise T. Daley (Melbourne University Press) 1966
New Zealand Shipwrecks, Ingram & Wheatley. (A.H. Reed) 1961
The Newcastle Packets, J.H.M. Abbott (Currawong Publishing) 1943
The River Trade, G. Painter (Turton & Armstrong) 1979
Port of Sydney, Journal of the M.S.B. of N.S.W. — quarterly
Royal Australian Navy 1939–1942, and 1942–1945 (2 vols) (the Official History) G.H. Gill (Australian War Memorial) 1957 & 1968
Ships in Australian Waters, Williams & Serle, (A. & R.) 1968
Ships of Today, Frank Norton (A. & R.) 1958
Shipwrecks at Port Phillip Heads, P.J. Williams & R. Serle (Maritime Historical Publications) 1963

Steamships Registered at Sydney Prior to 1900, R.H. Parsons, 1961
Union Fleet, I.J. Farquhar (N.Z. Ship and Marine Society) 1968
The Vanished Fleet, T.K. Fitchett (Rigby) 1977
Veteran Ships of Australia and New Zealand, G. Andrews (Reed) (1976)
Workhorses in Australian Waters, Mike Richards (Turton & Armstrong) 1988
S.S. Yoncala — Dive to the Past, M. Gleeson (Turton & Armstrong) 1987
Wrecks at Apollo Bay, J.K. Loney, (Loney) 1971
Wrecks on the Gippsland Coast, J.K. Loney (Loney) 1971
Wrecks on the North Coast N.S.W., J.K. Loney (Loney) 1976
Wrecks on the South Coast N.S.W.. J.K. Loney (Loney) 1976
Wrecks in Darwin Waters, Tom Lewis (Turton & Armstrong) 1991

Also: the various Historical Societies to be found in most of the larger towns on the North Coast all put out some very interesting booklets describing the history of their respective towns. These are readily available on payment of a small fee.

S.S. "Oakland stuck on the breakwater at Ballina early in 1903. She had not long been repaired and refloated when she was lost off Cabbage Tree Island on 26 May that year.

Acknowledgement: Richmond River Historical Society.